LEGITIMACY

ARTHUR ISAK APPLBAUM

LEGITIMACY

The Right to Rule in a Wanton World

Harvard University Press
Cambridge, Massachusetts, and London, England   2019

First printing

Library of Congress Cataloging-in-Publication Data

Names: Applbaum, Arthur Isak, 1957– author.
Title: Legitimacy : the right to rule in a wanton world / Arthur Isak Applbaum.
Description: Cambridge, Massachusetts : Harvard University Press, 2019. | Includes
    bibliographical references and index.
Identifiers: LCCN 2019012121 | ISBN 9780674983465 (hardcover : alk. paper)
Subjects: LCSH: Legitimacy of governments. | Government accountability. | Political
    leadership. | Political ethics. | Despotism.
Classification: LCC JC497 .A55 2019 | DDC 320.01 / 1—dc23
LC record available at https://lccn.loc.gov/2019012121

For Emma and Sophie

Contents

LEGITIMACY

Introduction

The musings that became this book began at the time of the US presidential election won by George W. Bush, loser of the national popular vote whose Electoral College victory was vehemently contested. I finished writing with Donald Trump in the White House, another loser of the national popular vote, suspected of winning the election with the help of Russian intelligence operatives. In both elections, many on the losing side questioned the legitimacy of the winner. In between these fraught elections, foes of Barack Obama questioned his legitimate claim to the presidency by denying that he was America born. All three were accused of illegitimacy because, like children born out of wedlock, their terms in office were said to be conceived through improper procedure. Millions of citizens (though different millions) think them bastard presidents.

Procedural defects in title certainly can deprive a purported authority of legitimacy. The victors of bloody coups, rapacious conquests, and manifestly fraudulent elections might wield the physical power of office but miss the moral right to govern. We make a mistake, though, in thinking that the right to govern is won and lost only through procedure or pedigree, and we make another mistake in thinking that the greatest danger to legitimate democratic governance is a defective electoral system.

Among the important concepts that political philosophers argue about, few are as protean as legitimacy. All of our normative concepts are matters of vigorous and, one hopes, fruitful disagreement. But often enough, for a time, we gain clarity about what the disagreement is about. So, though we might disagree about what distributive justice demands—who falls within the scope of its claims, what goods and freedoms are subject to it, and what are the correct principles of just distribution—we might agree that distributive justice is about who has a moral entitlement to which goods and freedoms under conditions of scarcity or conflicting interests and values. When it comes to arguments about legitimacy, however, there is less agreement about what we are disagreeing about.

John Rawls draws the well-known distinction between concept and conception, where a concept marks off the arena of a disputed idea that is filled, through normative argument, by conflicting conceptions or theories with different content, criteria, or conditions.[1] Without some conceptual analysis, understood as the exercise of marking off apt boundaries for fruitful argument, there are two ways an argument might misfire: if we are too loose in specifying a concept, we risk talking past each other; if we are too strict, we risk begging the normative question. The distinction between a concept and its conceptions is not hard and fast. It might shift over time as ideas get settled and then unsettled again. It might shift in the course of a single conversation, as we struggle to clarify where we disagree, and make judgments about whether, for a particular question, ordinary linguistic usage is more or less illuminating than stipulative definition, or whether highly moralized thick terms are more or less useful than relatively thin descriptions. The test of an aptly drawn concept is its fruitfulness, which in part is a matter of steering between the twin risks of engaging in merely verbal disputes and of assuming one's conclusion.

In specifying the concept of legitimacy fruitfully, and in distinguishing the concept from its various conceptions, we might begin with the rough notion that the concept of legitimacy is about the right to rule. Various conceptions of legitimacy differ on what the necessary and sufficient conditions are for A to have the right to rule B in some context C, and differ on what the reasons are for such conditions. But neither having a right nor ruling are transparent notions. Is the right to rule a claim-right that entails a moral duty to obey or a mere liberty? Is the right of a legitimate ruler conclusory or merely presumptive? Does legitimacy come in degrees or is it a binary property? Is legitimacy a minimal threshold that binds or an aspirational ideal that guides? Are the criteria for legitimacy necessarily tied to notions of pedigree or procedure? Are the criteria for legitimacy necessarily tied to the beliefs or the wills of those subject to legitimate rule, so that only rulers who are believed to be legitimate, or who have the consent of those ruled, can be legitimate? How is legitimacy connected to other normative ideas such as justification, legality, and justice?

One might at first say that all of these fine questions should be left maximally open at the level of the concept, allowing different answers under different conceptions. But is this not too open-ended to be fruitful? In ordinary language, we say "legitimate argument," "legitimate self-defense," "legitimate theater," "legitimate daughter," "legitimate monarch," and "legitimate state," but beyond some vague notion of properness, these uses do not share much. Some might hold that a state, in virtue of its legitimacy, has an entitlement to be recognized by other states, standing as a party to international treaties, the right to control territory and forcefully defend its borders, immunity from outside interference, and the normative power to impose moral obligations on its inhabitants. But others hold that a legitimate state is simply one that is justified in exercising coercion. For some, a legitimate ruler simply is a lawful ruler. For others, a legitimate ruler must be a just ruler. The notions of legitimacy behind these positions diverge enough to call into question whether their proponents agree about what they are disagreeing about. The same term, of course, can come to refer to different concepts. If I claim that a "civil right" is a polite uppercut to the jaw (like John Locke's "civil respectful cudgeling"), I do not have a real disagreement with Martin Luther King Jr.[2] Leaving the concept of legitimacy maximally open may hide from our view the real disagreements.

This book aims to make room for two views about the concept of political legitimacy: the *substantive* account and the *power-liability* account. The substantive account claims that criteria of political legitimacy need not refer exclusively to pedigree or procedure. The power-liability account claims that political legitimacy is a form of moral power to change the normative circumstances of its subjects that entails moral liability, but is not necessarily a moral claim-right that entails moral duty. Nor does having moral power with respect to subjects necessarily require having causal power over those subjects. I argue for the conceptual possibility of the substantive and power-liability views, and make the case for their correctness. If they are correct, the normative implications are considerable: together, they sketch a distinctive view about the legitimacy of political institutions and our obligations towards them. The substantive account supports the legitimacy of constitutions that not only establish fair procedures but that also settle certain matters of substantive justice; the substantive account also supports the legitimacy of counter-majoritarian institutions and practices, such as judicial review and outcome-sensitive voting schemes, if they are necessary for the realization of a substantively just constitution. The substantive view supports, as well, stiffer standards for the legitimacy of governments and correspondingly lower thresholds for justified violations of state sovereignty. The power-liability account complements the substantive account in supporting an appealing interpretation of justified civil disobedience in the face of legitimate but unjust law at home and of justified human-rights interventions abroad. I believe that these two views are correct, but it is often thought that they are not only false but incoherent. Many hold that proper procedure or pedigree, on the one hand, and entailed duty, on the other, are built into the meaning of the concept of political legitimacy. One of my tasks is to loosen these conceptual strictures.

If indeed the most fruitful specification of the idea of legitimacy is that legitimacy is a normative power that entails liability but not necessarily obligation, and that the criteria for having legitimacy may be in part substantive, and not necessarily wholly procedural, then the conceptual terrain is open to allow for what I believe is the most plausible normative conception or theory of legitimacy, the *free group agency* account. One enduring puzzle of modern political philosophy is how to reconcile every individual's fundamental right to freedom with the inescapable need to subject one another to coercive law. On the free group agency view, A legitimately governs B only if A's governance of B realizes and protects B's freedom over time, and this is the case only when A is a free group agent that counts a free B as a constituent member of that group agent.

Since no procedure by itself can make free those who are not already free, the free group agency view requires substantive as well as procedural conditions for government to be legitimate. Three principles guide three different dimensions of public governance, which protect against three distinct threats to free agency and therefore legitimacy. *What* to decide is subject to a *liberty principle,* under which all citizens are entitled to the protection of basic rights and freedoms. When the liberty principle is seriously violated, government sinks to a tyranny by practice, and we are dominated by *inhumanity*. *Who* decides is subject to an *equality principle*, under which each citizen is to have equal say in selecting who bears decision-making powers. When the equality principle is seriously violated, government sinks to a tyranny without title, and we are dominated by *despotism*. *How* to decide is subject to an *agency principle*, under which decision-making powers are to be exercised by decision-makers who constitute a self-governing and independent group agent that counts all citizens as self-governing and independent members. When the agency principle is seriously violated, government sinks to a tyranny of unreason, and we are dominated by *wantonism*.

Two surprising conclusions follow from the free group agency view. First, one might have thought that collective self-governance entails an equal say for all citizens in choosing the substance of the laws and policies that govern us. Not so. Collective self-governance requires that we all have an equal say only in choosing *who* governs us. The implication is that many of our conventional views about representation, campaign promises, and electoral mandates are mistaken. The second is that the standard debate between small "l" liberals and small "d" democrats about the legitimacy of counter-majoritarian institutions and practices such as judicial review overlooks a third major threat to legitimate government. Yes, we can be tyrannized by losing our equal democratic say, and we can be tyrannized by violations of our basic freedoms. But we can also be tyrannized—and not merely burdened or inconvenienced—by the wanton misrule of incontinent, inconstant, and incoherent rulers, even when liberty and equality, as standardly understood, are secure. Rulers that cannot govern themselves cannot legitimately govern others.

PART I

Substance and Normative Power

CHAPTER 1

Legitimacy in a Bastard Kingdom

"Now, gods, stand up for bastards!"

This is the battle cry of Edmund, bastard son of the Earl of Gloucester in *King Lear* and one of the great early modern theorists of political legitimacy. Edmund is scheming to usurp the earldom with the invention of a forged letter that frames the legitimate heir, his half-brother Edgar. Edmund's political philosophy is laid out in his first soliloquy, which I quote in its entirety without much commentary at the start. Why I believe Edmund is a great theorist of legitimacy will become more clear over time:

> Thou, Nature, art my goddess; to thy law
> My services are bound. Wherefore should I
> Stand in the plague of custom and permit
> The curiosity of nations to deprive me,
> For that I am some twelve or fourteen moonshines
> Lag of a brother? Why bastard? Wherefore base?
> When my dimensions are as well compact,
> My mind as generous, and my shape as true,
> As honest madam's issue? Why brand they us
> With base? With baseness? Bastardy? Base, base?
> Who in the lusty stealth of nature take
> More composition and fierce quality
> Than doth, within a dull, stale, tired bed
> Go to th' creating a whole tribe of fops
> Got 'tween asleep and wake? Well, then,

> Legitimate Edgar, I must have your land.
> Our father's love is to the bastard Edmund
> As to th' legitimate. Fine word, "legitimate"!
> Well, my legitimate, if this letter speed
> And my invention thrive, Edmund the base
> Shall top th' legitimate. I grow; I prosper.
> Now, gods, stand up for bastards![1]

Edmund's case has been partially conceded by Gloucester, who has already told us that he is quite disposed to recognize Edmund. He's fond of the lad: "But I have, sir, a son by order of law, some year elder than this, who yet is no dearer in my account. Though this knave came something saucily to the world before he was sent for, yet was his mother fair, there was good sport at his making, and the whoreson must be acknowledged."[2] Though Edmund lacks one kind of pedigree, Gloucester grants that his affection for the young man confers standing of another sort. Edmund has a point.

I. From Kosovo to Palm Beach County

We will return to Edmund and his theory of legitimacy in a moment, but first consider a contemporary puzzle about legitimacy that comes about when we juxtapose responses to the 1999 NATO intervention in Kosovo and responses to the 2000 US presidential election. To understand the piece of the puzzle posed by Kosovo, we have to back up a bit to the fall of Srebrenica in 1995, and what I am going to sarcastically call the Srebrenica Doctrine. Srebrenica was a UN "safe area" that proved insufficiently safe for the eight thousand or so Bosnian Muslim men who were led to their slaughter under the supposed protection of a Dutch peacekeeping battalion. There were a lot of negligent mistakes made around Srebrenica, and arguably, there was some cold-hearted political strategy that led to the fall and the slaughter as well. But Srebrenica happened in part because UN officials were in the grip of an idea, the Srebrenica Doctrine, which has three prongs: immunity, neutrality, and multilateralism. In order to respect the sovereignty of nations and the immunity from interference that supposedly follows, the humanitarian intervener must avoid two sorts of partisanship: taking sides in a conflict and acting on one's own.

To ensure neutrality and multilateralism, multiple parties held the keys needed to unfetter would-be rescuers. The Bosnian Muslims were prevented from arming and defending themselves, lest the peacekeepers be seen as taking sides among armed combatants. Once the Serbian encroachment began, the besieged UN peacekeepers were repeatedly instructed to give ground rather than fight back. The NATO fighter pilots, who, after days of delay, eventually flew overhead and could have routed the Serbs rather easily, were hampered by rules of engagement that permitted only close air support in defense of the peacekeepers themselves, not the unarmed civilians the Dutch battalion was there to protect. To save Srebrenica from slaughter, too many people had to turn their keys, and though the military commander holding the NATO key was prepared to turn it, the diplobureaucrat holding the UN key was not.[3] To counterattack Serbian forces would violate the neutrality that the Srebrenica Doctrine maintained was a requirement of international law.

In the aftermath of Srebrenica comes the NATO intervention in Kosovo, a ten-week bombing campaign aimed at driving Serbian-dominated Yugoslav forces out of the Yugoslav province of Kosovo in order to end the persecution of the ethnic Albanians. Whatever one thinks about the moral case for intervening in Kosovo, one would have been hard-pressed to make a legal case before 2005, when "Responsibility to Protect" provisions were adopted by the United Nations.[4] Military intervention that took sides in an internal struggle within a sovereign nation appeared to be a straightforward violation of the UN Charter, and so, of international law. The illegality of the intervention at that time was recognized by the Independent International Commission on Kosovo chaired by Richard Goldstone, justice of the Constitutional Court of South Africa and chief prosecutor of the UN International Criminal Tribunals for the former Yugoslavia and for Rwanda. So the Commission's report uncouples the concept of legality from legitimacy: "Experience from the NATO intervention in Kosovo suggests the need to close the gap between legality and legitimacy."[5] There is a gap. "The intervention was not legal because it contravened the Charter prohibition on the unauthorized use of force."[6] Straightforwardly, in violating the UN Charter, the intervention was illegal.[7] Nonetheless,

> ... the question of whether the intervention was legitimate has to
> be answered, especially since Kosovo may provide a precedent for
> further intervention in the future. The Commission's answer has

been that the intervention was legitimate, but not legal, given existing international law. It was legitimate because it was un-avoidable: diplomatic options had been exhausted, and two sides were bent on a conflict which threatened to wreak humanitarian catastrophe and generate instability through the Balkan peninsula.[8]

The Goldstone report drives a wedge between legitimacy and legality, and goes on to offer an argument why, though illegal, the interveners still acted with legitimacy. Gloucester's whoreson does not simply take law-fulness as the standard. "Wherefore should I / Stand in the plague of custom and permit / The curiosity of nations to deprive me, / ... When my dimensions are as well compact, / My mind as generous, and my shape as true, / As honest madam's issue?" Edmund offers a substantive standard for the proper exercise of power whether or not it comports with the cu-rious customs of conventional law. So too, the Kosovo Commission: in its view, a wedge can be driven between legality and legitimacy, and the Kosovo intervention, though illegal, was nonetheless legitimate.

Now consider the same wedge turned around. The example takes us to the arithmetically challenged State of Florida after the 2000 presiden-tial election. A couple of days after the final Supreme Court decision that gave the presidency to George W. Bush, House Minority Leader Richard Gephardt was interviewed by Tim Russert on NBC's "Meet the Press." After an exchange in which Russert is trying hard to get Gephardt to con-cede that George W. Bush is legitimate, he asks,

"So George W. Bush is the legitimate forty-third president of the United States?"

Gephardt answers: "George W. Bush is the *next* President of the United States."

Russert: "But is he legitimate? Is he?"

Gephardt: "And we have to respect the presidency. We have to respect the law. And we have to work with him to try to solve the people's problems. That's the task in front of us now.

Russert: But why can't a leading Democrat say he is a legitimate president of the United States?"

Gephardt: He *is* the president of the United States."[9]

In both cases, we see commentators claiming that legitimacy and legality can come apart. The Kosovo intervention, though illegal, was legitimate, and the Bush presidency, though legal, was, arguably, illegitimate. Edmund drives yet another wedge, between legitimacy and pedigree, and challenges the idea that the criteria of legitimacy are procedural, not substantive: are not his dimensions as well compact, his mind as generous, and his shape as true as his brother's? What is this idea of legitimacy, that it can be used in these sorts of ways? Can legality, pedigree, and legitimacy indeed come apart?

Of course they can, but we must struggle against a certain linguistic history—legitimacy's baggage—to make two distinctions stick. The first is the distinction between *descriptive* legitimacy—the social fact that people believe some person or institution has the moral right to rule—and *normative* legitimacy—genuinely having the moral right to rule. These are two different notions, and we need to be clear about when we are using one, when we are using the other, and what, if anything, connects the two.

The other distinction is between the *word* legitimacy, the *concept* or idea of legitimacy, and particular *conceptions* of legitimacy, the content of the concept. "Fine word, 'legitimate'!" Edmund says with irony. It is a fine word, but we need to trace its changing senses over time to distinguish the word from the idea or ideas it expresses. One word, of course, can come to refer to different concepts (to a sailor, a "civil liberty" might mean a well-mannered shore leave) and different words ("authority" is legitimacy's closest cousin) can refer to the same concept. I have, a moment ago, offered a rough account of the concept of legitimacy by saying that it is the moral right to rule, but if we understand conceptual analysis as the exercise of marking off apt boundaries for fruitful argument so that we neither talk past each other nor beg the question, we may discover that this rough draft needs some editing. Finally, the concept or idea of legitimacy can be filled out in different ways. We can both agree that we are talking about the same idea, legitimacy, but disagree about its content: criteria for how you get legitimacy and what it gets you.

II. Descriptive and Normative Legitimacy

Contemporary political usage of legitimacy often is ambiguous or confused. Consider the US Supreme Court opinions surrounding *Bush v. Gore*.

Here is the dissent of Justice Stevens from the stay that temporarily stopped the Florida recount while its legality was being adjudicated:

> It is clear, however, that a stay should not be granted unless an applicant makes a substantial showing of a likelihood of irreparable harm. In this case, applicants have failed to carry that heavy burden. Counting every legally cast vote cannot constitute irreparable harm. On the other hand, there is a danger that a stay may cause irreparable harm to the respondents—and, more importantly, the public at large—because of the risk that "the entry of the stay would be tantamount to a decision on the merits in favor of the applicants." . . . Preventing the recount from being completed will inevitably cast a cloud on the legitimacy of the election.[10]

Does Stevens mean that preventing the recount will cloud our perceptions of legitimacy, so that we will hold mistaken or uncertain beliefs about who has the genuine right to rule, or does Stevens mean that thinking makes it so, and the cloud will threaten the genuine legitimacy, the genuine moral right to rule, of the purported winner?

Justice Scalia, responding to Stevens, clearly understands Stevens to be making a point about perceptions:

> The issue is not, as the dissent puts it, whether "[c]ounting every legally cast vote ca[n] constitute irreparable harm." One of the principal issues in the appeal we have accepted is precisely whether the votes that have been ordered to be counted are, under a reasonable interpretation of Florida law, "legally cast vote[s]." The counting of votes that are of questionable legality does in my view threaten irreparable harm to petitioner, and to the country, by casting a cloud upon what he claims to be the legitimacy of his election. Count first, and rule upon legality afterwards, is not a recipe for producing election results that have the public acceptance democratic stability requires.[11]

Of course counting legal votes causes no irreparable harm, but counting votes of questionable legality can, and this is so even if they are ultimately ruled to be illegal. How? By casting a cloud on Bush's *claim* of legitimacy, not on his legitimacy itself. As I read Scalia, you either have or don't have legitimacy regardless of what people think you have. Irreparable harm comes if a cloud is cast over the truth, and the public fails to accept Bush's genuinely legitimate rule. Scalia recognizes the gap between descriptive and normative legitimacy. Count first and rule on legality afterwards is a recipe for perceived illegitimacy, but not for genuine illegitimacy. Though the Supreme Court was divided about the effects of the recount on perceptions of legitimacy, it agreed that legitimacy and perceptions of legitimacy are separable ideas—or so it seems.

But now consider Justice Breyer's understanding of legitimacy in his dissent from the final decision that gave the presidency to Bush. Breyer is commenting on the disputed Electoral College count in the Hayes-Tilden presidential election of 1876, which was decided by an *ad hoc* election commission appointed by Congress made up of five senators, five congressmen, and five Supreme Court justices. The commission split along partisan lines, and Justice Bradley cast the deciding vote for Hayes, apparently on technical, apolitical grounds:

> The relevance of this history lies in the fact that the participation
> in the work of the electoral commission by five Justices, including
> Justice Bradley, did not lend that process legitimacy. Nor did it
> assure the public the process had worked fairly guided by the law.
> Rather, it simply embroiled members of the Court in partisan
> conflict thereby undermining respect for the judicial process.[12]

On Breyer's telling, several Supreme Court justices who had genuine legitimacy on their bench tried but failed to lend this property to a new, *ad hoc* deliberative body, the election commission. Why would one think that this lending could succeed, and why did it fail? We can't be sure, but Breyer here apparently holds that thinking does make it so, and genuine legitimacy just *is* perceived legitimacy. If enough people had believed that Justice Bradley, respected and authoritative in his own domain, was acting with proper warrant in this new domain, then the legitimacy of the Supreme Court would have been successfully borrowed by the election commission, but as it turns out, enough people didn't believe this.

Many press accounts of Florida's election controversy either fail to differentiate normative and descriptive legitimacy or else implicitly suppose that normative legitimacy just *is* descriptive legitimacy. Consider this *Los Angeles Times* headline: "Bush Has Legitimacy, But It's Fragile."[13] Pause a moment and guess what sort of story would generate such a lead. . . . The story reports the findings of a poll taken shortly after the

Supreme Court ruling, in which 52 percent answered "Yes" to the following question: "Did Bush win the election legitimately?" He has legitimacy, because a majority says so, but his legitimacy is fragile, because it is a narrow majority. What Bush has is legitimacy—presumably, the genuine article. He has it, not because he received more valid votes than Gore in Florida, or because *Bush v. Gore* was correctly decided, or because Supreme Court decisions have moral authority even when mistakenly decided. He has genuine legitimacy because 52 percent *believe* that he received more valid votes or *believe* the case was correctly decided or *believe* that even mistaken courts are authoritative—even if these beliefs are false. Should 3 percent of the public change their minds—influenced by some fine point about statistical sampling, perhaps, or by a law review article on federalism, or by a political philosophy book about legitimacy—this fragile legitimacy would crumble, and Bush would revert to a bastard president.

This conflation of legitimacy itself and beliefs about it—between the normative and the descriptive—may have had its start in the social theory of Max Weber. I do not think that Weber himself suffers from this conflation. It is fairly clear that his account of legitimacy is an exercise in descriptive social science, not normative political philosophy, and the object of description is the social fact that people have *beliefs* about the normative grounds of legitimacy:

> But custom, personal advantage, purely affectual or ideal motives of solidarity, do not form a sufficiently reliable basis for a given domination. In addition there is normally a further element, the belief in legitimacy [*Legitimitätsglaube*]. Experience shows that in no instance does domination voluntarily limit itself to the appeal to material or affectual or ideal motives as a basis for its continuance. In addition every such system attempts to establish and to cultivate the belief in its legitimacy.[14]

Famously, Weber describes three pure types of grounds claimed by rulers to cultivate belief in their legitimacy: rational-legal grounds, traditional grounds, and charismatic grounds. These are introduced as legitimacy claims [*Legitimitätsanspruch*], not as normative criteria.[15] But Weber usually drops the references to beliefs about legitimacy or claims to legitimacy, and simply labels these grounds pure types of "legitimate domination [*legitime Herrschaft*]."[16]

After Weber, "legitimacy" enters into the lexicon of social science as a descriptive term with unexamined normative entailments. This has had two unfortunate consequences. Either the full-throated normative question about whether a ruler has genuine moral legitimacy becomes difficult to articulate, or—worse—the normative question is thought to be answered directly by empirical observation, so that legitimate rule just is rule believed to be legitimate.

But it is a conceptual confusion to hold that "legitimate" simply means "believed to be legitimate," for descriptive legitimacy is parasitic on the conceptually prior idea of normative legitimacy. What is supposed to be the content of these beliefs about legitimacy? Consider: when the objects of this social-scientific description, the members of some political society, believe that a rule or a ruler is legitimate, they are not (or not simply) engaging in their *own* social-scientific description of each other's beliefs. If that were so, when the citizens polled by the *Los Angeles Times* were asked "Is Bush legitimate?" each would have to answer "I don't yet know—I haven't seen the results of this very poll." What descriptive legitimacy describes are views about *normative* legitimacy. (This is so, by the way, even if normative legitimacy does not exist, which would be the case if various forms of moral skepticism or anarchism were true. Unicorns do not exist either, but the idea of a unicorn does, and therefore one's beliefs about what a unicorn is can be mistaken.)

This is not to assert that the social fact of what people take to be morally legitimate cannot figure in as a condition for having moral legitimacy. It is not incoherent to hold that an authority is morally legitimate if and only if most people (for whatever reason) believe the authority is morally legitimate. But note that this is a claim about the normative criteria for having moral legitimacy—a particular conception—not a claim about the meaning of moral legitimacy, which is conceptually more primitive than social facts about beliefs about it. Though not incoherent, such a claim is mistaken. In most cultures, over most of history, women believed that their husbands had legitimate authority over them, but that didn't make it so. Similarly, the fact that people in a society believe that their rulers have legitimate authority, or the fact that the rulers of other societies believe that the rulers of the society in question have legitimate authority, doesn't make it so.

Furthermore, it does seem that a conception of normative legitimacy that is wholly a function of beliefs about legitimacy fails the test of transparency, in that it depends on some people holding a different, mistaken conception. Suppose a two-member polity is subjected to the rule of an outside ruler. Both members believe that the correct conception of legitimacy is that the ruler is genuinely legitimate just in case the other believes the ruler to be legitimate, and illegitimate just in case the other believes the ruler to be illegitimate. Neither has independent beliefs about the legitimacy or illegitimacy of the ruler, nothing else counts for or against legitimacy, and it is common knowledge between the two that this is their conception. Then there are two stable normative equilibria, legitimacy and illegitimacy, and this is so because there are two stable epistemic equilibria: both members believing the ruler to be legitimate and both believing the ruler to be illegitimate. But there are no grounds whatsoever for choosing between the two equilibria. As specified, neither the members nor their conception can deliver an answer to the question "Is this ruler legitimate or illegitimate?"

This result generalizes to the N-person case in which the conception of legitimacy that everyone holds is that the ruler is legitimate if and only if n or greater out of N persons believe the ruler to be legitimate, for n greater than zero and less than N. To tip one way or another, there need to be exogenous beliefs about legitimacy or exogenous presumptions in favor of inferring beliefs in legitimacy that are precluded by the theory. For even if we suppose that each member of this society subscribes to the general conception that genuine legitimacy is wholly a function of beliefs about legitimacy, but they hold varying specific values for the critical threshold n, ranging from the minimal threshold of $n = 1$ up to the demanding threshold of $n = N - 1$, the cascade that will bring about unanimous justified belief in legitimacy (or, symmetrically, illegitimacy) cannot get started unless one person believes that the ruler is legitimate (or illegitimate). But this cannot happen if all form beliefs about legitimacy in accordance with their conception: the cascade depends on someone believing in the legitimacy or illegitimacy of the ruler on mistaken grounds, or on making a mistake in inference about the beliefs of others.

In some games with multiple equilibria, aren't some strategies dominant? Yes, but this is not a game of strategy in which players choose actions to their rational advantage. What to believe here is given by one's normative theory and that is not a matter of choice. Pascal's wager notwithstanding, a rational person cannot choose to believe. One can choose to *consent,* and on a normative account of legitimacy in which only consent matters, with the added assumption that it is to the rational advantage of each (or, on Kant's view, the duty of each) to live under legitimate rule, choosing to consent and thereby making the ruler legitimate is indeed a dominant strategy. But now consent, and not belief in legitimacy, is doing the work.

The appeal of taking perceived legitimacy as a sufficient condition for genuine legitimacy may arise from conflating perceived legitimacy with consent. An obvious way that belief in legitimacy and consent can come apart is when the belief has been fraudulently manufactured. If I agree to be governed by the winner of an election who actually stuffed the ballot boxes, or if I agree to be governed by the prophet of the one true god who actually is a fraudulent huckster, I have not genuinely consented. Perceived legitimacy and consent can also come apart in a deeper way. I can believe that a government has the right to govern us without our consent without that belief itself constituting consent. When the bastard Edmund's nonfictional contemporary James I of England argued for the divine right of kings, he explicitly denied that the legitimacy of his power depended on any sort of consent. The royally mandated instructional text *God and the King* insisted that the king has no superior besides God, the bond of allegiance from his subjects is inviolable, and it cannot be dissolved by tyranny, infidelity, heresy, apostasy, or acts of the pope.[17] Now imagine you are an English subject taught to believe that the king is God's lieutenant on earth, answerable to God alone. You chafe at James's violations of his subjects' liberties, and have the mischievous thought that if your consent mattered, you would not grant it, but, alas, you believe that consent doesn't matter. I think it odd to say that a person whose belief in the legitimacy of a ruler depends on the belief that one's consent is irrelevant to legitimacy has consented to be ruled.

More plausibly, descriptive legitimacy might be a necessary but not sufficient condition of normative legitimacy. This would be so if some measure of effectiveness were a condition for the justified exercise of coercive control, and the perception of justification were necessary for effectiveness. We will explore this point in Chapter 3, "All Foundings Are Forced."

Rather than Weber, we should return to the usage of Rousseau. When Rousseau in the opening lines of *The Social Contract* famously writes, "Man is born free, and everywhere he is in chains. . . . How did this change occur? I do not know. What can make it legitimate [*légitime*]? I believe I can answer this question," he is using legitimacy in the full-throated normative sense, a sense that is both historically and conceptually prior to Weber's.[18] For Rousseau, legitimacy does not simply mean the social fact of legality. What are our chains, if not existing legal and political institutions? Though everywhere we are under law, the legitimacy of such law for Rousseau is an open question, not a tautology. Again, one can make the substantive moral argument that the social fact of valid law is a necessary and sufficient condition for legitimate law, but this is a normative claim, not an analytic definition. For Rousseau, legitimate doesn't simply mean legal. Henceforth, when I refer to legitimacy unmodified, I mean normative, not descriptive, legitimacy.

III. Word, Concept, and Conception

Let us now turn to the second set of distinctions: the word legitimacy, the concept or idea of legitimacy, and particular conceptions of legitimacy—the content of the concept. I will begin by making an elementary and obvious point about words and concepts that has, in our case, an insufficiently appreciated implication. Take the word "bank." You say a bank is a good place to put your money, and I say not unless you like your dollars soggy. You mean the financial institution and I mean the side of a river, and we do not have a real disagreement between us. As with the polite boxer's "civil right," we are using the same word to refer to two different concepts, and so we are talking past each other. What conceptual analysis does is help figure out when we are having a real disagreement and when we are just talking past each other.

With banks, however, there is an etymological twist. "Bank" first means a raised mound of earth, as in a riverbank. By analogy, the word comes also to mean a long platform, table, or raised set of stalls—what looks like a riverbank. From there, we get the stalls or the tables of moneychangers, eventually followed by the financial institutions we call banks. So riverbanks and money banks have a common linguistic history. We might imagine some simple soul schlepping along, as etymological baggage, the idea that banks have to have something to do with raised mounds. He might think that, to really be a bank, there must be a teller behind a counter, or somewhere in the basement vault there must be a raised mound of bullion. An internet website whose deposits are simply entries in a database cannot be a bank. That, he says, is a conceptual error. This is, of course, foolish. Perhaps a substantive argument can be mounted in defense of tellers and gold deposits, but it will not be an argument about the proper meaning of the word bank.

The word "legitimacy" also comes with baggage, and if we want conceptual clarity, we had better pack lightly. The connection between actual political rule and rightful political rule has, of course, always been a central question in political philosophy, and one that takes on a special urgency during the religious strife of the early modern period, when so much of our current political vocabulary is shaped. But "legitimate" and "illegitimate" as the normative terms of art that characterize this connection arrive late on the scene, and, because of earlier uses, nearly always present problems of interpretation.

A striking shift in the normative terminology used to refer to rightful rulers began during the French Wars of Religion in the late sixteenth century. Before, the term "legitimacy" simply meant lawfulness, so that a "legitimate king" was a lawful king and a "legitimate law" was a redundancy. Around that time, legitimacy began to be used as a normative property that law and lawful rulers could have or fail to have, so that, by Rousseau, the open normative question of the legitimacy of law can be posed in so many words.

To be clear, the question was never unaskable; the change that I am flagging is terminological, not conceptual, or at least, not unambiguously conceptual. What begins to happen around the French Wars of Religion, and is firmly in place by Rousseau's time, is that the question is askable in so many words. In between, however, depending on the conceptual map and normative commitments of the writer—in particular, depending on the author's position on the connections between God's law, natural law, positive law, and morality—"legitimate" may mean simply lawful (if valid positive law can be at odds with natural law or morality), simply rightful (if morality can be at odds with valid positive law), lawful because rightful (if valid law simply is the natural law), or rightful because lawful (if the command of God or of the sovereign creates moral obligation). Alternatively, the author may be deploying a concept that simply does not distinguish lawful from rightful.

We should not, however, be too quick to suppose that early modern writers divided their conceptual space in ways that are distant from ours. Many years ago, I was taught that Buddhism was utterly transformed when it migrated from India to China because the Chinese had no word for zero, and so could not conceive of nothingness. I thought this profound, perhaps because a sophomore lacks the concept of sophomoric. But consider: Hongren, the fifth patriarch of Chan, has one robe and one bowl. He gives them to Huineng, choosing him as the sixth patriarch. How many robes and bowls are left in the fifth patriarch's head?

The source of any strangeness about the use of terms may be closer to the surface, in a different account of the content of, and criteria for, recognizing legal and moral rights and duties. For example, the king's prerogative to contravene common and statutory law was defended by Stuart absolutists in two ways, which showed two different ways of understanding the connection between valid law and legitimacy. On one account, the king's exercise of his prerogative was legitimate because it was lawful, since the king's command made new law; on another account, the king's prerogative was the legitimate exercise of an extralegal power, which morally overrode, but did not become, the law.[19] This intramural disagreement among royal absolutists is best understood as substantive, not conceptual. There is a difference between the view that "legitimate" simply means lawful and the view that the necessary and sufficient condition for being legitimate is this other property, lawfulness. If we fail to make this distinction, we are liable to misinterpret the thought of the writer.

The earliest work I have found that uses "legitimacy" as the primary normative term of art by which to evaluate rulers is the *Vindiciae Contra Tyrannos,* a remarkable contribution to the Huguenot resistance literature published in 1579 but probably written around 1575. The weight of recent scholarship attributes this justification of resistance to tyranny to Philippe du Plessis-Mornay (1549–1623), a young Protestant aristocrat who served Henri of Navarre as a military officer, diplomat, and counselor—though authorship may have been shared with his older friend, Hubert Languet (1518–1581).[20] Written in the aftermath of the St. Bartholomew's Day Massacres of 1572, the *Vindiciae* is the most developed and the most influential of the French Protestant works of political thought that address the question of justified resistance. It is not the most original—that distinction goes to either François Hotman's *Francogallia* or Théodore Beza's *Right of Magistrates.* But unlike Hotman, Beza, or the major absolutist writer of the day, Bodin, the *Vindiciae* repeatedly deploys the term legitimacy as a normative property of rulers that does not simply mean legality or procedural correctness.

As Edmund's complaint attests, the term legitimacy also comes down to us with the sense of proper birth. A legitimate child is a child born of a lawful marriage. Almost all instances of *legitimus* in medieval scholarship on Roman law concern the laws of inheritance. In a world where kings are the lawful rulers and the firstborn legitimate son ordinarily is the proper successor to the throne, political legitimacy can seem to be inextricably a matter of pedigree or procedure, a property of rulers who are not bastard kings. Commentators on *Lear* standardly point out that Edmund confuses primogeniture with bastardy when he complains,

> . . . Wherefore should I
> Stand in the plague of custom and permit
> The curiosity of nations to deprive me,
> For that I am some twelve or fourteen moonshines
> Lag of a brother? . . .

But Edmund is not confused—he is taking aim, not merely at the status of natural children in England, but at pedigreed conceptions of *political* legitimacy in the customary law of nations. Edmund doesn't simply want to be acknowledged. He wants to rule.

In commenting on the 2000 election, William F. Buckley captured (and lampooned) the sensibility that ties political legitimacy too tightly to paternity:

> Never mind, for the moment, whether the true Florida count will
> be ascertainable. . . . What can be generated here is a mood: Is that
> man really the father of that child? . . . Did "the people" really bear
> George W. Bush as president? . . . What is raised is the question of
> legitimacy as rising from the loins of "the people": the ultimate
> mystique of self-government, the transubstantiation of the single
> voter who, begetting a majority, creates a legitimate government.[21]

You can almost hear the irony of Edmund. Fine word, legitimate!

IV. Tyrants without Title and Tyrants by Practice

What was the normative term of art employed to refer to rightful or wrongful rule before the switch in meaning of legitimacy and illegitimacy? The ancient and medieval term was *tyranny*. Tyranny named a wrongful or improper regime, and tyrant named a wrongful or improper ruler. While the term legitimacy gains currency as a normative attribute of regimes and rulers in the early modern period, the term tyranny loses some of its normative force. Tyranny becomes in Machiavelli a descriptive term of a type of regime, not a normative attribute of regimes, and Hobbes demotes the term tyranny entirely to epithet: "one and the same *monarch* is given the name *King* to honour him, the name of *Tyrant* to damn him."[22]

The most articulated account of tyranny is to be found in the treatise *De Tyrannia* by the prominent fourteenth century Italian jurist, Bartolus of Sassoferrato.[23] He systematizes the accounts found in Aristotle and Aquinas, and in turn is the source for Mornay's *Vindiciae Contra Tyrannos*. Bartolus draws a crucial distinction between two conditions for tyranny: the tyrant by defect in title and the tyrant by practice.[24] A ruler can fail to have the right to rule for two different reasons: he can gain power through improper means or he can exercise power improperly. A ruler who oppresses his subjects, or who impoverishes or brings suffering upon his people, commits acts of tyranny, and so is a tyrant, even if he has gained his title through lawful procedures or proper pedigree. Bartolus is clear that, though there are two different criteria for becoming a tyrant, both result equally in tyrants that have equal normative standing: their commands do not obligate, and it is morally permissible to resist their rule with force (within limits).

One reason why the *Vindiciae Contra Tyrannos* is such a fascinating transitional work is that Mornay fully accepts these two conditions for wrongful rule—tyranny without title and tyranny by practice—and also considers both types of tyrant to lack the property of legitimacy. So, on Mornay's account, a king could have lawful title to the throne—that is, not be illegitimate in the pedigreed sense that bastards are illegitimate—and could have promulgated conventionally lawful commands, but nonetheless fail to be a legitimate ruler because the substantive content of his commands is unjust to his subjects in ways that meet Mornay's conditions of tyranny by practice.

Why this intellectual history lesson? Because an account of the linguistic baggage that comes along with the term legitimacy provides a plausible error theory for why, in both popular usage and in quite a bit of contemporary political philosophy, legitimacy is closely and exclusively tied to pedigree or procedure. This, I believe, is to make either the mistake of what I shall call *conceptual proceduralism* or the mistake of *normative proceduralism*. Conceptual proceduralism is the mistaken view that "legitimate" simply means "procedurally proper." On this view, it is incoherent to claim that law enacted in compliance with proper procedures by lawmakers that have proper title can be illegitimate in virtue of the substantive content of the resulting law. We may disagree about what makes for proper title: I may think only the first-born son of the previous king anointed by the prophet of the one true god is the legitimate ruler, and you may think only legislators elected freely and fairly under the provisions of a democratic constitution are legitimate. But if we are using the concept of legitimacy correctly, we must agree that legitimacy is a content-independent matter. The content of legislation may be just or unjust, good or bad; but legitimacy is an attribute of title and procedure.

In contrast, my view is that the concept of legitimacy is quite a bit thinner and less restrictive: it refers simply to the moral right to rule. (More precisely, legitimacy is the moral *power* to rule, using power in the Hohfeldian sense, and not necessarily a moral *claim-right*. I argue for this view in Chapter 2, "Legitimacy without the Duty to Obey.") Normative argument, not conceptual analysis, is required to determine whether the content of the concept, the necessary and sufficient conditions for having legitimacy, makes reference solely to pedigree and procedure or also includes substantive criteria. When Mornay declares that tyrants by practice, though they have lawful title, are illegitimate, he may be wrong, but he is not incoherent.

Normative proceduralism, in contrast, is a mistake about the correct normative conception of legitimacy. On this view, although it is not incoherent to hold that the substantive content of laws and policies matter to their legitimacy, it is incorrect, because according to the right normative conception, the necessary and sufficient conditions for having legitimacy turn out to be entirely matters of title and procedure, and not matters of substantive goodness or justice.

I argue for three claims. First, I aim to make conceptual room for what I shall call the *substantive* account of political legitimacy by showing why conceptual proceduralism is mistaken. Second, I will begin to fill in the space so created by arguing that a substantive account of political legitimacy is not only conceptually possible, but is normatively attractive—and so normative proceduralism is mistaken. Third, I will argue that, despite our deep intuitions, the procedure of consent cannot ground political legitimacy.

V. Against Conceptual Proceduralism

I propose to check lawfulness and pedigree, the two pieces of conceptual baggage just discussed, at the door. The connections, if any, between legitimate rule, lawful rule, and pedigreed rulers are not conceptually necessary—they are not built into the very idea of legitimacy. Rather, such connections are features of particular conceptions of legitimacy—the content and criteria of the concept—that must be established through moral argument. The concept of legitimacy—in our rough draft, the moral right to rule—puts fewer constraints on possible conceptions than one might at first think. When I claim that a ruler is legitimate just in case he is God's anointed lieutenant on earth, and you claim a ruler is legitimate just in case she protects the basic rights and liberties of her subjects, we disagree about the criteria for having moral legitimacy, but we agree, roughly, about what the disagreement is about. Unlike with riverbanks and money banks, we are not talking past each other.

The concept of legitimacy itself makes no essential reference to procedure or pedigree, so "a government is morally legitimate if and only if it is morally good" is a possible conception. Edmund offers another possible substantive conception: "Why bastard? Wherefore base? / When my dimensions are as well compact, / My mind as generous, and my shape as true, / As honest madam's issue?" Why are you reaching for pedigreed criteria for political legitimacy? Look at me! I've got all these fine features. Why shouldn't the right to rule follow from the qualities of the ruler, rather than his origins?

But neither does the concept make an essential reference to substantive goodness, justness, or all-things-considered moral correctness. Possible conceptions of legitimacy can refer exclusively to an authoritative text, or a line of familial descent, or the enactments of a legislative body. Particular conceptions of legitimacy might specify either some procedure or some substantive attribute or both as necessary or sufficient conditions. If legitimacy is the right to rule, there are many coherent ways to fill in the conditions for having that right.

Legitimacy is usefully distinguished from two other concepts: justice, on the one hand, and legal validity, on the other. On some conceptions, these concepts are coextensive: one could hold the view that a law is valid if and only if it is legitimate, and one could hold that a law is legitimate if and only if it is substantively just. But the three concepts pick out three different properties that a law can have. In particular, we should resist the temptation to see legitimacy as merely justice-lite. One might, in the end, conclude that a legitimate legal system is simply the system that comes as close to justice as is feasible under the circumstances, but that is the conclusion of a normative argument, not a conceptual starting point.[25]

The concept of valid law makes no essential reference to moral justification. Valid law refers simply to the institutional fact of the matter of what counts as the law for those who are subject to it. If validity is an institutional fact, it depends on shared understandings. It is quite plausible to suppose that cultures would include a shared understanding of normative legitimacy as a condition of legal validity, even if such a condition is not a formal requirement for having a shared understanding about valid law. But what a culture considers to be legitimate is not, by itself, legitimate. Cultural understandings about legitimacy can be mistaken. It may be a social fact about a people that their laws are valid only if widely believed to be legitimate, and they may in fact believe their laws to be legitimate, and yet their laws, though valid, may fail to be legitimate.[26] If this is baffling to your ear, you are not yet tuned to my distinction between descriptive and normative legitimacy.

One could argue that built into the very concept of legal validity is the claim of normative legitimacy—Weber's *Legitimitätsanspruch*—or beliefs about normative legitimacy—*Legitimitätsglaube*. This may be so, but neither the *claim* of normative legitimacy by rulers nor the *belief* by the ruled that this claim succeeds gets us all the way to normative legitimacy, for such claims and beliefs can be mistaken.

On particular conceptions of legal validity, laws are valid only if they are morally legitimate, or only if they are just. But valid law doesn't simply mean morally legitimate law or just law. A natural lawyer and a legal positivist disagree about what counts as valid law, but they agree about what they are disagreeing about. If the Kosovo Report is mistaken, and there is no wedge to be driven between legality and legitimacy, it is not a conceptual error that Justice Goldstone has made. To defeat the Kosovo Report, one has to provide a moral argument. If Richard Gephardt errs in suggesting that George W. Bush, though legal, is not legitimate, it is not a conceptual error. To show that Gephardt is mistaken, one has to provide a moral argument to demonstrate that the content of legitimacy is not what he supposes it is.

Conceptual proceduralism is guilty of prematurely closing off an open normative question. Suppose you hold that a ruler who engages in massive human rights atrocities becomes illegitimate, even if elected to office in a fair democratic procedure, and even if the massive atrocities are not violations of the conventional laws of the land. It would be question-begging of me to insist that you are misusing the concept of legitimacy, and to claim that a legitimate ruler *just is* a ruler who is properly selected and conventionally lawful. The idea of the right to rule marks off fruitful space for disagreement; since at least Rousseau, the name of that idea has been "legitimacy." We are not talking past each other: we are having a normative disagreement about the content of the concept.

VI. Against Normative Proceduralism

Recall that normative proceduralism is the claim that the necessary and sufficient conditions for having political legitimacy—that is, the right to rule—turn out to be entirely matters of title and procedure, and not matters of goodness or justice or some other substantive consideration. The well-known and standard argument for normative proceduralism is that disagreement about the goodness or justice of rules and rulers is pervasive and permanent. In the face of such substantive disagreement, the only way to live together fairly and peacefully is by appeal to procedural criteria for settling our substantive differences. If instead we were to hold that the legitimacy of our institutions depended on substantive standards, but disagreed about what those substantive standards were or whether they were met, we would have no way to go forward together that didn't involve, in some combination, mutual disrespect, resentment, political instability, or even violence. Citizens will of course not only disagree about the values government should realize and the purposes government should pursue, but also disagree about which procedures are more or less likely to realize these values and achieve these purposes. But how are we to resolve our disagreements about the procedures themselves other than by following our procedures for changing our procedures?

The two procedural criteria that have demonstrated quite a bit of acceptance and robustness in the face of substantive disagreement are, in some combination, the rule of law and majority rule. These two criteria are fitted together in some way, so that legitimate law is law chosen, in accordance with the laws of lawmaking, by lawmakers chosen by majorities in accordance with the laws of choosing lawmakers that in turn have been chosen by lawmakers who themselves have been chosen by majorities in accordance with laws. Nothing, however, can guarantee that a set of existing procedures will be judged by all citizens to properly satisfy the criteria of the rule of law and majority rule, and nothing can guarantee that all citizens will hold that the rule of law and majority rule are the correct and only standards. If normative proceduralism is to be internally consistent, it cannot appeal to an external account of what the rule of law or majority rule or any other criterion requires as the *final* arbiters of legitimacy—that would involve adopting a substantive standard as a test of the legitimacy of a procedure. If normative proceduralism is correct, then if we disagree about procedural criteria, there is no alternative to relying on some higher-order procedure or another, under the jurisdiction of some procedurally established institution or another, to decide whether political practices are legitimate. Constitutions need to be adopted and amended, legislation enacted, and legal cases decided by some procedure. When justices of the Supreme Court—the exemplar of a countermajoritarian institution—disagree on the substance of law, they settle their disagreements by the procedure of majority rule.[27]

Now, the case against. This argument for normative proceduralism confuses methods for achieving legitimacy and criteria of legitimacy. Of course, as a pragmatic matter, political decisions need to be made one way or another, by some actors or others, and some ways of making decisions by some actors are more likely than other ways by other actors to result in laws and policies that satisfy the criteria of legitimacy. What more can we expect of political actors than that the best method of decision be employed? Perhaps nothing more, but that is consistent with the possibility of failure: the best method for achieving legitimacy can still misfire. Now, something important may follow from the observation that, *ex ante*, the most that we can demand of political actors is that they follow the correct procedures and employ the best methods of decision. If they do so, that might exempt them from blame or criticism of a certain sort. But it does not follow that their mistakes are legitimate. We haven't yet explored what legitimacy gets you, but if legitimacy gets you a claim to obedience, or at least some measure of respect, deference, or immunity from interference, following the correct procedures cannot ensure that achievement.

A perspicuous way to put this point borrows a distinction made by Nomy Arpaly in a different context.[28] There is a difference between the contents of a user's manual for an intendedly legitimate actor and a theory of legitimacy containing necessary and sufficient conditions for legitimate action. Critics of a substantive conception of legitimacy rightly insist that, *ex ante,* an actor who aims to act legitimately should in effect follow the best instruction manual for legitimate actors, and that manual cannot help but be procedural. I don't deny this, but from the first-person, *ex ante* point of view, one ought to follow not only the legitimate actor's manual but also the just and good actor's manuals, which ordinarily are more demanding. Although I have made space for actions that are unjust but legitimate, no political actor reasoning from the first-person point of view may reasonably argue that he is morally permitted to commit an all-things-considered moral wrong on the grounds that he is legitimately empowered to make such mistakes. Rather, one must not intend to make moral mistakes.

So for whom are judgments of legitimacy binding constraints on action? One important case is the political actor with a plan for substantively just or good action who asks herself, from the *ex ante* first-person point of view, if she has the proper authority to carry out her plan. She cannot escape using the legitimate actor's manual. But judgments of legitimacy have their primary bite from the second- and third-person perspectives. Legitimacy arises as a problem for subjects, observers, and implementers who judge a political action or instruction to be unjust or bad. From those perspectives, however, the legitimacy of an observed actor *can* be evaluated on other than procedural grounds. They can say to the actor, even if it is so that no method other than the one you followed had a better chance of generating legitimate law, still, you failed to generate legitimate law. The practical upshot of such an evaluation from the point of view of the second or third party may justify disobedience, resistance, or intervention. *Ex post,* the actor herself can occupy second- or third-person perspectives on her past actions, and evaluate whether she succeeded or failed. The practical upshot of such an evaluation from the *ex post* point of view of the actor may require remorse, revision, or remedy. So following the best method for producing legitimate law doesn't *constitute* legitimate law any more than following the best recipe for crème brûlée constitutes crème brûlée. The proof of the pudding is in the eating.

This argument for a substantive conception rejects what we might call, paraphrasing John Rawls, *pure procedural legitimacy*—the claim that the results of some actual legislative procedures necessarily have legitimate authority, whatever the law's content. There is much to be said for *hypothetical* pure proceduralism in contemporary moral and political philosophy, of course, the most prominent examples being Rawls's constructivism and T. M. Scanlon's contractualism.[29] But this approach employs philosophical imagination to construct idealized hypothetical agents with idealized motivations or intentions or in idealized choice situations in order to model or represent a moral idea that is instantiated by what would be unanimously endorsed under the idealizations. *Actual* pure procedural legitimacy is the very different idea that there is some set of actual procedures that, when followed by actual agents with actual motivations and intentions, has legitimate authority over actual subjects, no matter what content results.[30] I've already concluded that it is question-begging to hold that actual pure proceduralism is a conceptual necessity. Considered as a normative claim, actual pure procedural legitimacy rests on a mistake about its own grounds of justification.

Rawls defines a pure procedure as a procedure for which "there is no independent criterion for the right result."[31] The example he gives is gambling. "If a number of persons engage in a series of fair bets, the distribution of cash after the last bet is fair, or at least not unfair, whatever this distribution is."[32] Let's unpack this. There is a normative standard, fairness. There is a procedure, playing a game of chance in accordance with its rules, and these rules are subject to background conditions that, on some account of what fairness requires, make the game fair. Notice how much turns on the off-stage conditions of what makes a procedure fair. In the gambling example, Rawls gives a non-exhaustive list of conditions for a fair bet: that it is entered into voluntarily, that no one cheats, that the expected gain for each player is zero. We might and he might have added other conditions: that the parties be well-informed; that neither party is exploited (on some theory of exploitation); that the stakes not require wrongdoing (as in Russian roulette or Faustian bargains). The point is that one needs to feed an external theory of fairness into the specification of the procedure before it is the case that the procedure constitutes fairness, whatever the outcome is. The content of this theory of fairness is the conclusion of a philosophical argument, not a choice endogenous to the actual procedure. Rawls does not say that what makes a game of chance a pure procedure is that gamblers follow rules they believe to be fair, or even that gamblers have a procedure they believe to be fair for writing the procedures of gambling they believe to be fair. Rather, the outcome of a gamble is fair when, on the *correct* account of fairness, the rules are fair.

What is the parallel construction of pure procedural legitimacy? There is a normative standard, legitimacy, which, on our rough draft of the concept, is the moral right to rule. There is a procedure, enacting laws in accordance with the rules of legislating, subject to background conditions that, on some account of what legitimacy requires, constitute a legitimate procedure. What are these legitimacy-making background conditions? As with fair gambling, we need to feed an external theory of legitimacy into the specification of the procedure before it can be the case that legislative procedures constitute legitimate law, whatever the content of the laws are. The bare-bones concept of legitimacy, understood as the right to rule, isn't yet such a theory. Perhaps we discover the correct conception of legitimacy through the philosophical method of a hypothetical armchair procedure, or through some other way of reasoning, but it is not a choice endogenous to the actual procedures of the voters, legislators, and constitutional framers in question. There is always a place to stand from which we can ask if those who follow a recipe for crème brûlée succeed in making crème brûlée.

Rawls supplies us with a much larger and more important example of pure procedural justice than gambling. He holds that economic outcomes for particular individuals are fair, whatever they may be, on the condition that these outcomes are the result of institutions that satisfy his theory of justice. That is, when the basic structure of society guarantees equal basic rights and liberties, provides fair equality of opportunity, and arranges inequalities of wealth and income for the greatest benefit of the least advantaged, then the distributive shares of individuals resulting from the workings of these institutions are fair, whatever they might be. But again, the fairness-making background conditions are given by philosophical reflection, not by actual legislative procedures. On his four-stage sequence, a particular outcome is fair, whatever it might be, if it results from laws that hypothetical legislators would enact in conformity with a constitution that hypothetical constitutional framers would ratify in conformity with principles of justice that hypothetical contractors would adopt in the original position.[33] Rawls clearly rejects the view that actual democratic decision-making itself is a pure procedure. After arguing that parties at the constitutional stage of the original position would adopt some form of majority rule, but "agree to put up with unjust laws only under some conditions," he says, "It is evident from the preceding remarks that the procedure of majority rule, however it is defined, has a subordinate place as a procedural device."[34] What follows? "There is nothing to the view, then, that what the majority wills is right. In fact, none of the traditional conceptions of justice have held this doctrine, maintaining always that the outcome of voting is subject to political principles."[35] Rather, with one limited exception, the best that actual procedures aiming to frame a constitution or write legislation can do is be what Rawls calls an *imperfect procedure*. "The characteristic mark of imperfect procedural justice is that while there is an independent criterion for the correct outcome, there is no feasible procedure which is sure to lead to it."[36] Substitute legitimacy for justice, and this describes our predicament.

The exception, and the closest Rawls comes to suggesting that democracy itself is a pure procedure, is when he acknowledges that the test of what justice requires of legislation is sometimes indeterminate. When actual legislation is within the range of laws that could have been chosen by ideal, rational legislators (that is to say, within a range acceptable by his theory of justice), "we must fall back upon a notion of quasi-pure procedural justice," meaning that, within the range the theory allows, we are to consider the law just, whatever it may be.[37] When this is so, "the decision of the majority is practically authoritative, though not definitive."[38] On this we can agree, but it is hardly an endorsement of normative proceduralism. For such legislation to have legitimate authority, notice how constrained it is by conclusions about a substantive theory of justice and a substantive ideal constitution that are not themselves the outcomes of an actual pure procedure.

For a pure procedural account of legitimacy to succeed, the normative proceduralist would have to defend a theory of legitimacy that treated the actual rule-making procedures of a political society as somehow self-legitimating. Such a theory would have to avoid not only external criteria to test particular legislative outcomes, but avoid external criteria to test the procedure itself. Such an account wouldn't be a conception of normative legitimacy at all, but something very different—a social scientific account of descriptive legitimacy. But perhaps there can be external normative criteria that are pump-priming or self-replicating, in that, once a procedure meets it, all downstream procedures enacted in accord with it are legitimate, whatever their content. There is such a self-replicating theory of normative legitimacy, and it is so widely held and deeply revered, that you must be wondering why it has taken me so long to mention it. Do we not hold it to be a self-evident truth that governments derive their just powers from the consent of the governed? It remains for me to show that governments not only do not derive their legitimacy from consent, but cannot.

VII. Legitimacy without the Consent of the Governed

The founding document of the United States declares:

> We hold these Truths to be self-evident, that all Men are created equal, that they are endowed by their Creator with certain unalienable Rights, that among these are Life, Liberty and the Pursuit of Happiness—That to secure these Rights, Governments are instituted among Men, deriving their just Powers from the Consent of the Governed. . . . [39]

Only a cynic, fool, or liar would deny being moved by these words, but they are not all truths, much less self-evident truths. Thomas Jefferson's rough draft shows multiple cross-outs and insertions here, making the claim to self-evidence amusingly self-effacing. My purpose, however, is not to take on the assertion of self-evidence, but to examine the truth of the claim that governments derive their just powers from the consent of the governed.

We hold two intuitions about legitimacy rather deeply, though not literally. The first is that political legitimacy requires, in some sense, the consent of the governed. The second is that political legitimacy is acquired only through proper pedigree or procedure. Together, we might call these intuitions the *consensual pedigree folk theory*. Any account of political legitimacy needs to explain how an authority's right to govern attaches to a particular subject. The folk theory's answer is that each individual subject consents (in some way) to be governed by an authority who has the proper pedigree (in some way), where properness traces back to some earlier collective agreements among some predecessors. The two prongs of the theory, consent and pedigree, need each other: consent unbounded by pedigree is unstable; pedigree free of consent is oppressive. Theory of course is too strong. Few upon reflection hold that political societies are founded only upon the explicit consent of individuals who unanimously contract to institute procedures of governance by majority rule. Nonetheless, the folk theory still exerts pull on us, and will continue to do so until a better alternative is found.

Consider a first pass at posing with some precision the opening claim of the Declaration of Independence, that "Governments are instituted among Men, deriving their just Powers from the consent of the Governed":

Declaration
1. Governments are legitimate if they are instituted so that they derive their just powers from the consent of the governed.
2. Democracies are instituted so that they derive their just powers from the consent of the governed.
   Therefore:
3. Democracies are legitimate.[40]

Echoing the two prongs of the consensual pedigree folk theory, governments are instituted and the normative power of this institution derives from consent. But this formulation is not sufficiently explicit about who is consenting to what, so consider:

Individual *Ab Ovo* Consent
1. A government is legitimate with respect to an individual if it derives its powers from that individual's genuine consent to an original social contract among other founding contractors.
2. Democracies derive their powers from the genuine consent of such individuals to such an original social contract.
   Therefore:
3. Democracies are legitimate.

Locke gamely insists that such consensual founding moments actually happened, and if there is no record in history of such a social contract, no matter: we do not doubt that the soldiers of Salmanasser or Xerxes were once children, though history does not record it.[41] Of course, no reader needs to be convinced that this is not how legitimate governments are actually founded. Facticity aside, the deeper problem here is possibility. Consider a conversation that might have occurred in the summer of 1776:

> *Reg:* There is no pedigreed procedure by which a band of malcontent planters and merchants gathered in Philadelphia has the normative power to declare the independence of thirteen colonies from the British crown.

> *Reb:* The men who are assembled in Philadelphia are authorized representatives of their respective colonial assemblies and together constitute the Continental Congress.

> *Reg:* There is no pedigreed procedure by which the assemblies of British colonies have the normative power to constitute such a congress and grant it authority to revolt against the crown.

> *Reb:* But that's what a revolution *is:* a discontinuity in pedigreed procedure!

> *Reg:* Then by what newly invented procedure does a band of malcontent planters and merchants sent by thirteen other bands of malcontent planters and merchants have the normative power to speak for the free and enslaved, landed and landless, European, African, and Indian, male and female inhabitants of the land? Like the Baron Münchausen, the so-called Continental Congress attempts to lift itself out of the swamp by its own hair.

The infinite regress fatal to the consensual pedigree folk theory is easily seen: before the results of any procedure can count as granting consent of the governed, that procedure needs to be enacted by an earlier procedure that grants the consent of the governed, and that consent-granting procedure must itself be enacted by a consent-granting procedure, and so on down the bottomless turtle stack. Members of the Continental Congress recognized the problem. The Dunlap Broadside, the version of the Declaration printed on the night of July 4 and pasted into the Congress journal, is entitled "A DECLARATION BY THE REPRESENTATIVES OF THE UNITED STATES OF AMERICA, IN GENERAL CONGRESS ASSEMBLED." The July 19 resolution that the declaration be fairly engrossed on parchment and signed by every member of Congress changes the title to "The unanimous declaration of the thirteen United States of America." Now the document boldly asserts that the states themselves, not merely their representatives whose pedigree might be questioned, have declared independence, and the states have done so unanimously, not by some other counting procedure whose pedigree might be questioned. Still, the questions remain.

Would the actual contemporaneous unanimity contemplated by Locke block the procedural regress? Consider:

The Godfather

Michael explains to his girlfriend, Kay, how his father, Don Corleone, convinced Johnny Fontane's band leader to release him from his commitments:

Michael: My father made him an offer he couldn't refuse.

Kay: What was that?

Michael: Luca Brasi held a gun to his head, and my father assured him that either his brains or his signature would be on the contract.[42]

Michael says that the Godfather makes an offer that could not be refused, but for that reason it could not be *accepted,* if by acceptance we mean genuinely informed and free acceptance. For consent to ordinary transactions, coerced consent does not change the normative situation of the person tokening consent in that it does not permit what had been prohibited or require what had been optional. Against a lawless background, all agreements are in a sense coerced, because without law, our rights against others are indeterminate and insecure. If a revolution indeed is a discontinuity in pedigreed procedure, then the relations of one to another are—for a time—lawless, and so subject to each other's fear or favor. Hobbes famously bites this bullet, claiming not only that coerced agreements bind but that *only* coerced agreements bind. But then Hobbes thinks that liberty is compatible with necessity in the way that water is free to run downhill. We might want more out of freedom than that.[43]

Perhaps we err in trying to locate the consent of the governed in the consent of each individual. Consider:

Group *Ab Ovo* Consent

1. Governments are legitimate if they derive their powers from The People's genuine consent to an original social contract.

2. Democracies derive their powers from The People's genuine consent to an original contract.
Therefore:
3. Democracies are legitimate.

But this will not do. How are The People constituted, if not through some sort of pedigreed procedure to which they have consented through some pedigreed procedure? Again, we face turtles all the way down.

Maybe a consensual account of founding moments is an insolvable blind alley. Still, perhaps the genuine consent of individual citizens in an ongoing political society, however formed, is both necessary and sufficient for its legitimacy. Consider:

Individual *In Medias Res* Consent
1. A government is legitimate with respect to an individual if it derives its powers from that individual's genuine consent to join in an existing social contract.
2. Democracies derive their powers from the genuine consent of such individuals to such existing social contracts.
Therefore:
3. Democracies are legitimate.

If we suppose that, in a way that still needs to be explained, the existing social contract creates a lawful condition, individuals who token consent *in medias res* are not coerced by a lawless state of nature, but their consent may still be defective in some way. No one today has a real alternative to living within the jurisdiction of one state or another, most of us cannot lawfully choose our country of citizenship, and even for those of us who can, leaving one's culture and language of origin is for most not a reasonable option. But I wish to focus on another difficulty, which is that those who invoke *in medias res* consent typically deny that such consent can be refused. Consider:

Johnny and Consent
In elementary school, Johnny read in the Declaration of Independence that governments derive "their just powers from the consent of the governed." Ever since, Johnny has worn a sign around his neck that says, "I do not consent to be governed." Johnny is now an adult. Has Johnny consented to be governed?

Note that I am not asking if the United States has "just powers" to govern Johnny, or if Johnny has a moral obligation to obey US law. Perhaps it does and he does for reasons that do not depend on his consent. Rather, I am asking if, despite his denial, he has given genuine consent.

Most of us do not give express consent to be governed. Unless one is a naturalized citizen, a government official, or a soldier, the opportunity to give express consent does not usually arise. So perhaps when it comes to consent to be governed, the ordinary default that only "yes" means yes is reversed, and consent is presumed. But surely, then, it must be possible to rebut the presumption, or else "no" also means yes. Has Johnny rebutted the presumption? If not in this way, then what would he have to do to rebut it? If there is no way for Johnny to rebut it, then there must be two kinds of consent: the consent that we consent to and the consent that we do not consent to—the offers that we can possibly refuse and the offers that we cannot possibly refuse. Genuine consent has great normative power: it permits actions that otherwise are forbidden and it requires actions that otherwise are optional. Consent turns what would be theft into gift and slaves into employees. It obligates us to show up or pay up, though we have changed our minds about how to spend our time or money. Is it not deeply unsettling to attribute these great normative powers to this second kind of consent, a consent that cannot possibly be withheld?

Perhaps Johnny has given *tacit* consent, because he has accepted the benefits of citizenship. So consider:

Johnny and Tacit Consent

In high school, Johnny read Locke:

> The difficulty is, what ought to be look'd upon as a *tacit Consent,* and how far it binds, *i.e.* how far any one shall be looked on to have consented, and thereby submitted to any Government, where he has made no Expressions of it at all. And to this I say, that every Man, that hath any Possession, or Enjoyment, of any part of the Dominions of any Government, doth thereby give his *tacit Consent,* and is as far forth obliged to Obedience to the Laws of that Government, during such Enjoyment, as any one under it; whether this his Possession be of Land, to him and his Heirs for ever, or a Lodging only for a Week; or whether it be barely travelling freely on the Highway.[44]

Ever since, before enjoying his possessions or traveling freely on the highway, Johnny has worn a sign around his neck that says, "I do not tacitly consent to submit to this government, and no one should infer from my enjoyment of my possessions or from my traveling freely on the highway that I have given my tacit consent." Johnny is now an adult. Has Johnny tacitly consented to be governed?

If tacit consent is a species of genuine consent, and if genuine consent is to have the normative power we attribute to it, then withholding tacit consent must be possible too. Perhaps the way tacit consent is supposed to work is that enjoying the benefits of citizenship is *evidence* of consent. If so, then such evidence must be rebuttable in some way. Perhaps traveling freely on the highway *tokens* consent, in that it is the socially recognized symbol of consent, the way that tugging on one's ear in an auction house tokens a bid. If so, then there must be a way for Johnny to refrain from such tokening short of remaining housebound for the rest of his life or deporting himself, neither of which are uncoerced alternatives. Or perhaps traveling freely on the highway *constitutes* consent, and it does so independent of any intention Johnny has. But then the worry that there are two kinds of consent returns, the kind that one has consented to and the kind that one has not. If so, it is hard to resist the well-known quip that tacit consent isn't worth the paper it's not written on.[45] Again, it could be that enjoying the benefits of citizenship creates political obligation. The fair play argument of H. L. A. Hart and John Rawls astutely notices that one can be obligated by the voluntary acceptance of benefits, else one is a free-rider.[46] But then it is unfairness, not consent, that is doing the normative work.

VIII.   From the Actual Egg to the Middle of a Possible Thing

Since their origin, social contract accounts of political legitimacy have changed in two complementary but distinguishable ways: first, the *ab ovo* question of how a legitimate political order is founded has been replaced by the *in medias res* question of what makes an ongoing political order legitimate. Second, the condition of actual consent, and the consequent specification of a contractual primal scene, has been replaced by conditions of possible or hypothetical consent, and the consequent specification of a philosophically convincing model of idealized agreement. The two developments are complementary, for once actual consent is seen as unnecessary (and perhaps insufficient) to ground political legitimacy, the search for both the normative specification of a legitimate founding and its historical moment may be called off. Says Rawls, "Political society is not, and cannot be, an association. We do not enter it voluntarily. Rather we simply find ourselves in a particular political society at a particular moment in time."[47] Indeed, for Kant, the search must be called off. "A people should not *inquire* with any practical aim in view into the origin of the supreme authority to which it is subject."[48]

For both Kant and Rawls, the double move away from actual consent at some historical founding moment is no concession to realist politics. Since almost all of the earth's inhabitants already live in ongoing political societies, the *in medias res* question is our question, and since almost all of the earth's inhabitants have no real alternative to living out their lives within the political society in which they are born, let alone the option of living outside of any political society, voluntary actual consent is not an option. The claim is not that most inhabitants do not consent, or will not consent. To have the conditions of legitimacy influenced by such facts indeed would be a concession, and therefore be political in the wrong way. Rather, if consent is a transaction between independent persons, rather than simply an approving mental state, inhabitants *cannot* give genuine consent: the background conditions make unforced consent impossible for most of us.

Why is consent thought to be so important? Genuine consent is normatively powerful: it sometimes transforms moral prohibitions into permissions, and permissions into requirements. It has this power because sometimes consent protects and extends our freedom. But consent doesn't always protect and extend our freedom, and consent isn't always needed to protect and extend our freedom. As Scanlon notes, we are prone to give consent outsized importance because sometimes, to permit one's treatment of another, consent is the last, most visible condition to be satisfied, obscuring from our view background conditions that often are necessary and sometimes are sufficient.[49]

To push this thought further, when individual consent does have normative power to permit and to obligate, it is not because consent is a potent content-independent procedure, but because consent changes the substantive content of actions and treatments. The clearest example of this is sex, where genuine consent is not a content-independent justificatory procedure, but a powerful transformer of content and meaning that differentiates lovemaking from rape. Having cautioned against letting our terms drive our concepts, I shouldn't make too much of the observation that "consensual rape" is an impossibility. But nor do I think it an accident that we employ thick, highly moralized, indeed, almost conclusory normative terms, such as "rape" and "murder," in cases where procedural authorization fails to provide sufficient justification. Consenting to be killed for thrills provides the would-be killer with no moral permission. Just as consent does not universally permit, it doesn't universally obligate. We do not generally enforce genuinely consensual personal service contracts by specific performance.

The solution to the puzzle of how individual self-governance and individual freedom are compatible with coercive law will be an *in medias res* solution, and it need not make and keep us free by way of consent. Even if the consent of the governed were possible, it would not be sufficient to underwrite a government's just powers. There is no pure procedure for legitimacy, in that the results of consensual or pedigreed procedures, whatever their content, are sufficient to create a right to rule. This follows from the crème brûlée account: the proof of the pudding is in the eating. If political legitimacy must meet both procedural and substantive criteria, then majoritarian practices and institutions do not guarantee legitimacy, and counter-majoritarian practices and institutions need not undermine legitimacy. The "Will of the People," insofar as the notion picks out something with normative power, is neither temporally nor conceptually prior to the institutions of governance that are said to speak for it. Either what can possibly count as the will of the people, or what gives the will of the people normative power, is constrained by substantive standards, so the design of legitimate institutions not only may but must be sensitive in some way to the realization of those substantive standards. Yes, I said it: to be legitimate, democratic procedures must be rigged.

This chapter has made conceptual room for substantive accounts of legitimacy. The most plausible conceptions, I believe, have both procedural criteria that specify a required connection between the governors and the governed, and substantive criteria that require the protection of at least a short list of basic rights and liberties. The connection between governors and governed cannot be consensual, and needn't be majoritarian, which is why substantive constraints on majority rule are not affronts to democracy. The procedure of majority rule is neither self-enacting nor self-justifying. This is a normative view in need of moral argument, rather than an entailment of the concept of legitimacy itself. I begin to develop this normative view, which I call the free group agency conception, in Chapter 3, "All Foundings Are Forced," and if you are eager to get to my moral argument you might want to skip ahead. I, however, am duty-bound to finish clearing the conceptual ground. Chapter 2, "Legitimacy without the Duty to Obey," explains why legitimacy is best understood as a moral power that entails moral liability, rather than a moral right that entails a moral duty.

Legitimacy without the Duty to Obey

The previous chapter argued that, despite the linguistic and historical association of the word illegitimacy with bastardy, the idea of political legitimacy is not essentially tied to notions of procedure or pedigree. Those who hold that governments and laws must meet substantive criteria to be legitimate are not making a conceptual mistake. This chapter presents the second plank in my analysis of the concept of legitimacy, the claim that legitimate authority does not necessarily entail for its subjects a moral duty to obey. I do not deny that, ordinarily, we have moral obligations to comply with legitimate laws, but why this is so and when this is so must be established by moral argument, not by definition. So I also reject the view that political legitimacy is merely the justified use of coercion. The claim that the exercise of legitimate authority entails the duty to obey is too strong, and the claim that the exercise of legitimate authority is merely command backed by permissible force is too weak. Mine is a Goldilocks view: legitimate authority is a moral power (which is more than mere permission) to create moral liabilities (but not necessarily moral duties).

Compared with the standard alternatives, the power-liability view gives us an explanation that makes better sense of the complicated judgments responsible citizens make when they confront legal demands that are either tragic or trifling. On the one hand, we need to explain why a conscientious citizen does not engage in civil disobedience lightly. On the other hand, we need to explain why driving five miles above the speed limit on a six-lane highway isn't invariably an immoral action that expresses contempt for our fellow citizens. What I mean by moral power and moral liability is the task ahead.

I. Must Legitimacy Entail Duty?

One standard view is that political legitimacy entails two other normative relations: the moral obligation of those legitimately ruled by the ruler to obey, and the moral immunity of the ruler from coercive interference in the exercise and enforcement of legitimate rule. On this view, it is incoherent to hold that an authority is legitimate, but that those subject to the authority are not morally obligated to comply with its commands, or that others are not morally disabled from stopping the legitimate authority from exercising its legitimate powers. To think that legitimate commands do not necessarily obligate is like thinking that parenthood does not necessitate children.

One important proponent of this view, John Simmons, claims that "state legitimacy is the logical correlate of various obligations, including subjects' political obligations."[1] If, as Simmons holds, a subject's consent or something like it is a necessary condition for a state to be legitimate with respect to that subject, then indeed a tight (but still, not airtight) connection between legitimacy and obligation would follow. For ordinarily, to what would the subject consent, if not to political obligation? But the consent of the governed is not itself a conceptual requirement of legitimacy: the view that a ruler is legitimate if and only if he has been anointed by the one true god is a mistake, but not a logical contradiction. So Simmons's view should be understood as a normative conception of legitimacy. Simmons thinks that rival conceptions of what makes a particular state legitimate with respect to particular subjects suffer from not being sufficiently distinguishable from accounts of what justifies the state—that is, accounts of what must be the case for the exercise of coercion by the state to be morally permissible. As will be explained shortly, I agree that legitimate authority is not merely justified coercion, and Simmons surely is correct that a complete account of legitimacy must connect particular subjects to particular authorities. But it does not follow that consent to obligation is the only possible way to make this connection.

I said earlier that it is a virtue in conceptual analysis to seek the least restrictive specification of a concept that is still useful and fruitful, because if we do not, we risk making two mistakes. The first is to misdescribe a genuine disagreement as a semantic misunderstanding. The second is to dismiss rival moral arguments too quickly as logical mistakes. In this case, the dismissal indeed is too quick. If the exercise of legitimate authority creates moral obligation, this is so for moral reasons. If legitimate authorities have immunity, it is not an analytic truth.

Joseph Raz is the contemporary philosopher who has made the strongest case for a conceptual connection between legitimate authority and obligation (though he has not, to my knowledge, taken a stand on immunity). Raz has convincingly argued that the exercise of legitimate authority by an actor entails some change in the normative situation or status of another. Otherwise, having authority cannot be distinguished from merely having a moral permission to causally affect another. To use one of Raz's examples, having the liberty to burn rubbish in my backyard despite the objections of my neighbor does not give me legitimate authority over my neighbor.[2] When we invoke legitimate authority, we ascribe to the actor something more powerful than merely a liberty or privilege. Raz says that this power is the power to obligate.[3]

I think Raz is right that legitimate authority is more powerful than mere permission, and it is a deep insight of his to recognize that this something more is the power to change the normative situation of others. But there may be other ways that legitimate authorities can change the normative situation of others aside from obligating them. If normative changes short of obligation can be found, then room is made for the commonly held view that disobeying legitimate law is not always morally wrong, and that sometimes one may disobey the law while still, in some sense, recognizing its claims.

Consider, for example, civil disobedience. If legitimate authority entails a dispositive duty to obey, civil disobedience disappears as a poignant moral phenomenon. If the authority is legitimate, disobedience is not justified. If, by assumption, disobedience is justified, then the authority that is disobeyed cannot have been legitimate. The Rawlsian account of nonviolent civil disobedience as an illegal practice that nonetheless expresses respect for and fidelity to the laws of a nearly just democratic society that has fallen short of its own aspirations is, on the legitimacy-entails-duty view, misconceived. When disobedience is justified, the authority that is disobeyed is not legitimate, is not due respect, and so presumably is a fair target for even sharper tactics of dissent, such as militant resistance or subversion. There may be other moral reasons to refrain from sharper tactics, but if any disobedience is justified, respect for democratic authority is not among those reasons. If you consider civil disobedience, when the conditions that justify it are met, to be an important form of dissent midway between lawful protest and armed insurrection, then you had better hope that there is some way to drive a wedge between legitimate authority and moral obligation. The way to drive the wedge is to recognize that the power of a legitimate authority to change the normative situation of the subject is not necessarily the power to obligate. But what else can that power be?

II. Legitimacy as a Hohfeldian Power

To get at what I think is the correct conceptual account of legitimacy, we need to return to the well-known analytic jurisprudence that Wesley Hohfeld developed early in the twentieth century.[4] Hohfeld distinguished four legal advantages that A can have in relation to B, which, correlatively, entail four legal disadvantages of B in relation to A. If A has a *right* (or, more specifically, a claim-right) against B, B has a correlative *duty* to A; if A has a *privilege* (or liberty, or permission, or justification-right) with respect to B, B has *no-right* against A; if A has a *power* with respect to B, B faces a *liability* from A; and if A has an *immunity* from B, B has a *disability* with respect to A.[5] Each legal advantage also has its negation: having a *claim-right* is the opposite of having *no-right*; a *privilege* is the opposite of a *duty*; a *power* is the opposite of a *disability*; and an *immunity* is the opposite of a *liability*. Hohfeld's elegant scheme was formulated to show the connection between legal concepts, but, with some minor tinkering, it illuminates connections between moral concepts as well: if A has a *moral* claim-right against B, then B has a correlative *moral* duty to honor the claim, and so on. These relationships are shown in Table 1.

On my account, legitimacy is a kind of *moral* power, the power to create and enforce *nonmoral* (or perhaps I should say not yet moral) prescriptions and social facts.[6] A legitimate authority has the moral power to author legal, institutional, or conventional rights and duties, powers and liabilities, and create social facts and mechanisms of coordination that change

Table 1   Hohfeldian Legal Relationships
Vertical pairs are correlatives. Diagonal pairs are opposites.

RIGHT	PRIVILEGE		POWER	IMMUNITY
DUTY	NO-RIGHT		LIABILITY	DISABILITY

Source: Wesley Newcomb Hohfeld, "Fundamental Legal Conceptions as Applied in Judicial Reasoning," *Yale Law Journal* 26 (1917).

the legal, institutional, and conventional situation or status of subjects. In what way, though, does the exercise of this moral power change the *moral* situation or status of the subject? If Hohfeld's scheme is correct, when A has a moral power with respect to B, and thereby can strip B of an institutional right, impose upon B an institutional duty, or change some social fact relevant to B, then B must have a correlative *moral liability*. What is this liability? It is that B's *moral* claims against some other subject, C, or against the legitimate authority, A, can be changed by A. By A's decree, C might gain a moral privilege not previously held to act against B's interests (even if B is not burdened with a moral duty to allow such action by C), and B may be subject to morally justified enforcement of its institutional duties to A or to C. But a moral liability is not a moral duty, and an institutional duty is not a moral duty. Raz's requirement that the exercise of legitimate authority change the normative situation of the subject of that authority is satisfied because B is now subject to a moral liability—the justified loss of moral claims against C and the morally justified enforcement of institutional duties by A. It is not conceptually necessary that, if A exercises legitimate authority in imposing upon B an institutional duty, B has a moral duty to comply.

To be clear: it is tautologically the case that if A succeeds in imposing upon B an institutional duty, B has an *institutional* duty to comply. It is no part of my view that valid law simply is a declaration of the ruler's will backed by threat, morally justified or not. Valid law generates, among other legal advantages and disadvantages, valid legal obligations. At issue is whether valid legal obligations are of necessity moral obligations. The power-liability account says no: whether hypothetical imperatives are also moral imperatives is a conceptually open question to be settled by substantive moral argument in light of morally relevant empirical circumstances.

How are we to understand a moral liability that is not yet a moral duty? Note that the opposite of a liability is an immunity: the subject of legitimate authority has no moral immunity against the loss of legal rights and the subsequent detrimental exercise of privileges by others, or the imposition of legal duties and their enforcement, and this limits the sort of justified complaints the subject can make. When such legal privileges are granted and exercised by others, or when legal duties are imposed and enforced, the subject can complain that the law is mistaken, stupid, or unfair, but he cannot justifiably complain that the law is an unauthorized abuse of power. He can complain that he has been wronged in one way, but not in another: if legitimate, this is the sort of mistake about right and wrong that is the authority's to make. As a conceptual matter, a legitimate law need not be a just law.

III. An Objection from Overridden Duties

Why not account for justified violations of legitimate law by introducing duties that are overridden or outweighed? That way, legitimate authority always entails duty, but not always dispositive duty. Sometimes, the duty is only presumptive or *prima facie* or *pro tanto*. Whatever the merits of this response, it is not one that Raz can offer. According to Raz, legitimate authority can be restricted in scope and predicated over particular actors, actions, circumstances, and reasons, but within its scope, the directive of a legitimate authority is an exclusionary reason that preempts the primary reasons that count for and against the directive. Of nonexcluded reasons that properly count against obedience, Raz says, "They determine the conditions of legitimacy of the authority and the limits of its rightful power."[7] An authority that oversteps, and claims to preempt reasons over which it has no jurisdiction, has not only failed to generate a dispositive duty. It has also, in exceeding "the limits of its rightful power," failed to be legitimate. If at this point one insists on calling such a directive a presumptive, *prima facie,* or *pro tanto* duty, then one should also call the authority that gave the directive merely presumptively, *prima facie,* or *pro tanto* legitimate. When, all things considered, subjects are not morally required to obey, then, all things considered, the authority was not morally permitted to command.

But perhaps Raz is mistaken about the preemption thesis, and legitimate authority does not entail dispositive moral duty. Why can we not then say that legitimate authority entails presumptive moral duty that sometimes is outweighed or overridden by other moral reasons? I think Kant has the correct account of apparent conflicts of moral duty: duties are conclusory. *Grounds* for duties can be overridden and outweighed, but a specified duty, if it is a duty, is not overrideable or outweighable. We may be misled by a false temporal story we tell, under which unforeseen circumstances come up to override. But the correct way to think about these circumstances is that they are exceptions built in from the start.

The main intuition that supports the moral duties-in-conflict view is the phenomenon of moral remainder, the notion that, even if one has acted rightly in the face of conflicting claims, sometimes something is still owed on the unmet claim. That there can be normatively genuine moral remainder is not in dispute, but I think that it can be accounted for in various ways without resort to genuine duties-in-conflict. One such way is to distinguish between the inviolability of rights and the inviolability of persons. Persons are not dispositively inviolable, but the right of a person not to be violated, when that right is properly specified, is dispositively inviolable.[8] Another is to recognize that the reasons that counted in favor of a rebutted duty are sufficient to create a genuine subordinate duty, such as the duty to compensate or express regret. A judgment in favor of this interpretation is that our intuition that the victim is owed compensation in remainder situations is usually stronger than our intuition that the burden of compensation must fall on the agent causing the harm.

Consider the case of a hiker stranded in a snowstorm who breaks into an empty cabin and burns the furniture to survive. Joel Feinberg offers this example to show that the rights of the cabin owner have been infringed, for clearly the hiker owes compensation.[9] But if compensation for the loss of the furniture came from a general fund for such purposes, the cabin owner would not have any further complaint against the hiker. The hiker needn't feel or express guilt or remorse (though gratitude and regret are in order). We would not see the decision to freeze to death rather than break into the cabin as supererogatory, rather than neurotic.

IV. Two Objections from Reduction

The power-liability account is distinct: it neither reduces to the view that political legitimacy amounts merely to a justification-right, a moral permission to use coercion, nor collapses back into the view that political legitimacy amounts to a claim-right that entails a duty to obey. The view that legitimate authority is merely a justification-right often is identified with the position advanced in a much-cited article by Robert Ladenson.[10] But Ladenson's view is considerably more sweeping. His main claim has three steps. If power (here understood as a causal, not a normative property) is the ability to make a person do what one wishes, and governmental power is power sufficient to maintain peace among members of a social group and protect them from outsiders, then:

1. Governmental authority is the effectively uncontested exercise of governmental power plus the right to rule;
2. The right to rule is held by those who possess governmental power and who have the acceptance of those they presume to govern; and
3. The right to rule is a justification-right (that is, a Hohfeldian privilege), not a claim-right (which would entail a correlative duty to obey).[11]

Clearly, there is nothing in the power-liability account that I have presented that requires endorsing either step (1) or (2): the power-liability view by itself does not take a stand on the necessity for legitimacy of effective power (in its causal sense) or on the joint sufficiency of effective power and acceptance by the governed. So the only part of Ladenson's view that needs to be addressed here is (3): that the right to rule is merely a justification-right. Accepting this proposition alone does not make one's view Ladenson's, so I needn't say anything more on that score. The challenge to me is to show that a moral power is more than, and does not simply reduce to, a justification-right, a mere privilege to use coercion, but also to show that a moral power is less than, and does not simply reduce to, an obligation-entailing claim-right.

The argument for reduction goes something like this: legal authorities have legal powers that correlate with legal liabilities. If legitimate authority does not entail moral obligation, then legitimate legal authorities do not have moral powers. They merely have a moral privilege to exercise their legal powers. So, legitimate authority is nothing more than a justification-right to issue and enforce commands. Only if the legal powers, when exercised, have moral force, is the legal power a moral power. But what is this moral force, other than the creation of *moral* rights and duties? So there is no room for a distinctive power-entailing-liability view of legitimacy: either legitimacy is merely a justification-right or it is a claim-right that entails obligation. There is nothing in between.

The reply to this objection is that the creation of a legal right or duty by a legal power can change the normative situation of a subject of the legal right or duty by changing his moral rights and privileges and powers and immunities even when no moral duty to obey the legal power has been generated. Having the power to change these moral statuses is moral power. Although all such moral powers can also be said to be moral privileges to exercise legal powers—hence the temptation toward reduction—not all moral privileges to exercise legal powers are moral powers because the exercise of legal power does not always affect moral rights and privileges. The difference matters because we should expect that the criteria for having a morally justified privilege to exercise an institutional power that does not affect moral rights and privileges (altering the rules of Quidditch) are less demanding than the criteria for having a moral power that operates via institutional powers (altering the rules of private property). Powers and privileges are not redundant ideas, and the subsequent streamlining of Hohfeld's scheme by the deontic logicians provided no illumination in legal and political philosophy. Although one can attempt to circumvent using the idea of a moral power by reducing all such situations to moral privileges to exercise institutional power, an important distinction would be lost.

Consider now the objection that the power-liability view collapses into the legitimacy-entails-duty view. Says Raz, "In every case the explanation of the normative effect of the exercise of authority leads back, sometimes through very circuitous routes, to the imposition of duties either by the authority itself or by some other persons."[12] But collapse threatens only if the normative change to which the subject of authority is liable always leads back to the imposition of a duty *on the subject* to obey *the authority's command.* Even simple moral permissions come along with a duty not to interfere with the exercise of the permission in some way or another—not by conceptual necessity, but by a sort of practical necessity if the permission is not to be futile. Consider again Raz's example that distinguishes a mere permission from authority: if A has the liberty to burn rubbish in his yard abutting B, that does not give A authority over B. A's permission does not entail a general duty of B to comply with A's plan. B may exercise certain permissions in remedy: she may set up a fan to blow the smoke back into A's yard, for instance. But B may not spray her garden hose over the fence to extinguish A's fire, or harass the neighbor by reporting a fire to the fire department. So even a mere permission generates at least some minimal duties of noninterference if the permission is to play a role in the mutual regulation of conduct. I say mutual regulation, for if B is an utterly passive moral patient who cannot take countermeasures, then A does not need further normative constraints on B for A's permission to be effective. But morality, in the first instance, is constructed for moral agents, not patients.

Notice, however, that Raz's example still makes its point: the burner of rubbish does not have authority over the neighbor. So, while it is true that on the power-liability view, the exercise of legitimate authority by A over B imposes on B not only liability for enforcement and punishment, but also a duty not to take certain measures of resistance to enforcement and punishment, this does not collapse the power-liability view into the right-duty view of legitimacy. Yes, the exercise of normative power does entail some duties that regulate resistance, and so correlatively some claim-rights against certain measures of resistance, but it does not entail a duty to comply with the command. It is not necessary, to establish the power-liability view as an independent third interpretation of legitimacy alongside of the legitimacy-entails-duty view and the command-backed-by-permissible-force view, that the exercise of legitimate authority leaves everyone's duties completely unchanged; all that needs to be shown is that a legitimate command does not entail a duty to comply with that command.

This has all been rather abstract, so perhaps some examples will help. I offer two: the first illustrating a legitimate authority's moral power to change the normative relations between two other parties and the second illustrating the moral power to enforce and punish.

V. Beachowner and Clamdigger

In a coastal jurisdiction, beachfront property extends to the mean high tide line, and all are permitted to walk, boat, or fish below that line. Houses on the beach are set far apart and are separated by blueberry barrens and rocky ledges. Here and there, paths that cut through the barrens and around the ledges have been used by the townspeople for as long as anyone can remember to get down to the shore. For many generations, Clamdigger's family has used one of these paths down to a clam flat below the high tide line. Because the ledges here go right down into the water, this clam flat is accessible by land only from this path. Although this particular path has never been subject to adjudication, in this jurisdiction courts have ruled in similar cases that such paths are public rights-of-way by custom and adverse possession. The property Clamdigger's path runs across has recently been purchased by Beachowner, who strung a chain across the entrance to the path with a "No Trespassing" sign hanging from it. The town, siding with Clamdigger, litigated, but Beachowner won the lawsuit, successfully defended on appeal, and so the sign and chain remained. Suppose that on the legal merits, and on whatever is your favored account of legal interpretation, the case was wrongly decided: on a positivist account, the substantive result is not supported by the legal materials; on a Dworkinian account, the substantive result is not supported by the appropriate moral reading of the law. Nonetheless, suppose as well, on whatever is your favored account of legal interpretation, that the ruling is valid law, in that the courts have authoritatively determined the parties' legal claims.

Clamdigger does not deny the validity of the legal ruling. He concedes that Beachowner now has the legal right to block access to the path and that he would violate a legal duty if he used the path without permission. Neither does Clamdigger deny the legitimate authority of the legal ruling, on his view of what legitimate authority entails. He accepts that the court had the moral power to rule as it did and that, though mistaken in one sense, the court is not mistaken in another: it has not abused its power. This is the sort of mistake the court has the moral privilege to make. He concedes that he is addressed by the ruling and, in a way that needs to be spelled out, is its subject, and that therefore the ruling changes his normative situation. What Clamdigger denies—not because of a general denial that law obligates, but because of the specific attributes of this case— is that he has a moral duty to obey the ruling. So Clamdigger skips over the chain and walks down the path to dig clams as he has always done. My question is not whether Clamdigger is making a moral mistake—he may indeed be—but whether he is making a conceptual mistake. Clamdigger's view is that the court ruling is morally legitimate, but does not morally obligate him. Must he be holding incoherent beliefs about the concept of legitimacy?

The answer turns on whether the moral power of the court to change Clamdigger's normative situation, and correlatively, his moral liability to such change, can be explicated in a way that does not cash out, either directly or circuitously, in a moral duty to obey the court order. So consider the normative relationships between Beachowner and Clamdigger under the legal interpretation that was authoritative prior to the court ruling. Before, Clamdigger had a moral claim-right against Beachowner not to have his right-of-way blocked, and Beachowner had a correlative moral duty not to block Clamdigger. One might hold that the court ruling completely reverses this, so that Clamdigger now has the moral duty and Beachowner the claim-right. But there is another possibility that still counts as a change in their normative situation: the ruling could grant Beachowner only a moral privilege to put up the chain, and Clamdigger only a moral privilege to jump the chain. As we saw earlier in the discussion of Raz's Rubbish-Burner case, Clamdigger's privilege is not unbounded: before, he might have had a privilege to rip down the chain blocking the path, and perhaps now he has a new moral duty not to damage the chain while climbing over; both before and after, he has a moral duty not to use violence against Beachowner's person. Beachowner is entitled to use stronger measures: he may build a high fence, or post a guard (but not set a man-trap or plant landmines). No doubt one can tell stories of other circuitous duties and their correlative claim-rights. But these are not the sorts of duties that are needed for the legitimacy-entails-duty view to succeed: the court has ordered Clamdigger off of the path, and that precise duty, whether directly or circuitously, is the one Clamdigger, without contradiction, denies. The court has attempted to grant Beachowner a moral claim-right, the right not to have his land crossed without his permission, but, again without contradiction, Clamdigger claims that the court has achieved only something weaker: it has succeeded in granting Beachowner only a moral privilege to attempt to prevent the crossing of his land. If the supposed injustice to Clamdigger were greater, Clamdigger might have viewed the law as without any normative effect whatsoever and held that Beachowner is still under a moral duty not to block access. But Clamdigger has taken a more nuanced view of what substantively mistaken but legitimate law accomplishes here. I am not arguing for the moral attractiveness of this construal. I am well aware of the instability and uncertainty that positing such misfirings of authority creates, of the difficulties that arise from letting us be judges in our own cases, of the need for procedural finality to settle substantive disagreement, and the like. But the question before us is a different one: is Clamdigger making a conceptual error in holding that the court is a legitimate authority, in that it has the moral power to change his normative situation so that what was his moral claim-right now is merely a moral privilege, but does not, under the circumstances, have the moral power to impose a moral duty? The answer is that he makes no such conceptual mistake.

Notice that this conclusion does not depend on the particular reason that authority misfires here: that a determination of law is substantively mistaken. If Beachowner's property right over the path had been established by legislation, or even constitutional amendment, so that the legal validity of the law's substance were uncontested, Clamdigger would still not be making a conceptual mistake if he held that he is not obligated because of the substantive unfairness of a law whose substantive validity is not in question. Notice, as well, that this account in no way depends on the command-backed-by-justified-force view of authority that Raz quite rightly dismisses as inadequate. No appeal has been made to any permission the court has to enforce or punish; what the exercise of the court's normative power has changed is the normative relations between the two parties, and that would be the case even if legal rulings in this jurisdiction were merely unenforceable pronouncements of what the law requires (an odd stipulation for municipal law, but not so odd for international law). So the normative relation of the court to the parties is poorly captured by reducing it to a permission with respect to the parties. What the court has is the normative power to change the normative permissions that hold between the parties.

VI. Motorist and the Long Red Light

Consider now an illustration of the power-liability view that does appeal to enforcement, but blocks the reduction to mere command backed by permissible force. For many years, at the outskirts of town, a stop sign regulated traffic at a sparsely traveled intersection with unobstructed views of flat desert for hundreds of yards in all directions. The town council, under pressure after a highly publicized fatal accident at a stop sign at a very busy intersection in the center of town (and taking advantage of a temporary price reduction offered by the local distributor of traffic control equipment), has decided to replace every stop sign under its jurisdiction with a traffic light and to post "No Turn on Red" signs at every one. It turns out that this model of traffic light is a bargain because the lights are preset to change at long intervals and their timing mechanisms are cumbersome to reprogram. Motorist, who wishes to turn right at the sparsely traveled intersection, approaches just as the light turns red. She knows from prior experience that she is in for a very long wait. It is a clear day. No pedestrians, bicyclists, or other cars are in sight. Taking great care, she turns on red. Police Officer, on a motorcycle hidden behind a cactus, stops Motorist and writes her a ticket, which she accepts and pays ruefully, but without resentment. She pays, not because she fears the consequences of not paying, but because she believes that she ought to. Next time, she takes a long hard look at the cactus before turning on red.

The elaboration of this old chestnut is meant to sketch the violation of legitimate but foolish law. The faulty considerations upon which traffic regulation in this town is based are not intended to amount to illegitimate corruption. And the faultiness is intended to be, at least *ex post,* common knowledge and uncontroversial. If this hypothetical specification suggests something else to you, rearrange the facts to fit an example of a law that is uncontroversially legitimate and uncontroversially foolish. But it is not my purpose to give an example that tests our convictions about the moral obligation to obey foolish but legitimate laws. I believe that there ordinarily is such an obligation, and until convinced that a red light actually is broken, I will sit at it, my thinning patience fortified by thoughts of respect for my fellow citizens. Rather, the purpose of the example is to make plausible two claims: that such an obligation is no conceptual entailment of the law's legitimacy, but that legitimacy is not merely command backed by justified force.

Motorist denies that, under the circumstances, she has a moral duty not to turn on red, accepts that Police Officer is justified in ticketing her, and accepts that she ought to pay the fine. Is this a coherent set of positions? Does her view entail that the town council and Police Officer do not have the moral power to enforce traffic law but, like Rubbish-Burner, have merely a moral permission, and so do not have legitimate authority over her? Alternatively, does her recognition that she ought to pay the fine reduce to a moral duty to obey the law? Neither construal is necessary. Motorist can consistently hold that the town has the moral power to impose upon her traffic fines—correlatively, that she is morally liable to have traffic fines imposed upon her—but not the moral power to impose upon her a moral duty to obey this traffic regulation. Her recognition that she ought to pay the fine would follow from a substantive moral argument, rather than a conceptual analysis, of what minimal respect for legitimate law requires. Although this is not a case of civil disobedience, such an argument could make use of the ideas employed in defining and justifying civil disobedience: the outer limits of fidelity to the law, a natural duty to support just institutions, and the willingness to accept punishment as a demonstration of good faith. Still, she can deny reduction to the legitimacy-entails-duty view, because the exercise of legitimate authority has misfired, in that it fails to impose the moral duty that it sets out to impose: she retains the moral privilege to turn on red. Such an argument may not succeed, but if it is defeated, it will be on substantive moral grounds, not by demonstrating a contradiction.

Note that Motorist is to be distinguished from Bad Person Motorist, who recognizes no moral reason to pay fines, and does so only when it is in her interests to do so.[13] Bad Person Motorist's conception of legitimate authority does appear to be no more demanding than the command backed by justified force view. But Motorist pays her fines even if she could successfully evade them and, in doing so, recognizes her moral liability. If you are not persuaded, substitute Honor System Motorist. Honor System Motorist doesn't simply recognize that she ought to pay traffic fines when caught. She voluntarily mails in the applicable fine every time she turns on red. Her normative view is that respect for legitimate law requires that one should pay the penalty for every violation, whether enforced or not, but that there are circumstances under which there is no moral duty to obey the law in the first instance.

The views of neither Motorist nor Bad Person Motorist nor Honor System Motorist could reasonably be held about all legitimate law, whether *malum in se* or *malum prohibitum*. The ends of fair social cooperation are not served if all laws are treated merely as price schedules, whether paid voluntarily or under threat. But some laws (parking meter ordinances perhaps) are, or have become, mere price schedules, and recognizing that this is so does not endanger their standing as authoritative—if you deny a moral obligation to vacate a parking space before the meter expires, there is no conceptual entailment between legitimacy and duty that you fail to recognize. Motorist, like Clamdigger, judges that, under certain circumstances, particular legitimate legal duties that she is subject to are not, for her, moral duties, but merely moral liabilities imposed by a moral power to which she is subject. Her mistake, if she is making one, is not conceptual.

VII. A Holmsean Objection

Consider an objection suggested by the Motorist illustration.[14] Perhaps the duty claimed by the legitimacy-entails-duty view is disjunctive: legitimate law imposes on its subjects a duty either to comply or to accept the legal consequences. This, famously, is Oliver Wendell Holmes's analysis of the legal duty that a contract imposes. According to Holmes, there is no duty not to breach a contract. Rather, there is a disjunctive legal duty either to perform the contract or to compensate for breach.[15] This is a legal formulation, not a moral one; the moral parallel would be the view that legitimate law entails a moral duty that has the following disjunctive structure: either obey the law or accept the legal penalty. So the legitimacy-entails-liability view collapses back into the legitimacy-entails-duty view. Nothing in Raz's account prevents the entailed moral duty from having such a structure.

To reply, first note that, as a formal matter, a disjunctive duty can have even more disjuncts. Legitimate law could impose a moral duty either to obey the law, or to pay the legal penalty upon breaking the law, or to go to prison upon refusing to pay the legal penalty, or to not use violence resisting capture upon refusing to go to prison, or to not accuse the police of improper use of force when they use violence in return. Now, not only has the legitimacy-entails-duty view subsumed the legitimacy-entails liability view, it has also subsumed the legitimacy-as-justified-coercion view, and that should tell us that something is awry with the disjunctive strategy. Raz and Ladenson, Kant and Hobbes mean to disagree.

Whether or not Holmes gives a correct analysis of the legal duties that contract law imposes, legal duties are not in general disjunctive in that way. There aren't two ways to comply with one's legal duties concerning murder, either to not commit murder or to go to prison if convicted. There aren't two ways to comply with one's legal duties concerning taxes, either to report income truthfully or to pay penalties for underpayment if audited. Nor are there two ways to comply with one's legal duties concerning torts, either to not act negligently or to pay damages. Where legal duties track prior moral duties, the prior moral duties surely are not disjunctive. We do not comply with the natural moral duties concerning murder and negligent injury by accepting punishment after killing and by paying compensation after harming. I have argued elsewhere that, even if Holmes is correct about the disjunction in the law of contracts, this does not render the moral obligation to keep the underlying promise disjunctive.[16] So legal duties are not in general disjunctive, and neither are prior moral duties, at least not the perfect duties. (The imperfect moral duties can be thought of as disjuncts, but one should not conflate duties of moral remainder with disjunctive duties.) Therefore, the view that legitimate law entails a moral duty that contains the disjunct, "either comply with the (nondisjunctive) legal duty or accept the legal consequences," though coherent, is not perspicacious.

VIII. Distinguishing Power from Permission

Consider the distinction between moral power and moral permission more closely. Someone who has merely a moral permission to use force does not have a moral power to change the normative situation. A permission is a static normative advantage: one has it or not, one may or may not be able to delegate or assign it, and we needn't have any control over when and how a permission is first granted or acquired or when and how it can be lost or taken away. A normative power, in contrast, is the ability to bring into existence or change other normative statuses, such as permissions. A power is a normative status that is generative of other normative statuses: it enables.

This distinction is obscured when the authority and the enforcer are the same entity. When they are different, as is the case with the town council and the police officer, it is more clear that the authority changes the normative status of both the enforcer and the subject. The authority, exercising its moral power with respect to the subject, grants the enforcer a moral permission (and perhaps a moral duty) to enforce; the subject was morally liable to having her normative status changed by such enactment, and she is now morally liable for specific enforcement. Power is the ability to enact. This is why legitimate authority typically is exercised through speech acts (and why Hobbes, invoking his whimsical method of argument by etymology, sees authorities as the *authors* of the actions of their agents). The status change must be enacted—the power exercised—before enforcement against the subject is permitted. In authority as mere permission, the authority says to the agent of enforcement: "I am permitted to force that subject to comply, and you are my agent. On my behalf, force that subject to comply." In legitimacy as normative power, the authority says to the agent of enforcement: "I have the power to make it the case that you are permitted to force that subject to comply. I hereby invoke that power. Force that subject to comply." This can be so even if the authority itself never has permission to enforce. The members of the city council may not have the power to grant themselves permission to write traffic tickets. If they have the power, they still have to grant it to themselves. President Richard Nixon had the power to order Attorney General Elliot Richardson to dismiss Special Prosecutor Archibald Cox, but did not have permission to do so himself, hence the drama of what became known as the Saturday Night Massacre.

The power-liability view explains what is especially wrong with the abuse of force by officials and with extra-legal vigilantism, even when the actions taken track what a properly authorized outcome would have been, and this explains why the victims of the improper use of force by officials have a serious complaint even when they get what should have been coming to them through proper channels. Our special horror of these abuses is not explained fully by the fear of arbitrary and mistaken application of force. Even if exactly the same enforcement from some other official were properly authorized, we would still be rightly indignant if the enforcing official were not properly authorized, for we have moral immunity from the exercise of unauthorized powers. Nor is it simply that a public official did wrong: we don't have the same horrified reaction to an official who misuses his office for personal gain without exercising force or coercion over subjects. The morally liable subject still is morally inviolable until the power to which she is liable is invoked. Not so under the account that reduces all moral powers to moral permissions to exercise legal powers. Under that account, the subject never is inviolable with respect to the authority, because the authority already has permission to use force, and the subject already has the correlative no-right against force. On the two views, compare how many moral mistakes Henry II's four knights make when they act upon "Will no one rid me of this meddlesome priest?"

When Motorist considers herself free to turn on red and Police Officer free to ticket her, she need not view legitimate authorities merely as entities that have moral permission (over some domain) to force her (in certain ways). That would leave her normative status unchanged once the city council had an initial moral permission to regulate traffic. Enactment and enforcement would then be rearrangements of legal advantages and disadvantages, not moral ones. She still could be morally wronged by the council and by the police, but such a wrong would trace back to some overstepping of the initial conditions of and on the moral permission. In contrast, on the power-liability view, the city council has an initial moral power to regulate traffic, and Motorist is liable to that power. Her normative situation changes depending on how that power is exercised.

Apart from the power of enforcement and punishment, the city council's power to regulate traffic also gives it the power to change normative relations between other parties, as did the court in Clamdigger. Motorists may have acquired specific moral duties of care to one another that they didn't have before, because others will act in reasonable reliance on the new traffic signs. Motorists who ignore the sign are legally liable under tort law, for turning on red may reasonably be taken to be conclusory with respect to legal judgments of negligence. The moral case may be different: someone who turns on red may have exerted all due moral care but, because of freakish circumstances, causes damage (say a balloonist at that moment falls out of the sky). Still, she has no moral complaint about legal liability.

Now, it would be quite odd for a lawmaker to defend creating and enforcing an unjust or foolish law on the grounds that it is legitimate. Surely, from the first-personal perspective, I am morally prohibited from issuing an unjust law and have good reason not to issue a foolish law, even if I have the legitimate authority to do so. But this shows that legitimacy is primarily a practical judgment made from the second- or third-person perspective: it governs how you, the moral patient, should react to my unjust or unwise moral agency, whether lesser officials should enforce, and whether third parties should intervene. Or, to put it another way, the question of legitimacy arises when there is disagreement about the justice or goodness of an authority's command. Raz holds that to judge an authority legitimate is simply to judge that the subjects of that authority have a moral duty to obey it. I hold that to judge an authority legitimate is simply to judge that the subjects of that authority are morally liable—that is, not morally immune—from the exercise of a moral power to impose and enforce conventional duties and change relevant social facts in ways that change the subject's normative situation. The circumstances under which subjects face a moral duty as well remains an open question. To answer, we need a normative conception of legitimate authority, which is the task for the remaining chapters of this book.

IX. On Immunity

What about the reigning orthodoxy in international law, that a legitimate authority has immunity from outside intervention? Again, if Hohfeld's scheme holds up, having a moral power is not the same as, and does not entail, having a moral immunity. When A exercises a moral power over B, and imposes upon B an institutional duty, this imposes upon B a morally justified liability to enforcement, which is the opposite of a moral immunity from enforcement. Just because B lacks moral immunity from A, however, does not entail that A has moral immunity from the interference of some third party, C. There is no conceptual route from having legitimacy—having moral power—to having moral immunity. Nor does having legal immunity under international law entail having moral immunity. These all are connections that will have to be established by moral argument, not conceptual analysis.

One such argument is that respect for less-than-just laws, policies, and practices abroad follows from the respect owed to members of a political community who have collectively decided, in a way collectively acceptable to them, how to govern themselves. A political community that fails to have just practices may reasonably claim that the offending practices are still *their* practices, and that, within bounds, mistakes about what justice demands are theirs to make. I said within bounds: the bounds are marked by whether interference would be disrespectful to those most burdened by unjust practices because, nonetheless, they reasonably endorse the practices as their own. Surely, if those burdened correctly held the burdensome practices imposed upon them to be genuine moral duties, outsiders would have no cause to interfere for *their* sake.

This, I think, is how to avoid the unappealing conclusion that Rawls's *Law of Peoples* requires liberal societies to be deaf to the cries of unjustly treated minorities inside illiberal but decent hierarchical societies.[17] Among the requirements for a decent society are that its laws impose *bona fide* moral obligations on its subjects, that basic human rights, including some measure of liberty of conscience, be secured, and that the society be well-ordered, meaning that it be stable for the right reasons. Now, since Rawls clearly rejects moral relativism, exactly how law that is unjust is supposed to generate genuine moral obligation in decent societies isn't clear. It must have something to do with nearly universal and genuine endorsement of the illiberal conception of justice in that society sufficient to reproduce that conception from one generation to the next without resort to repression (which is ruled out by the requirements of human rights, liberty of conscience, and stability for the right reasons). But if these conditions are all satisfied, the unjustly treated will not be crying out to liberal ears. The reason they will not isn't that they have been silenced or brainwashed, but that they (mistakenly but reasonably in light of the burdens of judgment applicable across cultures) do not consider their treatment to be unjust, or they (perhaps correctly, or perhaps mistakenly but reasonably) do not consider their treatment sufficiently unjust to justify illegal activity. Conversely, an illiberal society that has a significant minority crying out for help from liberal quarters doesn't meet the criteria of a decent hierarchical society, and so wouldn't be immune from interference. Other readers of Rawls might reasonably (but mistakenly) take my reading to be too charitable.

Recall, however, that legitimate authority to impose an *institutional* duty does not entail a *moral* duty to comply. Governors (or the majority, or the powerful) may be sufficiently connected to the will and interests of the governed (or the minority, or the weak) to pass the threshold of legitimate authority, but not sufficiently connected to make the burdensome practices the practices of the burdened, and generate in them genuine moral duties to obey. Contrary to Raz, justified civil disobedience against a legitimate authority is not an empty category. Unjustly treated minorities can be forgiven if they reject a reified account of "We" in "We the People" under which their injuries are self-inflicted. When this is so, it shows no disrespect to *them* for outsiders to intervene on their behalf. Legitimacy and moral immunity can come apart, legitimacy and moral duty can come apart, and therefore duty and immunity can stand and fall together. When oppressed minorities and dissenters aren't morally obligated to obey unjust but legitimate authority, outsiders aren't morally disabled from helpful meddling on their behalf. What forms of meddling are morally permitted are shaped and constrained by the respect owed to an unjust but legitimate regime by outsiders, but it isn't at all clear why this should be any greater than the respect owed by unjustly burdened insiders.

X. What If Everyone Did *What?*

We now can interpret and evaluate Justice Goldstone's claim, cited in Chapter 1, that NATO's intervention in Kosovo, though illegal, was legitimate. Milošević's Yugoslavia claimed the legal power to impose binding legal duties on the Kosovars, who had no legal right of resistance. Under international law, Yugoslavia had standing as a sovereign state immune from intervention. NATO's member states are bound by international law—or, to put it in a more cumbersome but precise way, international law has the power to impose legal duties and other legal disadvantages on states, and one such disadvantage is that states are legally disabled from intervening in the internal affairs of other sovereign states.

When subjected to even minimally demanding criteria of moral legitimacy, however, Milošević's Yugoslavia fails miserably. Having amply demonstrated their capacity for slaughter, rape, and ethnic cleansing on a grand scale in Bosnia, Serbian nationalists had begun operations in Kosovo. The Kosovars were deprived of their most basic political freedoms and faced massive human rights violations. It would be perverse to maintain the fiction that the Milošević regime impersonated the will or protected the basic interests of its Kosovar citizens. The rump Yugoslav state did not constitute a normative group that counted the Kosovars as members. Surely the Kosovars had the moral right to defend themselves.

Did the United States and other member states of NATO have moral permission to intervene on their behalf? If the United States is subject to legitimate international law that immunizes Yugoslavia against interference, and if Raz is correct that legitimate authority entails moral obligation, then the answer is no. For the answer to be yes, either the international law that grants Yugoslavia immunity must not be legitimate, or Raz must be mistaken. Of the three claims—(1) NATO's intervention to prevent massive human rights violations in Kosovo was morally permitted, (2) international law prohibiting such intervention is legitimate, and (3) legitimacy entails moral obligation—at most two can hold. I am more sure of the truth of (1) than I am of anything else in this chapter, even if that requires giving up (2). But one does not need to give up (2) if one gives up (3) in favor of the power-liability view of legitimacy.

On the power-liability view, international law, insofar as it is legitimate, is a kind of moral power to create and enforce nonmoral legal obligations, and this entails that those subject to these legal obligations face moral liability, but not necessarily moral obligation. So the Hohfeldian picture of the moral relationships looks like this: Milošević has no legitimate moral power over the Kosovars, and the Kosovars have no moral duties to the Yugoslav regime. Yugoslavia has no moral immunity from intervention, and outsiders are not morally disabled from aiding the Kosovars. Insofar as international bodies such as the United Nations are legitimate, they have the moral power to create nonmoral legal rules, and states that are subject to those rules are morally liable to enforcement, sanction, or censure. But, by analogy to domestic civil disobedience and conscientious refusal, conditions can be specified under which an actor is morally justified in violating such rules. When those conditions are met, it does not follow that the law that is justifiably violated is illegitimate law.

There are important disanalogies to civil disobedience too—perhaps the most important that we are here contemplating the use of violence, and violence is constitutive of a rejection of legitimacy. But note that the target of violence here is Milošević's regime, not the United Nations. If, counterfactually, the only way to save Srebrenica were to attack the UN peacekeepers, such a strike *would* be incompatible with the view that the UN had legitimate authority in Srebrenica. The general point is that tactics of dissent express views about the authority that is resisted, and so the justification of dissent will depend in part on a proper match with the normative status of the authority. Civil disobedience in a nearly just democracy requires tactics that, by appealing to the sense of justice of the mistaken majority, express sufficient respect for one's fellow citizens.[18] Tyrants are owed no such respect.

Specifying the necessary and sufficient conditions for justified disobedience of international law is a task for another time; here I will simply assert that protecting a large civilian population from massacre, systematic rape, and massive dislocation will easily meet any plausible test of justified disobedience. How international conventions that legally prohibit such intervention can meet the test of legitimate law is not so easily supposed in the absence of a well-worked-out normative theory of international law, which I do not have. But any normative theory of legitimate law, municipal or international, will need to acknowledge the irreducible asymmetry between the perspective of the legislator whose task is to frame an *ex ante* institutional rule that anticipates bad judgment and bad will, and the perspective of the agent exercising principled moral judgment *ex post*. One way that space for justified disobedience of legitimate law opens up is in the gap between these two perspectives.

Failure to appreciate the difference between institutional rules and moral principles is at the bottom of a lot of ill-considered legal and moral reasoning. Consider this *non sequitur* by UN Secretary General Kofi Annan, made in the years between the Srebrenica massacre and the Kosovo intervention:

> Can we really afford to let each state be the judge of its own right, or duty, to intervene in another state's internal conflict? If we do, will we not be forced to legitimize Hitler's championship of the Sudeten Germans, or Soviet intervention in Afghanistan?[19]

Now, it is unclear whether the judgments, rights, duties, and legitimization in question here are moral or legal, but on any construal, the answer to the second question is a resounding "No!" Each state's judging its own right or duty (whether legal or moral) is consistent with objective standards for such judgments, and a state that fails to properly meet those standards, either mistakenly or willfully, can in turn be judged (whether legally or morally) and held to account. An individual judging her right to use force in self-defense, a manufacturer judging its right to impose reasonable risks on consumers, a legislature judging its right to enact constitutionally questionable legislation, are all subject to judgment for the exercise of judgment. Does Kofi Annan think that if a person being mugged has the right to defend herself without obtaining a court order first, every claim of self-defense, no matter how groundless, must be accepted on its face? To be fair, I must stress that the lecture from which Annan's quote is taken is a forceful defense of intervention in a state's internal affairs in cases of extreme violation of human rights—but only on the authority of the UN Security Council.

Now, there may indeed be good reasons to have a procedural international rule that says:

No state may intervene in another state's internal conflict without the explicit approval of the UN Security Council,

and this rule may have advantages over some substantive rule, such as:

No state may intervene in another state's internal conflict except to prevent imminent humanitarian disaster and only when peaceful means have no reasonable chance of success.

But it is obvious that a substantive rule does not legitimize Hitler's armed robbery of Czechoslovakia or the Soviet's imperial misadventure in Afghanistan any more than the procedural rule legitimizes a claim that the Security Council approved some action when in fact it did not. Any criterion can be invoked disingenuously. The empirical prediction that a criterion will be invoked and misapplied disingenuously or mistakenly, and that misapplication will lead to bad consequences, counts against writing that criterion into a rule. If, predictably, more unjustified acts of aggression will occur under the substantive rule than under the procedural rule, that is a reason to enact the procedural rule. But if, predictably, fewer justified humanitarian interventions will occur under the procedural rule than under the substantive rule, that is a reason to enact the substantive rule. Either way, we are never "forced to legitimize" the exercise of judgment by a state, if the phrase means something like disabled from challenging the legitimacy of a state's actions.

Proponents of pure procedural legitimacy and of strict duties of obedience sometimes talk as if their critics are guilty of a practical contradiction, as if the substantive account and the power-liability account propose maxims that fail the test of universalizability. But as typically invoked, the "What if everyone did it?" objection confuses moral principles with institutional rules. True, a candidate for a moral principle that fails the test of universalizability probably fails as a moral principle. But the proper retort to the objection "What if everyone did it?" is "What if everyone did *what?*" Without contradiction, one can put forward substantive criteria for the illegitimacy of states and the permissibility of humanitarian intervention, including unilateral, extralegal intervention, that are not simply self-dealing, and wouldn't be self-defeating if other state actors did the same, where "doing the same" is acting in accordance with precisely those substantive criteria. It is no embarrassment to a correctly formulated moral principle that disaster would result if others acted on some different, incorrectly formulated principle, either through error or cynicism. Moral reasoning is paralyzed if one's commitment to the soundness of a moral argument is undermined by the fact that one's argument could be misunderstood, misapplied, and misused by others.

In contrast with moral principles, the bad consequences of incorrect interpretation and misapplication do count against an institutional rule, just as the unavoidable overinclusiveness and underinclusiveness of *correct* interpretation and application counts for and against a particular formulation of an institutional rule. Rules, as Fredrick Schauer has convincingly argued, are to be understood as entrenched generalizations, and so are necessarily overinclusive or underinclusive with respect to their underlying justifications, even when properly interpreted and applied.[20] Moral principles are generalizations too, but not entrenched generalizations. If a piece of moral reasoning pitched at a certain level of generality does not accord with our considered judgments about particular cases, that puts pressure on the specification or ordering of moral principles that gave the discordant answer, and consistency demands that something give: we either revise the specification or ordering of our principles or revise our judgment about particular cases. The pursuit of reflective equilibrium, as Rawls calls this method, is one of the few tools in the philosopher's kit.[21] So, it is always an embarrassment to a candidate for a moral principle that, when correctly applied, it gives the wrong answer, but it is never an embarrassment to the correct moral principle that, when incorrectly applied, it gives the wrong answer. It needn't be an embarrassment to an institutional rule that, when correctly applied, it gives the wrong answer, and it sometimes is an embarrassment to an institutional rule that, when incorrectly applied, it gives the wrong answer.

The way these considerations of interpretation and application of institutional rules count is through their empirical consequences, not through some hypothetical generalization. One asks the empirical question, "Will the promulgation and enforcement of this formulation of the rule predictably lead to more serious misapplications than some other formulation of the rule?" and not the hypothetical question "What if everyone misapplied the rule?" Institutional rules requiring procedural criteria and those permitting substantive criteria are held to the same empirical test.

What is properly subjected to a universalizability test is one's specification of the normative conception of legitimacy, with its criteria for legitimate and illegitimate governments and its criteria governing when actors are morally permitted to disobey institutional rules in defense of human rights. Once the necessary conceptual links between legitimacy and pedigree or procedure and between the legitimate authority of law and the moral obligation to obey it are broken, whether such a specification contains substantive criteria or permits disobedience becomes an open moral question settled by moral argument and judgment. Appeals to authority obviously will not settle questions about the moral powers of that same authority, and since it is authority all the way up, it is judgment—including substantive judgment—all the way down. This, in his way, is what Edmund told us at the start:

> Thou, Nature, art my goddess; to thy law
> My services are bound.[22]

PART II

Free Group Agency

CHAPTER 3

All Foundings Are Forced

One of the central challenges of modern political philosophy is to reconcile our compelling claim to personal freedom with the inescapable need to subject one another to coercive law. The early social contract tradition attempted the reconciliation by invoking the consent of the governed: if I am free when I govern myself, then we are free when we agree to collectively govern ourselves. Stated this baldly, however, an obvious fallacy of composition threatens. Popular governments can, and regularly do, violate the freedoms of their citizens, and it adds insult to injury to tell the victims that these violations are self-inflicted. Our personal freedoms need more protection than a purely procedural account of collective self-governance provides, so pure procedures are not self-legitimating.

In Chapter 1, with the help of some archeology of ideas, we created conceptual space for a substantive normative conception of legitimacy. I then concluded that, in general, pure procedural accounts fail as normative conceptions of legitimacy, and that in particular, actual consent cannot make governments legitimate. Substantive normative conceptions that condition legitimacy on the realization of certain standards of justice and goodness, and so recognize the possibility of tyranny by practice even when rulers have proper title, are more promising. Substantive normative conceptions still must meet the challenge of how to connect particular authorities to particular subjects, though. A completely hypothetical construction can tell us what the constitution and laws of a legitimate government ought to contain, but until a theory specifies how actual governments and laws become the governments and laws of actual particular citizens, it is incomplete. In Chapter 2, I agreed with Simmons and Raz that legitimate authority is not simply morally justified coercion. Legitimate authorities change the normative circumstances of the subjects they properly address, so we need an account of who is properly addressed by an authority and why.

The aim of this chapter is to articulate a substantive normative conception of legitimacy that both remedies the defects of pure procedural accounts and explains the connection between the governed and their governors. As will become clear, my answer is still very much in the spirit of the social contract tradition, though the idea of membership in a free group agent, rather than consent of the governed, bears the weight of the argument. On this view, A legitimately governs B only if A's governance of B realizes and protects B's freedom over time, and this is the case only when A is a free group agent that counts a free B as a constituent member of that group agent. The heroic (though, in the end, heartbreaking) 2011 uprising in Libya provides us with an historical foil. Tracing both the factual and counterfactual paths of that rebellion out of tyranny and towards a legitimate government will help us illuminate the account.

I. Claiming Legitimacy in Libya

On March 5, 2011, after its first meeting in Benghazi, the newly formed and self-appointed "National Transitional Council of the Republic of Libya" proclaimed itself "the only legitimate body representing the people of Libya and the Libyan state."[1] Five days later, after consultations with a couple of defected Libyan diplomats who may have been freelancing, the French Foreign Ministry announced that France recognized the National Transitional Council as "the legitimate representative of the Libyan people."[2] The council was led by a man who, before the uprising, was Qaddafi's minister of justice, and comprised an assortment of lawyers, businessmen, professors, and other defectors from the Libyan government. Unlike its neighbor Egypt, Libya lacked much of an organized opposition before the seemingly spontaneous uprising of February 15. The mostly young protesters transformed themselves into loose bands of fighters without plan. Their early successes in the eastern cities from Benghazi to Tobruk and in the towns surrounding Tripoli should be attributed to the early panic and disarray of Muammar Qaddafi's loyalists as much as to the rebels' unquestioned courage. Three squabbling ex-generals claimed to command a few thousand untrained, ill-equipped, ragtag fighters, along with perhaps one thousand army defectors, all the while disputing each other's authority.[3]

The *de facto* success of any popular uprising or *coup d'état* depends on the probability of reaching a self-fulfilling equilibrium: will enough actors judge quickly enough that the rebellion will succeed for them to risk joining in, thereby collectively assuring the success that each predicted? The strategy of every rational revolutionary or junta therefore is to assemble, before reaching the fatal point of no return, as much of a winning coalition as possible without detection by the regime in power. History perhaps will show this to be an overstatement, but the Libyan revolution at its start was no one's rational strategy, much less the strategy of the worthy members-to-be of the National Transitional Council. They did not plan the uprising, they did not trigger it, and—on the day that they announced themselves to be the only legitimate body representing the Libyan people—they did not control it. On no plausible account of how a people or a state come to be represented could the council claim to have represented the Libyan people or state on the fifth of March: they were not rightful successors to authority on any account of pedigreed succession; they were not chosen in any procedure, either customary or newly invented, by the people they claimed to represent; they did not secure the basic rights and liberties of the people they claimed to represent; they were not better guides to the practical reasons that applied to individual Libyans than were those individuals themselves; and they did not even control the territory of most of the people for whom they claimed to speak.

All this is so, not because the tyrant had some superior claim to pedigree, consent, rights protection, or normative guidance. Had Qaddafi set sail to his Elba early in the uprising, leaving factional chaos behind, the council would have faced no lower hurdle of justification. No Law of the Conservation of the General Will exists, such that legitimacy may neither be created nor destroyed, only changed from form to form. So suppose that, whatever is the correct view of justified revolution against a tyrannical regime, Libya on March 5 was a legitimacy-free zone: a Hobbesian condition of mere nature, a Lockean state of war, a Kantian barbarism.

The claim to title of the National Transitional Council still appears to be unmoored.

Yet there was strategic logic in France's early recognition of the council as the legitimate representative of the Libyan people: saying so might make it so. Under the right conditions, recognition of legitimacy is also self-fulfilling. Despite the rather vaporous existence of the National Transitional Council, its claim to speak for the revolution was widely accepted both at home and abroad. No other group arose to question its leadership. Alas, France made its declaration just as the Qaddafi regime was regaining its footing, on the day that would turn out to be the rebels' most extensive advance for quite some time. Qaddafi's forces pushed the rebels back to the outskirts of Benghazi, triggering the UN Security Council's authorization of a no-fly zone on March 17. NATO airstrikes thwarted Qaddafi's advance on Benghazi but could not, from the air, turn the rebels into an effective fighting force. On the factual ground, the conflict stalemated for quite some time. Not until October 20, 2011, with the killing of Colonel Muammar Qaddafi, did Libya's revolutionaries achieve their long-anticipated military victory.

On normative grounds, despite our deep admiration and empathy for those who rise up against tyranny, we must fret about how the normative power to govern Libya is created and conferred on this or any other ruling body or its successors. The source of this anxiety is easily placed. The twin intuitions of the consensual pedigree folk theory, that political legitimacy requires, in some sense, the consent of the governed and is acquired only through proper pedigree or procedure, continue to tickle our moral imaginations. But the National Transitional Council of the Republic of Libya did not and could not rule with the consent of those it purported to govern, and did not and could not have acquired its powers through proper pedigree.

When left underspecified, the folk theory provides some sorry comfort *in medias res.* No, perhaps actual consent isn't possible for us and wasn't possible for past generations, but don't we endorse or accept the authority of our government in some way? And don't we do so, even when we oppose our officeholders and disagree with their laws and policies, because the officeholders were installed and their laws and policies enacted through proper procedures? And aren't those procedures proper because they were endorsed or accepted in the past? Yes, it's turtles all the way down, but aren't they *our* turtles? The folk theory, however, faces a sharp problem in *ab ovo* founding moments, for the riddle no longer is which came first, the procedural chicken or the consensual egg. Neither has come.

Why do we need to answer the question of *ab ovo* legitimacy at all? Why not say that the only answerable questions about legitimacy are posable *in medias res,* and while a revolution is underway, legitimacy, like division by zero, is undefined? One reason is pragmatic: Libyas repeatedly happen. Of the 193 current members of the United Nations, only two existed as independent states before the publication of Kant's *Metaphysics of Morals* in 1797 and have not since had ruptures in governance caused by revolution, coup, or occupation. Another reason is philosophical: as Kant understood well, thinking about the contradictions of legitimacy *ab ovo* in abstraction from existing political institutions is one way to construct an account of legitimacy *in medias res.*

II. Free Group Agency

I wish to present an alternative to the folk theory of political legitimacy that acknowledges the tug of our intuitions about consent and pedigreed procedure, but avoids at least some of the puzzles that arise when one tries to get specific about what is meant by consent and pedigree. To develop the view, I begin by offering a merely suggestive formulation and then tighten it up a bit as I go along. My claim is that an account of political legitimacy must solve the puzzle of how free moral agents can remain free even when subjected to coercive governance. The solution, roughly, is that free moral agents remain free only when they are governed by a free group agent of which they are constituent members. A legitimately governs B only when A governs B in such a way that both A and B remain free moral agents over time. This is so only when A's governance of B realizes and protects B's freedom over time, and this in turn is so only when A is a free group agent that counts a free B as a member. Over grown-ups of sound mind, the only legitimate governance is collective self-governance. My task is to specify this old commonplace in an illuminating way.

What is a moral agent? On this account, a moral agent is an entity that is the proximate locus of respect and responsibility: an agent can make genuine moral claims on others, and others can make genuine moral claims on an agent. I take it to be a conceptual truth that anything that can be held to be properly responsible is (or at one time was) capable of action. To count as an action (and not merely an event or a behavior), the agent who performed it must have three capacities or their functional equivalents: (1) considering: the capacity to respond to reasons for action, endorsing some and rejecting others; (2) willing: the capacity to choose to act (or not act) in ways guided by the relevant reasons; and (3) doing: the capacity to behave in ways guided by one's choices.[4] Only entities that have these three capacities of considering, willing, and doing, and whose behaviors follow from the exercise of these capacities, can be said to have the unity required to be agents capable of action.

What is a *free* moral agent? For our purposes, agents must be sufficiently free in both internal and external senses of freedom. The conception of internal freedom put to use here is freedom as competent self-governance. Self-governance simply is a degree of autonomy, but to avoid confusion with thicker and more demanding accounts of autonomy, such as Kant's, I shall often use the less lofty term. To be a competent self-governing agent is to have the three capacities of action to some adequate degree. Note that room is left over for an impaired agent: one who has enough minimal capacity for considering, willing, and doing to count as some sort of agent, rather than merely an event-generator like the wind or a lower animal, but not enough capacity to count as a competent self-governing agent. So an internally free agent is a competent self-governing agent.

Although Kant's conception of inner freedom is too demanding to follow here, his conception of outer freedom is especially fitting. Agents have external freedom when they are independent of the domination of others.[5] External freedom, on this view, is not a matter of being unconstrained by circumstances, so that the fewer options one has, the less freedom one has, whatever the source of constraint. Rather, the conception of external freedom used here considers a person to be free if his choice of ends is not subject to the control of another person. External freedom is violated when one person's innate powers or properly acquired means are destroyed or unilaterally appropriated by another person's choices.

On these conceptions of internal and external freedom, we now say that A legitimately governs B only when A governs B in such a way that both A and B remain *self-governing and independent* moral agents over time. This is so only when A's governance of B realizes and protects B's self-governance and independence over time, and this in turn is so only when A is a self-governing and independent group agent that counts a self-governing and independent B as a member.

What is a *group* agent? Note that the account of agency above made no reference to mental states, so need not be restricted to a natural person with a wet brain between her ears. A group is capable of unified action if, together, it possesses in requisite measure the three capacities of considering, willing, and doing. I want nothing to do with spooky accounts of the general will here. A group agent is not a metaphysical entity, and collective willing is not a psychological state in some group mind. Yet neither is a group agent a simple aggregation of the preferences of individuals. To be fully capable of self-governing shared agency, individuals have to be properly constituted, incorporated, represented, or personated. A natural individual is capable of agency, of willing ends, when there is a unity of the self, the capacity for reflecting on desires and for endorsing some and not others, for making choices, and for engaging in behaviors that are guided by one's considerations and choices. When a collection of individuals has this unity of will and capacity for second-order reflection, it is capable of group action and what comes along with action: the group itself is a proper subject for moral evaluation. (The conditions under which such evaluation properly distributes to the individual constituent actors is a further question.) Without a shared will, there are only the individual wills of individual persons, which may show statistical regularities, may be coordinated in various ways, and which always result in some vector that is the consequence of individual actions, but none of this makes for shared agency. To use Christine Korsgaard's image, a bag filled with mice will move, but the bag cannot act. This is the difference between the results of a public opinion poll and the results of an election: a public opinion poll is a mere aggregation of individual preferences. An election (when the conditions for its legitimacy are met) is a performative, the speech act of a shared agent.

Can there be *normative* groups, understood as groups that are bearers of respect and responsibility, and if so, what properties must they have? First, if the idea of a normative group is to be taken seriously, then all of the moral claims a normative group can make and all of the moral claims that can be made against it cannot merely be direct pass-throughs for the separate and several moral claims by and on the natural individual persons who make up the normative group. If that were so, talk of a normative group would simply be a convenient shorthand, a manner of speaking.

Yet the idea of a normative group should not be taken seriously in the wrong way and be given moral standing unconnected to the moral standing of the natural persons that constitute it.[6] In ways that are often complex, claims against a normative group distribute into claims of some sort against at least some of its members; claims against one set of individual members sometimes generate claims against the normative group as a whole, and these in turn may distribute onto a different set of individual members; at least some claims by individual members generate claims by the normative group; and at least some of the claims of individuals can be discharged by satisfying claims made by the normative group (even though the substance of the claim of the natural person may fail to have been met).

In short, if normative groups are possible, any normative status they have must be in virtue of the normative status of natural persons. If groups in some measure are owed respect and can be held responsible in some ways, this is because they are made up of natural persons who are owed respect and can be held responsible. But there is no simple reduction or one-to-one correspondence from the claims attached to persons and the claims attached to groups.

A complete account of group agency would show how individual capacities for and instances of considering, willing, and doing can combine to constitute an entity with sufficient unity of the right sort to count as an agent that itself considers, wills, and acts. I do not have a complete account of agency, individual or collective, but I have already offered one necessary condition: agents must be sufficiently free in both the internal and external senses of freedom. They must be competent enough and independent enough. A natural agent must have an adequate set of freedoms necessary to have the three capacities of considering, willing, and doing, and a collective agent must be made up of sufficiently free natural agents whose individual capacities for considering, willing, and doing mesh in a way that renders the collectivity sufficiently free to have the capacities of considering, willing, and doing. Similarly, a free natural agent must be independent—that is, not dominated by the choices of others. To be independent, a group agent must make and keep the natural agents that make it up free of individual domination. Natural agents who are dominated by the unilateral will of others are dependent on the purposes of those others, and so cannot count as active members of the group agent whose considerations, choices, and acts are their own. An independent group agent also must itself be free from domination by external forces.

Sovereignty, in the standard way that idea is understood in international law, is neither necessary nor sufficient for a group agent to be independent. A government whose sovereignty is made complicated by issues of federalism, subsidiarity, and international governance can be independent in an uncomplicated way. Nor do I mean to deny that group agents that are unambiguously subject to the authority of the state, such as associations, universities, churches, and corporations, are legitimate with respect to those over whom they claim some sort of normative power (though the extent of those powers must necessarily be circumscribed). A group agent is independent if it is not dominated by outside forces, where domination is the wrongful subjection to the will of another. Just as individual agents can be independent though subject to legitimate law, so too political group agents can be independent though subject to legitimate law in a federal or international legal system. Internal and external freedom are connected in the following way: at least some of the rights and liberties that are necessary for freedom as independence are also constitutive or instrumental preconditions for freedom as self-governance.

A natural individual can fail to be a moral agent in degree, hence the notion of an impaired or incompetent person. Children and those who are seriously mentally ill or mentally impaired are still persons. Similarly, shared agency can fail in degree. So the account of normative groups would also specify the minimal capacities for considering, willing, and doing that make a collectivity an agent at all, and, as with individual natural agents, specify the thresholds that distinguish competent from incompetent collective agency. An aggregation of individuals that does not meet even minimal threshold conditions does not count as a shared agent at all, and so does not count as a normative group at all. A collective agent can fail the test of sufficient freedom, either because the natural persons that make it up are not sufficiently free, or because their individual capacities for considering, willing, and doing have not combined in the ways needed to form a collective agent that is sufficiently free. Something similar goes for external freedom: natural agents can be independent—that is, undominated by the unilateral choice of others—in both degree and in kind, in some contexts but not in others. So too for the group agents they constitute. So not all normative groups are already free.

III. Constitution and Conscription

So far, I have said little about what the conditions for shared agency are. How does an aggregation of individual "I"s somehow go *POOF!* and become "We," a unified moral agent capable of shared action and that is the proper proximate subject of moral appraisal? Two sorts of answers are needed. One answer should be sufficiently general so that, when we look at aggregations as diverse as marriages, string ensembles, baseball teams, street demonstrations, universities, hospitals, business enterprises, professions, organized crime families, ethnic groups, political societies, and governments, we are able to say which have the capacity for shared agency and which do not. Then we need an answer that is sufficiently specific to the kind of aggregation in question, so that we can specify the necessary and sufficient conditions for success as a shared agent of that kind. Conditions for succeeding at "playing the Mendelssohn Octet" may be different than conditions for succeeding at "amending the Constitution."

For A to be a group agent that counts B as a member, two sorts of conditions need to be satisfied. First, we need *constitutive* conditions: in what way is A formed to possess the capacities for moral agency? Second, we need *conscriptive* conditions: why and how does A's power to govern come to apply to B? One might have thought that, if the answer to the question of legitimate governance is collective self-governance, constitution and conscription are not separate ideas: a group agent simply is constituted by its members. Not so. Though constitution and conscription are simultaneous, at least initially, they are conceptually distinct achievements that have conceptually distinct success conditions. To see this, think of how a new member joins an existing group. Even if one says that a group agent is reconstituted each time a new member joins, different members can attach to the group in different ways.

Constitution

How are group agents *constituted?* Unified, shared agency can come about in at least three general ways. Every plausible account of which I know follows these three routes, either singly or in combination.

Meshed Aims and Plans. The structurally simplest route to the constitution of a group agent is through the intermeshing of aims and plans.[7] Very roughly, a "we" is formed that plays Mendelssohn when each of us aims to play the piece together, knowing that each of us has that aim, and with each of us planning to (and knowing that each plans to) adjust our actions (tempo, pitch, dynamics, phrasing) to mesh with the actions of others as necessary to support each other to achieve our shared aim. Because no organizational or procedural structure needs to be relied upon for the intermeshing of aims and plans, the paradigm cases are face-to-face, small scale, and synchronic (although more complicated collective agency is not precluded). Note how this simple collective agent succeeds at being the proximate locus of responsibility. The octet itself is a proper subject of evaluation, to be praised or criticized, and this praise and criticism to some extent distributes onto the individual players in a way that is not simply an evaluation of the individual contribution of each. This is captured by locutions such as "We did it!" after a good performance: "we," all together, the weakest player and the strongest, did one thing, "it." But note too that, if the intermeshing of aims and plans is the only route to shared agency relied upon here, if the eight string players are a subset of a larger chamber orchestra, the woodwinds and horns who stayed home did not "play the Mendelssohn Octet." For the stay-at-home players to be authors of this action in any way, so that some sort of responsibility for the performance could distribute on to them, recourse to one of the other two routes to shared agency is needed.

Representation. The second route to the constitution of a group agent relies upon representation and impersonation. Hobbes of course is the great propounder of the view that unity of agency is achieved only through the unity of the representative:

> A Multitude of men, are made *One* Person, when they are by one man, or one Person, Represented; so that it be done with the consent of every one of that Multitude in particular. For it is the *Unity* of the Representer, not the *Unity* of the Represented, that maketh the Person *One*. And it is the Representer that beareth the Person, and but one Person: And *Unity*, cannot otherwise be understood, in Multitude.[8]

A shared agent is formed and can act as one only if each of many individuals severally authorizes a person to represent each, or, in Hobbes's phrase, to impersonate each.[9] The core idea here is that, under certain conditions, A can act for B in a way that makes B the author of the action, and so the proper locus of responsibility for the action. Via this route, collective agency comes about when one agent is authorized to act in the same way on behalf of each of many. There need not be coordination or intermeshing of the plans of the many, or even common knowledge of the multiple representation (although one might make authorization contingent on the authorization of others, in which case common knowledge would be necessary). Notice how the route of intermeshing plans and the route of representation can combine. A multitude of unmeshed individuals can be represented by a team with intermeshed plans, or we can together, through an intermeshed plan, appoint a single natural representative to act for us.

Procedure. The third route to the constitution of a group agent relies on procedures, practices, or organizational structures. The various capacities of considering, willing, and doing are functionally accomplished by the combined efforts of many, though perhaps no one natural person has considered, willed, or acted in a way that matches the shared action. Indeed, one tempting test of whether a procedure constitutes a shared agent is that the outcomes of the procedure meet some appealing standards of rationality even when the collective choice is at odds with the individual choices appealingly aggregated.[10] A mechanism that produced an authoritative decision or action out of (and sensitive to) practical inputs of individual agents would be such a procedure. A shared action produced by a procedure could be relatively simple, such as friends choosing a movie by majority vote, or as complex as the rendering of law in a legal system in which the admission of evidence, factual determinations given the evidence, legal rulings given the factual findings, and appellate review given this and other precedential legal rulings are produced by many actors, not one of whom may will the outcome for a consistent set of factual and legal reasons.

To illustrate how a procedure can constitute a group agent that rationally makes choices that no natural member would make, consider a hypothetical. Suppose the National Transitional Council is considering, before he is captured and killed, whether to put Colonel Qaddafi on trial *in absentia* for war crimes, and suppose the decision depends on three considerations: Does the Council have lawful jurisdiction? Will international allies support a trial? Will remaining Qaddafi loyalists in the rebel-controlled territories remain peaceful? A trial will proceed only if all

Table 2   Group Agency Constituted by Procedure: Majority Rule

	Lawful Jurisdiction?	International Support?	Loyalists Peaceful?	Individual Judgment
Justice Minister	NO	YES	YES	**NO**
Foreign Minister	YES	NO	YES	**NO**
Defense Minister	YES	YES	NO	**NO**
Group Judgment by Criterion	**YES**	**YES**	**YES**	**Try Qaddafi?**

three questions are answered in the affirmative. Three council members are to make this decision: the justice minister, the foreign minister, and the defense minister. For each of the three questions, one of the ministers answers no, but the other two answer yes, as presented in Table 2.

On the individual judgment of each minister, Qaddafi should not be tried, so if the decision procedure were to aggregate individual conclusions, the judgment would be unanimous: no trial. Instead, the decision procedure is to render a collective judgment on each of the three considerations by majority rule. Since two of the three answer yes to each question, the group renders a judgment that Qaddafi should be tried. Some may think this conclusion paradoxical or even irrational, but there is another interpretation: the result confirms the existence of group agency, for here is a rational decision-making procedure demonstrating the capacity for considering and willing that produces a judgment of the group that does not match the judgment of any single natural agent.

Group agency constituted by procedure does not depend on majority rule for the choice of procedure. Suppose instead that the procedure followed by the Council is a division of labor, so that each minister determines the answer to the question under his area of expertise. Change as well the answers the ministers give to the three questions, so that each minister answers yes to the question in his area of expertise, but no to the other two questions, as presented in Table 3.

Again, the group judgment is to proceed with the trial, since each minister answers the question in his area of expertise in the affirmative, even though the individual judgment of each minister is not to proceed.

Complex instances of shared agency typically will rely on all three routes of constitution. A corporation or association might form through the

Table 3   Group Agency Constituted by Procedure: Division of Labor

	Lawful Jurisdiction?	International Support?	Loyalists Peaceful?	Individual Judgment
Justice Minister	YES	NO	NO	**NO**
Foreign Minister	NO	YES	NO	**NO**
Defense Minister	NO	NO	YES	**NO**
Group Judgment by Criterion	**YES**	**YES**	**YES**	**Try Qaddafi?**

intermeshing of the aims and plans of its founders, appoint representatives to make decisions through procedures, and then delegate the implementation of plans to intermeshed teams of workers. To make sense of "amending the Constitution" as an act of a shared agent, the web of intermeshed aims, representations, and procedures would have to be even more elaborate.

Conscription

What are the conditions for *conscription?* For each of these routes to the constitution of a group agent, we must ask what gives it its authority in Hobbes's sense: what makes any particular natural agent an author of the group agent's actions, and so a candidate for distributed responsibility? The mere existence of a procedure is not sufficient to create a shared agent out of those natural agents whose practical capacities and functionings are taken to be inputs. Your neighbors may, to your surprise, announce a procedure whereby each house on the block is to be painted the color preferred by the majority, and under that procedure, after duly taking your fondness for blue into account, the color of your house is to be changed from blue to yellow. Yet surely something more than the counting of your preference as an input must tie you to this procedure before you assume any authorship in, or responsibility for, the alleged shared agent that has arrived on your doorstep with cans of yellow paint. If instead of employing a procedure, your neighbors appointed as representative a natural agent to make the neighborhood painting decisions, what is she to you? Or if a neighbor appears with a couple of yellow paintbrushes in one hand and a shotgun in the other, you may find it prudent to join him in painting your house yellow and—one eye on the gun—take pains to do it right, meshing your plans with his. Although you would be taking the action of painting your house yellow, you would not, in any normatively important sense, have formed a shared agent to paint your house yellow.

What are we to say about string players in a concentration camp ordered to play Mendelssohn for the guards? Self-governing individual action can be nested inside a generally coercive background. An individual cellist ordered to play the Bach solo suites for the guards may be forced to do something she would not voluntarily choose to do, but, against that forced background, she may out of defiant pride, or simple pleasure amid misery, decide to exercise the discretion that remains hers to play her best, and then, again within limits, she is a responsible competent agent. So too, eight prison musicians may form a locally self-governing group agent whose purpose is survival, or defiant pride, or a bit of happiness amid the misery. They do not form a collective agent, however, with the guards. Is a collective agent formed with a guard who also is a good violinist and orders that the prisoners play with him? Under some circumstances and for some circumscribed purposes, yes. If, nested inside the larger coercive background, the prisoners have and exercise local self-governance in performance with the guard, then for purposes of aesthetic praise and criticism, they are acting collectively with him. If the guard also is a musical bully who demands obedience note by note under threat of punishment, then no. Either way, the prisoners do not form an all-purpose group agent with the guard that is responsible, as a group agent, for all of the consequences of the forced performance. Suppose the performance also served as the signal to commence atrocities elsewhere in the camp. Performing under those circumstances may or may not be excusable, but this is a direct assessment of responsibility to be made of each musician taken as an individual natural agent, rather than an assessment of distributed responsibility for the action of a group agent. Group agency is a normative ascription that supervenes on some descriptive facts, but is not itself a descriptive fact of the matter.

A natural agent can be conscripted into constituting a shared agent, and so share authorship in a shared agent's actions, in three ways. The first is if the natural agent, under uncoerced and informed circumstances, *consents* to constitute a group agent in this way for this purpose. Second, voluntary action short of consent could constitute participation in a collective agent if a version of the *fair play* principle applies, in which the natural agent voluntarily accepts the benefits of a mutually advantageous and fair cooperative venture under conditions where the benefit could have been refused.[11] The third way to conscript a natural agent is if commitment to constitute a shared agent in something like this way for this purpose is a *practical necessity*, in that it is either constitutive of, or a precondition for, acting upon the natural agent's prior uncoerced and informed commitments, and the natural agent, knowing that this is so, either cannot or will not give up these prior commitments. Says Kant, "Whoever wills the end also wills (insofar as reason has decisive influence on his actions) the indispensably necessary means to it that are within his power."[12] These are demanding conditions for authorship, but such demandingness is needed to attach a natural agent to an entity with the moral standing and powers of a group agent. Recall that a group agent is a proximate locus of respect and responsibility that both bears the moral claims made by and against its constituent members in some ways and distributes the moral claims made by and against it over its constituent members in some ways.

Three conditions for constitution and three conditions for conscription give nine ways of attaching a natural agent to a group agent, as shown on the grid in Table 4. I have suggestively filled each cell with a collectivity that arguably is a normative group that arguably is constituted and conscripted in one of the nine ways. I invite you to disagree with me. You may not be convinced that all of these nine groups are normative groups, bearers of respect and responsibility in virtue of their capacities for self-governing and independent shared agency. Or you may disagree that they constitute shared agents by the route I suggest or conscript members as authors in the way that I say. You might be correct on all counts. I have not given precise criteria for distinguishing free normative groups from impaired normative groups from groups that are not agents at all. Also,

Table 4   Constitution and Conscription

	Meshed Aims and Plans	Representation	Procedure
Consent	string quartet	symphony orchestra	legislature
Fair Play	ocean fishery	labor union	jury
Practical Necessity	lifeboat	army	electorate

complex group agents may be constituted in nested levels, so that the unity of agency is built up out of a combination of meshed aims and plans, representation, and procedure. So, too, conscription of members can occur by either consent, fair play, or practical necessity for different members, and for some members, conscription may be overdetermined. So I invite you to fill out the grid your way.

IV. Group Agency and Political Legitimacy

The kind of shared agency that is of greatest interest to us, of course, is political agency. Political action has profound effects on the freedom and interests of those subject to it because it nearly always involves coercion and seeks to change the normative status of its subjects by imposing duties or liabilities. Because of these high moral stakes, the conditions for successfully constituting a political "We" from a multitude of "I"s are going to have more moral content than what it takes to constitute a string ensemble. For how can a political people be *my* people unless, in some way, whoever speaks and acts for the people speaks and acts for me, representing in a morally adequate way both my will and my basic interests across the broad range of freedoms and goods that governments claim the right to regulate?

When the collective agent in question claims the normative power to coerce its constituent natural agents, the criterion that these natural agents be sufficiently free is threatened. Governments, by imposing and enforcing laws, appear to restrict the freedoms of the governed. So governments must either show that these restrictions on freedom nonetheless leave the governed sufficiently free or show that the enactment and enforcement of law does not, despite appearances, actually restrict freedom. One strategy for showing that restrictions on freedom leave natural agents sufficiently free is to show that restrictions are for the sake of realizing and protecting these same freedoms, for there is no condition of anarchy or other scheme of government under which these freedoms would be more inviolable or less violated, and so no other condition under which natural agents in general would have greater capacities for agency. One strategy for showing that apparently coercive law does not restrict freedom is to show how the subject of law can also be, from some normatively appropriate point of view, its willing author who therefore is not coerced. These are not two separable strategies, however, but two turns of the same justificatory argument. One of the central questions of modern political philosophy is how, if at all, collective self-governance is compatible with individual freedom. The correct answer, I believe, has both a substantive and a procedural component, because it needs to address agents both from their perspectives as subjects of law and their perspectives as authors of law. The agent viewed as the subject of coercive law must be given adequate justification, and the most promising strategy of justification is to show that equal and fully adequate freedom for all requires such limits on the freedom of each. The agent viewed as the author of coercive law must be free enough in the relevant ways to count as an author. Only if individuals are free enough to count as authors can the collective body constitute a shared agent. How free is free enough? No more constrained than is necessary to guarantee other constituent members of the collective body the freedoms they need to have the capacity to be authors. To establish that subjects also are authors, we do not look for free founding moments. Even if such foundings were not myths, they would not by themselves do the job needed. Rather, we look for virtuous circles in which subjects are free enough to have the capacity to be authors of collective acts, procedures, and institutions that realize and protect the freedoms that make them free enough to have the capacity to be authors.

I have been offering necessary conditions for collective political agency, but notice that these conditions do double duty as criteria for a normative conception of political legitimacy. This should come as no surprise. If the concept of political legitimacy is, roughly, the normative power to govern, then one plausible account of the criteria for the legitimacy of a government is that only governments constituted as shared agents authored by their subjects have the right to rule those subjects, because only then is the puzzle of how we can remain self-governing when governed by others solved. Yet note that, if the account of shared agency above is correct, then the correct account of political legitimacy has substantive as well as procedural requirements. Only free enough natural agents can constitute a shared agent, and no procedure can make a natural agent free enough who is not free enough already. This is why, to be legitimate, procedures of governance must be constrained by substantive preconditions (for example, constitutional rights that limit majority rule).

On the conception of political legitimacy that I believe is correct, the test of legitimate government is two-pronged, just as the test of shared political agency is two-pronged. There needs to be an adequate connection between the governors and the governed (the procedural prong), and there needs to be adequate protection of at least basic human rights (the substantive prong). At a minimum, legitimacy requires the political freedom and basic protection that are constitutive of, or instrumentally necessary for, the individual moral agency of the members. Hence, the criterion offered earlier, applied to political society: *A necessary condition for a free (enough) people is that it be made up of free (enough) persons.* We do not have to be too precise about the thresholds here. Perhaps something less than democracy will satisfy the political freedom prong, and perhaps something less than the full complement of liberal rights will satisfy the human rights prong. But on no plausible normative account of group agency, and therefore of legitimacy, does a tyrannical regime that recognizes no constraints on the arbitrary will of the tyrant and that systematically violates basic human rights personify the people it rules.

V. Constitution and Conscription in the Libyan Revolution

Social contract theory advanced under Kant and then Rawls when it let go of just-so stories about *ab ovo* foundings. Nonetheless, the world presents us with the chickens and eggs of legitimate governance. Was France (that normative group represented by Nicolas Sarkozy) to send the rebel diplomats home empty-handed or with the prize of recognition? We could say that, on March 10, it is too early for the question of legitimacy to arise. Libya either has returned to a state of nature or has never left it, there is no way to legitimately bootstrap oneself to legitimate governance, and all now is domination. We may predict whether a faction of dominators will triumph, we may predict whether a faction, once in empirical power, will treat the residents of Libya harshly or leniently, and so we may have reason to back one faction over another on humanitarian grounds. We may even predict which faction is more likely to satisfy the conditions of free group agency, and so legitimacy, in the future, and that gives us further reason to support its struggle. But being the best candidate for legitimate governance no more makes one legitimate than being the best candidate for president of the United States makes one president of the United States.

We might, however, be able to do more than just predict the outcome of a struggle over governance. We might be able to predict the course

Table 5   Constitution and Conscription in Libya

	Meshed Aims and Plans	Representation	Procedure
Consent	prominent rebels	Benghazi civil servants	Transitional Council
Fair Play	demonstrators	rebel army units	rebel army officers
Practical Necessity	besieged towns	all Libyans as subjects	all Libyans as citizens

through the routes of constitution and conscription that the likely winner is likely to take. And perhaps there are conditions under which a possible course that cascades through the routes of constitution and conscription is self-enacting: early successes do not merely predict later successes, but make it the case that later success has already happened. In Table 5, consider again our nine-cell grid, this time filled in with potential group agents in the Libyan rebellion.

Constitution by Meshed Aims and Plans

Begin with the structurally simplest route to group agency, constitution via meshed aims and plans. The surprising success of street demonstrations prompted a number of high-level defections from Qaddafi's government, the return of some exiles, and the emboldening of some dissident voices. These prominent, would-be leaders of the rebellion gathered in Benghazi, where demonstrators had forced out Qaddafi loyalists. We do not know exactly how these prominent Libyans jockeyed with each other to be heard and to gain a following in the crucial first days, but some subset does appear to have reached an agreement among themselves to claim leadership of the rebellion. The initial core may have recruited allies and elbowed out adversaries, but at some point, a relatively stable coterie was speaking with one voice. By meshing their aims and plans, they constituted the shared group of prominent rebels; the participants who constituted this group were conscripted by consent. Though the stakes were enormously higher, the process of group formation was probably no more complex than face-to-face schoolyard coalition-building and snubbing. Their shared aim was to lead the rebellion. That, of course, did not make them the rebellion's leaders or give them one shred of normative control over anyone but each other. But, like a string quartet, they did constitute a normative group capable of responsible action.

What of the demonstrators themselves? Those who took to the streets ought to have quickly recognized that they were engaging in a mutually advantageous cooperative venture whose aim was the reform or overthrow of Qaddafi's regime. Because the venture met with partial success, we can suppose that rules of coordination emerged among the crowd: when and how to communicate with each other, when and how to stand firm, when and how to retreat. So those who shared in these ends and shared in these means constituted a limited purpose group agent who performed the shared action of demonstrating. It is unlikely that they formed a *competent* agent with adequate capacities for unified, reason-guided action—surely they were unable to mesh their aims and plans with the unity of a string quartet—but nor did they simply remain a crowd. Rather, they formed a normative group, albeit an impaired one.

Who was conscripted into this shared agent? It is not necessary to suppose that only those demonstrators who voluntarily agreed that these be the rules of engagement and coordination count as members of the normative group. It is enough that these spontaneous conventions of coordination governed a great many of the demonstrators, and that the demonstration's success depended on a great many continuing to be governed by these conventions. Fairness would then require that a demonstrator who aimed at the demonstration's success and voluntarily engaged in protest side by side with those who were governed by the rules of engagement also be governed by these rules of engagement, and therefore count as a conscript to the group.

To be clear: on this argument, no one was obligated to demonstrate. But those who did demonstrate were conscripted as constitutive members of the group agent of demonstrators in virtue of their voluntarily sharing in the benefits of the coordination of others. I do not need to go so far as to say that the fair play principle *obligates* the voluntary demonstrator to comply with the cooperative rules. All I need to say here is that, in virtue of the fair play principle, voluntary demonstrators are normatively governed in some way by those rules, and that makes them participants in a (somewhat impaired) group agent.

What does it mean to be governed without necessarily being obligated? As we saw in Chapter 2, if A has a moral power with respect to B in context C, B correlatively faces a moral liability. What is this liability? B is liable to changes in his normative situation. Such changes could be a duty not to interfere with A (that is, a recognition of A's immunity), liability to A's use of force or coercion, liability to changes in one's rights against third parties, or liability to changes in normatively significant social facts. None of these normative changes are the same as being morally obligated to comply with A's commands.

Meanwhile, Misurata and the towns surrounding Tripoli that had initial success in throwing out government forces were under siege, suffering shelling and bombing by Qaddafi loyalists. No case of practical necessity is clearer: the physical survival of the residents of these towns was in jeopardy, and each individual had the same compelling aim of staying alive. The means to staying alive almost certainly demanded some level of organization and coordination: barricades needed to be manned, fires extinguished, wounds stanched. Insofar as these residents are guided by reason, if they will to survive, they must will the necessary means to survive. Add the usual universalization requirement that one may not make of oneself a special case, for we are not so foolish as to try to derive morality from rational self-interest alone. Then any modestly effective coordination mechanism that emerged is something the residents of these towns were reasonably compelled to join. This is no factual prediction: some may have cowered in basements or profiteered on the black market. And the conscription of others may be overdetermined, for they may also have consented or have voluntarily accepted offices in the resistance. But voluntary acts are not necessary to conscript the residents of a besieged town to its common defense.

Constitution by Representation

Consider now, more briefly, group agency in the Libyan rebellion constituted by representation. Following Hobbes, the wills of a multitude of authors can be unified in the person of their representative. Civil servants in Benghazi faced a choice: should they remain loyal to Qaddafi, or show up in the morning to work for the self-appointed rebel leaders? If they showed up to work, then they helped to constitute the emerging rebel institution of governance. Now at a scale larger than the face-to-face sharing of aims, this wider institution was constituted by representation: the individual wills of the rebel civil servants were represented by the rebel leaders, and insofar as civil servants took supervision from the leaders, they were demonstrating the effectiveness of this representation. How were the civil servants conscripted into the rebel institution? For many, their showing up for work tokened consent, but for all, their continued voluntary acceptance of the benefits of office connect them as participants in group agency by way of fair play, whether or not they consented.

A similar story can be told about rebel army units. Most were comprised of enthusiastic, untrained, poorly equipped young men. Some were defectors from Qaddafi's forces. For the uprising to have succeeded beyond a few days, they needed to have been organized under some command. Somehow, local commanders emerged. We know that, at the top, military command of the rebels was less than perfectly unified because generals were squabbling over the top post. But that did not prevent local units from constituting local group agents, unified by a commanding officer by way of representation. How are individual soldiers conscripted into the normative group of a fighting unit? All showed up to fight by consent. They need not, however, have consented to the command structure that emerged. Some may have shown up at the front having only the vaguest notions of military command and control. But a military venture cannot succeed unless it is organized as a rule-governed cooperative scheme, and the more disciplined among them did just that, subjecting themselves to the command of those who had the experience or nerve to put themselves forth as officers, thereby constituting a group agent via representation. At that point, a fighter who is voluntarily at the front can no longer go it alone. Consenting or not, he is conscripted into the shared agent through the fair play principle and is normatively governed by the local commanding officer who represents the will of the group. In the heat of an existential battle, he is conscripted by practical necessity as well.

Constitution by Procedure

As the institutional structures of the rebellion expanded, solidified, and matured, constitution by procedure took hold. When the self-appointed informal rebel leaders announced that they had become the self-appointed National Transitional Council, they were not simply giving themselves a fancy title. They were, as well, adopting procedures of decision-making for themselves and for those civil servants and fighters who took them as their representative. So meshed aims and plans as a route to constitute group agency among the rebel leaders was partly supplemented and partly replaced by a set of procedures to unify their capacities of considering, willing, and doing. How competent these procedures were is uncertain. But it is clear that, if the rebel normative group was to expand to cover cooperating civil servants and army units in the field, formality and complexity of constitution would be needed. The members of the National Transitional Council conscripted themselves to their own enterprise by consent. Once a large scale mutually advantageous cooperative venture of rebellion and governance is up and running, consent is not the only route of conscription. Imagine the situation of rebel army officers. Because they have volunteered for their positions and opportunities, it does not matter whether they have consented to join a normative group led by the National Transitional Council. The procedures of the council speak for them because they would be taking unfair advantage of the cooperative efforts of others if the council did not speak for them.

Conscription by Fair Play

Consider an objection to employing the principle of fair play to conscript membership in normative groups.[13] The fair play argument, as developed by Rawls, shows how one can acquire an obligation through the voluntary acceptance of the benefits of a cooperative scheme even if one has not consented to be obligated. Rawls himself retreated from the claim that fair play creates obligation to obey the law because most of us are not free to voluntarily accept or reject the benefits of political society. Do the actors that I imagine could be conscripted through fair play—demonstrators, Benghazi civil servants, and rebel army soldiers and officers—voluntarily accept the benefits created by the group agent to which they are supposedly conscripted? But some cannot avoid the benefits the group agent confers: a demonstrator may have done nothing to seek safety in numbers, though the crowd makes him safer. Others have no acceptable alternative to accepting the benefits: a soldier who rejects coordination on the battlefield puts his life in danger. Worse still, some are coerced by the group agent into accepting benefits because the group agent itself has rendered the actor's alternatives unacceptable: a civil servant might show up to work for the rebels because the rebels have made his preferred alternative, working for the Qaddafi regime, fatal.

The answer to this objection is built of several steps. First, note that I have been employing conceptions of freedom, consent, voluntariness, and coercion that are practical, not metaphysical, and partly normative, not purely descriptive or psychological. Consider the paradigmatic example of fair play: neighbors who form a cooperative venture to dig a new community well. If Adilah draws water from the well, the principle of fair play obligates her to do her fair share in the well's upkeep according to the rules of the cooperative venture, even if she has not consented to do so. But suppose that the neighbors who dug the new well wrongfully dumped the waste rock down Adilah's own well, blocking it. If Adilah has been deprived by her neighbors of a source of water to which she is entitled, then drawing water from the new well does not satisfy the criterion of voluntary acceptance of benefit under the fair play principle. The neighbors violate Adilah's moral baseline by destroying her well. On a normative conception of coercion, if she then consents to join the new cooperative, such consent is coerced. Similarly, if she does not consent but merely draws the water, her acceptance of benefit is not voluntary on a normative conception of voluntariness. To assess whether the neighbors present Adilah with a coercive threat or a voluntary offer, we do not compare the benefit of proposed membership in the cooperative scheme to Adilah's descriptive alternative, which is to go thirsty, but to the alternative morally owed to her by the neighbors, which is not to damage her well.[14] Similarly, in asking if Libyan demonstrators, civil servants, and soldiers voluntarily accept the benefits of a cooperative scheme, we assess whether they have benefited and whether the benefit has been voluntarily accepted in comparison with their normative baselines—how they ought to be treated—not their descriptive baselines—how they will be treated. Unlike Adilah, who has a prior entitlement to the water of her own well, Qaddafi's civil servants have no prior entitlement to a comfortable job in a tyrannical regime. So, though the rebellion worsens the civil servants' descriptive alternative to accepting the benefits of working for the rebels by eliminating the option of working for Qaddafi in safety, this worsening need not violate the civil servants' normative baseline. On a moralized conception of coercion, coming to work for the rebels in the morning is the acceptance of an offer, rather than submission to a threat.

How far does this appeal to moralized baselines go? If, as Kant holds, in a lawless condition every individual is subject to unilateral domination by every other, one might think that all of our interactions in a state of nature are mutually coercive and so incapable of being genuinely consensual in a normative sense. We are capable of psychological voluntariness, of course, in that it is possible to intentionally and successfully act on our desires. We can also be held responsible for many of our actions, in the sense that we can act in ways that are morally appraisable as blameworthy or praiseworthy (on those moral reasons, perhaps attenuated, that apply to us in a state of nature). But one might think that we cannot consensually *obligate* ourselves in a state of nature, and that wherever obligation via consent is impossible, obligation via fair play also is impossible, on the same ground. Both conclusions, however, are extravagant, for the upshot of mutual domination is not so drastic. The normatively voluntary action necessary to create consent and fair play obligations is possible in a lawless condition.

Outside of a civil condition, our rights are insecure in three ways: they cannot be legislated, they cannot be adjudicated, and there is no assurance that they will be enforced.[15] Because of these three defects, all agreements in a lawless condition are inherently unstable, and some may be so unstable that some offers will never be made, and if made, never accepted. But it does not follow that the genuine acceptance of an offer or of a benefit is conceptually or practically impossible. If someone has trusted you and performed first on an agreement, you cannot ordinarily claim lack of assurance or of adjudication as a justification for not performing second, at least on your unilateral interpretation of what performance requires. Yes, there is a sense in which we all wrong each other all of the time in a state of nature because we are failing in our duty to force each other into a civil condition. But I have not put you in this lawless condition and I cannot, on my own, remove you from it. Our situation is more like two would-be contractors who face an unjust background that neither has created. If A steals B's bicycle, that wrongful act does not disable B from contracting to buy C's bicycle. In the "smaller moral world" that exists between potential cooperators in a state of nature, the background condition of enduring coercion may be bracketed for many purposes.[16]

In one respect, establishing voluntariness in a lawless condition may be easier, rather than harder, than in a lawful condition. Without lawgiving and adjudication, what one is entitled to in a state of nature is underdetermined and therefore one's normative baseline is underdetermined. In a lawful condition, the moral baseline is shaped by what is allowed by actual legitimate law. In a lawless condition, what counts as a coercive threat rather than merely sharp bargaining is incompletely specified. One should not exaggerate: the state of nature is not a morality-free zone. But unlike in a lawful condition, where there is a presumption, rebuttable to be sure, of a rough correspondence between *ex ante* empirical baselines and normative baselines, there is no such presumption in a lawless condition.

Finally, recall that to conscript an actor into membership in a group agent, we do not need to establish that the actor is morally obligated to obey the directives of the group agent. Rather, all we need to establish is the weaker claim that the actor is liable to the normative power of the group agent—that the group agent legitimately governs the actor over some scope and in some jurisdiction of action. Recall again the constitutive properties of a normative group: an entity that is the proximate locus of respect and responsibility in virtue of its capacity for unified considering, deciding, and doing. An agent does not need to be morally obligated to obey group decisions in order for her individual actions to function as contributions to unified considering, deciding, and willing. Nor does an agent need to be morally obligated to obey in order to share, in some way, in the rights and responsibilities of the group that are distributed over its natural members. For those who still are repelled by the idea that one can be conscripted, without consent, into membership in a group, observe that membership entails, not moral obligation, but moral liability. A normative group, to be a normative group, need only claim the normative power to create and change the normative situation of its members in some ways, not in all ways. A group creates and changes institutional rights and duties in ways that change its members' moral liabilities. But this is just to say that the moral rights and responsibilities of normative groups are distributed over the natural actors that are members of the group.

Why doesn't my invocation of moralized conceptions of coercion to rescue conscription by fair play create the opposite difficulty?[17] I have titled this chapter "All Foundings Are Forced," but on moralized conceptions of freedom and coercion, if we each have a right to require each other to leave the state of nature and enter into a lawful condition, the physical means that we employ cannot count as coercion. A moment ago, we worried that it was impossible to enter into voluntary agreements with each other in a state of nature, but on a moralized baseline, it now appears to be impossible to force each other out of the state of nature. Indeed, on a moralized conception of coercion, to say that legitimate law is coercive is a contradiction: law can be legitimate or coercive, but not both.

The answer is to recognize that coercion is only a *partially* moralized concept. We mean two different things when we consider a concept moralized. We might mean that the conditions for the correct invocation of the concept are not purely descriptive, but involve moral considerations. Or we might mean that the concept, when correctly invoked, delivers a moral verdict. Unless one denies that the naturalistic fallacy is a fallacy, the moral considerations will have to come in somewhere, either early or late.[18] No morally relevant concept has purely descriptive conditions and also, when correctly invoked, delivers a dispositive moral verdict. But it doesn't follow that when a concept does have normative conditions, it must, when correctly used, deliver a dispositive moral verdict. "Murder" in contemporary English is dispositive—justified murder is a contradiction. In our entrenched linguistic usage, however, terms such as force, coercion, and deception are only partially moralized. They are morally suspect actions that call for justification, but are not dispositively wrong. So it is not a contradiction to speak of justified force, coercion, violence, and deception, and we would have to go through unacceptable linguistic contortions to restrict our use of those terms to actions that are dispositively forbidden.

Similarly, when we speak of freedom, we mean it in more or less moralized senses, and though there is always danger of equivocation, it isn't all that difficult to be clear. Sometimes when we speak of being free, we mean, in the descriptive sense, having unconstrained options. If there are tomatoes in the grocery store, and we have enough money, we are free to buy them. If the price of tomatoes goes up, we are able to buy fewer tomatoes, we have fewer options, so we are, in the descriptive sense, less free. This isn't a mistaken sense of freedom, but it leaves quite open what is morally important about being free in that way. If we are able to shoplift the expensive tomatoes without detection, our options have increased, and we are again more free in this descriptive sense. Against Mill's claim that "all restraint, *qua* restraint, is an evil," however, nothing of moral importance is lost in reducing the freedom of shoplifters to steal tomatoes.[19] On the view adopted in this book, the sort of freedom that is of great moral importance is freedom from being dominated by the unilateral will of others.[20] Therefore, the meaning of a well-known and crucial statement of Kant is perfectly clear, though he switches between moralized and descriptive senses of his terms mid-sentence. Here it is, with my annotations in brackets:

> If a certain use of [descriptive] freedom is itself a hindrance to [moralized] freedom in accordance with universal laws (i.e., wrong), [descriptive] coercion that is opposed to this (as a *hindering of a hindrance to* [moralized] *freedom*) is consistent with [moralized] freedom in accordance with universal laws, that is, it is right.[21]

Annotated, the title of this chapter is: "All Foundings Are [Descriptively] Forced."

VI. Constituting the Legitimate Representative of the Libyan People

The astute reader will have noted that I left the most difficult cells for last. I have shown how the institutions of rebellion can emerge, constituting (by the various routes of meshed aims, representation, and procedure), a group agent that conscripts rebels as its members. But a similar mechanism can account for the emergence of a Mafia crime family, the Church of Scientology, or Qaddafi's dictatorship. None legitimately govern a political people. What, if anything, connects the willing rebels and their institutions to all Libyans? What, if anything, can make the National Transitional Council's claim to be "the only legitimate body representing the people of Libya and the Libyan state" true?

Conscription by Consent?

We can rule out some answers. An entire people cannot constitute a normative group by the route of meshed aims and plans. No multitude at that scale can share the range of aims that must be set by a government, let alone mesh their plans to act as one. Only in a much smaller domain—a more limited context C—is unity without institutional structure possible. Nor can an entire people be conscripted into a normative group by way of consent. As said earlier, this is not simply an empirical claim, but most often a conceptual one. For almost everyone, consent *in medias res* cannot be genuine, because almost all find themselves without alternatives to life in one coercive regime or another. One can endorse one's political arrangements, and when we endorse morally endorsable political arrangements, we have reached, in Rawls's lovely but obscure phrase, "the outer limit of our freedom."[22] But if consent is a transaction between independent wills, endorsement of an unavoidable condition does not count as consent.

Ab ovo, however, attempts at consent occur against the backdrop of natural freedom in a state of nature. Why can't such attempts conceptually succeed? Over a smaller domain—a smaller context C, not fewer contractors—I have supposed that they can: the rebel leaders are assumed to have conscripted themselves to their joint plans through mutual consent. But, despite the obviously grave and widespread consequences of a rebellion, the joint project of a rebellion's instigators is quite limited, when properly understood. Their joint actions are instrumental and time-bound: to drive out Qaddafi and bring about the conditions under which a much greater process of constitution and conscription can occur. Legitimate collective self-governance is a condition in which three powers that every natural person has—the power to make one's own law, the power to interpret one's own law, and the power to coercively enforce one's own law—are combined in such a way that these powers are exercised together, not unilaterally. Any smaller contract that is executed under conditions of legitimate governance is constrained to comply with legitimate law. A smaller contract that is executed outside of conditions of legitimate governance—that is, in a state of nature—takes lawlessness as the background condition of things, but is not itself an attempted solution to lawlessness. The subject matter of smaller contracts is not the replacement of unilateral judgment and coercion by collective self-governance. When the rebel leaders successfully form the National Transitional Council, they are neither constituting collective self-governance for all Libyans (despite their claims), nor constituting a tiny lawful condition among a couple of dozen middle-aged men. They retain whatever natural rights of judgment and coercion they have in a state of nature. So what they consent to is quite shallow. There is no fundamental difference between a dozen persons in a state of nature consenting to start a revolution together and consenting to go to a movie together. Any such group agent is unstable and unenforceable, but factually possible to realize. Just as the movie-goers might find that they have succeeded in acting together to "go to a movie," so too the rebel leaders might find that they have succeeded in acting together to "overthrow Qaddafi," or to "set the conditions for the constitution of legitimate government." But they cannot, on their own, "constitute legitimate government." That can be the collective achievement of all Libyans only. Now we can see why collective self-governance *ab ovo* cannot be achieved through consent. A state of nature is a state of mutual domination, where each, as a self-legislator and self-judge, is entitled to coerce each. So a choice to replace this coercive lawless condition with a coercive lawful condition is no more consensual than the *in medias res* choice to accept the existing coercive lawful condition that one cannot avoid. Hence the conclusion that one can consent to go to the movies in both a state of nature and in a lawful condition, but one cannot consent to be in a lawful condition in either.

Fair play will not connect all Libyans to the National Transitional Council for much the same reason that consent will not. As Rawls ultimately recognized, ordinary citizens cannot voluntarily accept the benefits of a mutually advantageous scheme of social cooperation when they cannot refuse the benefits. Those who seek offices, positions, and other advantages from institutions and practices constituted by others may thereby count as constituent members themselves, but this condition does not hold for all.

Conscription by Practical Necessity

On the view proposed here, a government has political legitimacy only when it is a free group agent constituted by the free natural agents whom it governs, where freedom is understood as competent self-governance and independence. Two ways remain to achieve legitimate governance: conscripting all of the governed through practical necessity to constitute a group agent by representation and conscripting all of the governed through practical necessity to constitute a group agent by procedure. Earlier, I invoked practical necessity to conscript survivors of shipwrecks and victims of siege warfare into normative groups constituted for their survival. Is it not extravagant to claim that we are all, always, equally compelled by reason to be citizens? Hobbes may be right about nasty and brutish, but surely he exaggerates with short: anarchy is not invariably fatal.

The demands of practical necessity, however, are not limited to existential threats. Recall the formulation of a practical necessity: something that is constitutive of, or a precondition for, acting upon a moral agent's prior commitments that the agent either cannot or will not give up. A moral agent cannot possibly give up a commitment to internal freedom, understood as competence in the capacities of considering, willing, and doing, and still count as a moral agent. External freedom, understood as independence from domination, is in some measure at least a precondition for, and arguably constitutive of, internal freedom, for without bodily integrity and liberty of thought and expression, self-governing action is not possible. Practical necessity here is not to be understood simply as a demand of instrumental rationality, or even of prudence, but a requirement of agency itself. So it is not extravagant to conclude that institutions and procedures that guarantee freedom are practical necessities, as shown in the bottom right cell of Table 5. The offer of legitimate government—that is, the offer of institutions in which we are free enough to have the capacity to be authors of procedures and collective actions and that realize and protect the freedoms that make us free enough to have the capacity to be authors—is an offer we cannot refuse.

Is it possible to refuse something less? A benevolent despotism might offer its subjects something short of active citizenship. It might provide the rule of law, realize basic human rights, and promote the well-being of all, but be unwilling or unable to make the subjects of its decent-enough rule active authors of their own governance. If we are to consider a society governed by a benevolent despotism as a form of group agency, it can only be conceived as subjects constituted by representation and conscripted by practical necessity. This describes the bottom center cell of Table 5, but like hypothesized elements on the bottom row of the Periodic Table, it may not exist in nature. The problem is that, as described, the situation does not call for any action or transaction on the part of subjects at all, so there is nothing about the subject's will that is practically necessary. True, all subjects need the freedom that the despot provides (and more), but there is no need for the joining of wills to realize that freedom. Someone who gives me a gift may gratify my wish, but does not represent my will. The subjects of benevolent despots are, collectively, patients, not agents. Perhaps they form a group patient that bears respect, but not a group agent that bears responsibility. As a normative group they are, at best, seriously impaired. So benevolent despotisms do not exercise legitimate normative power over their subjects. I elaborate on this claim in Chapter 6, "Despotism."

VII. Are Legitimate Foundings Possible?

The National Transitional Council succeeded in organizing elections for a General National Congress tasked with writing a constitution, transferred its claimed normative powers to the newly elected body, and dissolved itself in August 2012. Alas, the militias that were able to defeat Qaddafi were not able to unify in peace, and Libya soon fractured into warring factions, with two rival governments claiming legitimacy and large portions of the country under the control of neither.

How could the National Transitional Council have genuinely become the only legitimate body representing the people of Libya? They would have had to be in a position to make an offer that the people of Libya *could not* refuse—a self-enacting offer that, once made, made it the case that all Libyans were collectively self-governing, competent, and independent citizens. Nothing is like that *ab ovo*.

This is not, however, a reason for complete despair. The other eight cells of Table 5 hint at what emerging governance could be like *in medias res.* So, though no assertion of political legitimacy is *self-enacting,* some assertions of political legitimacy can be *self-fulfilling.* Over time, first through small-scale consent and meshed aims and plans, then through fair play and representation, the actions of Libya's imperfect rulers and flawed institutions could conscript more Libyans into normative groups constituted for more encompassing contexts. The day may then arrive, after many tendentious assertions of the legitimating power of impossible consent of the governed through procedures of fantasized pedigree, that the people of Libya are free enough to participate in political institutions that make them free. And that will be enough.

I have said more than once that the puzzle of political legitimacy is primarily an *in medias res* question: though born free, when we wake up in the morning, whatever we do, we feel the chains of coercive legal institutions. Still, reflecting on the anomalous normative phenomenon of an *ab ovo* founding isolates, and so illuminates, the moving parts of constitution and conscription that might otherwise be hidden from our moral imagination. For the same reason, we turn from the case of revolution in Libya, where the constitution of free group agency might have gained

Libyans their freedom, to the bookended case of intervention in Iraq, whose only plausible justification depended on the diagnosis that external force alone could constitute the free group agent that would make Iraqis free. If this chapter has told a partly sunny story of how an independent and self-governing group agent that realizes and protects the independence and self-governance of its citizens might emerge from the political efforts of individual natural agents, Chapter 4 uses the gloomy story of a failed political society that either doesn't constitute a normative group agent at all or else is too impaired as an agent to make and keep its natural agents free.

Forcing a People to Be Free

Is forcing a people to be free possible, and if so, is it ever morally permissible? The question cries out for clarification: What is it to be a *people*? What is it for a people to be *forced*? And what is it for a people to be *free*? As with so many questions in political philosophy, the hardest task here is to ask the right one, so I will spend most of my time specifying and clarifying what I am asking. When the question is well posed, it will almost answer itself, or so I hope.

I. Operation Iraqi Freedom

The question in some form is provoked by the 2003 war in Iraq and one of its stated justifications: freeing the Iraqi people from tyranny. When "Operation Iraqi Freedom," as the war was called, began, President George W. Bush announced, "Our mission is clear: to disarm Iraq of weapons of mass destruction, to end Saddam Hussein's support for terrorism, and to free the Iraqi people."[1]

Now that it has been established beyond doubt that Iraq had no weapons of mass destruction at the time of the invasion, and now that President Bush has acknowledged that there was no evidence at all of a connection between the September 11 terrorist attacks and Saddam Hussein's regime, the freedom argument must bear all the weight of justification for both the invasion and the extended occupation that followed. The Bush administration's case for war initially had three legs. Could it have stood on one alone? And if "to free the Iraqi people" was a good enough reason to permit the forceful occupation of Iraq, in what way did the Iraqi people have to be free before such permission ran out?

To be clear, I am not asking about the motives or intentions of politicians and generals, but about right reasons. There are sound theoretical grounds for holding that the rightness and wrongness of actions (in contrast with the goodness and badness of actors) does not ordinarily turn on motives. But even if this is not so, the project of political ethics in the first instance is forward-looking and first-personal: the primary question is what we as political actors should do, and only secondarily how we should evaluate the actions of others. Insofar as we are asking the first-personal question, we are asking what reasons rightly govern our actions, not what motives cause our behavior. To put it another way: what should we, who in asking this question already are moved (or want to be moved) to do what is right, do next time the opportunity to force a people to be free arises?

Nor am I asking about the means that might be employed to depose a tyrant and suppress his supporters. From the negligent failure to prevent the looting of Baghdad to the sickening abuses of detainees in Abu Ghraib prison, the United States has much to answer for. The overall conduct of, and any particular incident in, a war and its aftermath may fail the appropriate criteria for *jus in bello,* justice *in* war. Although crucial to an overall moral assessment of the war in Iraq or any war, I set them aside in this discussion. My sole concern is the claim that forcing a people to be free can, under some conditions, satisfy the criteria for *jus ad bellum,* justice *of* war.

To make a related but different distinction, there are first-order moral considerations that matter to the justification of any war, what might be called the substantive merits of the case: how much death, destruction, and misery will be inflicted on their soldiers and ours, their civilians and ours, for what reasons and for whose benefit, for how long and at what cost and with what prospects of success? Then there are second-order moral considerations concerning who is to decide upon the first-order judgments: is the target government morally immune from intervention in this way for these reasons by virtue of the moral legitimacy of its rule? Does this candidate intervenor or some other candidate intervenor have the legitimacy to intervene in this way for these reasons? I will focus primarily on the first of these second-order questions, the legitimacy and consequent moral immunity of targets, rather than the legitimacy and the consequent moral powers, privileges, and duties of intervenors.

So I set aside, as well, the important question of who, if anyone, can and may force a people to be free. There may be good reason to conclude that an *ad hoc* coalition of the United States, Britain, and thirty-two other countries (from Italy's three thousand troops to the no doubt brave twenty-four person Moldovan fighting force) does not have legitimate authority to topple a regime and establish democracy, but some other actor—the United Nations or a regional treaty organization—does have such authority. My students often adamantly object to military intervention on the grounds that the usual intervenors are too arrogant or too hypocritical to be entrusted with such a mission, but they soften when I propose intervention by the CSSSC—the Coalition of Small Scandinavian States and Canada. My question is whether it is possible and permissible for *any* external actor to force a people to be free, not whether the United States is such an actor.

Nor will I consider here whether there are any circumstances under which forcing a people to be free is, or ought to be, lawful under international law. Moral principles are discoveries or constructions of reason, not enactments or conventions of political bodies, and sometimes there ought to be a gap between the prescriptions of morality and the prescriptions of institutional rules. Every rule, even when properly followed, will sometimes be either overinclusive or underinclusive with respect to its underlying purpose.[2] Also, because rules are not always properly followed, the formulation of the best rule takes into account the consequences of mistaken or manipulative misuse of the rule.

Finally, although the use of lethal force ordinarily is unavoidable in military interventions, force understood as violence is not my central concern. Even if Saddam Hussein's regime could have been toppled without a single shot or drop of blood, our question about forced freedom would still stand. Our main concern is about coercion, whether or not violence is employed. (To be more precise, violence is a presumptive wrong in need of justification for two reasons. First, violence physically harms its target. Second, violent force overwhelms the will of its target, either by physically preventing one from exercising one's will or by threatening severe harm if one does not submit to the will of the threatener. I am concerned here with violence insofar as it is employed to overwhelm the will of its target.) Is it possible to *coerce* a people to be free, to free a people against its will?

This investigation, then, isolates one claim that has been made in defense of the war in Iraq in order to explore general questions about the possibility and permissibility of forcing a people to be free. If freeing the Iraqi people indeed is the only remaining ground for the war, then establishing the possibility and permissibility of such forced freedom by some actor under some conditions is necessary to justify the war. Clearly, however, the success of this claim is not sufficient.

One might be tempted to complain about both the formality and narrowness of this exploration in light of the messier and wider moral and political issues that the US invasion and occupation have raised, and criticize philosophical fiddling while Fallujah burns. Following Montaigne, however, I make no apologies for making distinctions. "Should we not dare say of a thief that he has a fine leg? And if she is a whore, must she also necessarily have bad breath?"[3] If history judges the (mis)adventure in Iraq to be a moral disaster, we will not know if this is a necessary or contingent conclusion without such distinctions. The stakes are high: unwarranted generalizations about failures in Somalia played a part in the shameful neglect of Rwanda. When errors of both omission and commission might be catastrophic, we need more fine-grained distinctions, not fewer.

One response to the objection that an intervention aimed at freeing a people is impermissibly coercive is that, under the appropriate counterfactual, the people would have welcomed the intervention, and so were not coerced after all. Before the invasion of Iraq, Deputy Secretary of Defense Paul Wolfowitz was sure that, had there been some mechanism for showing support, the attack would have been supported:

> If the Iraqi people were free to demonstrate they would be on the streets in the millions now saying, "Why didn't you come sooner? Don't make us wait any longer." I don't think there's any question where the feelings of the Iraqi people are.[4]

Posing a slightly different hypothetical, he also said, "I'm absolutely sure that if you could take a free poll among Iraqis, they would say . . . 'Please come; please do the job, and do it quickly.'"[5]

We do not know what Iraqis would have said to pollsters before the war. Asking the question requires a careful posing of the counterfactual. We safely can guess how Iraqis would have answered an actual poll had they faced the prospect of arrest for answering wrongly, but that of course is not the counterfactual Wolfowitz had in mind. If the aim is to justify the invasion by appeal to implicit but actual consent, however, neither can the right counterfactual be "How would Iraqis answer a poll had they not had their political views shaped by decades of tyranny?"

Fortunately, we do not have to guess what Iraqis would have said, because we know what they *did* say soon after the invasion, and what they continue to say. The one indisputably enduring contribution of Western democracy to Iraq is the public opinion poll, and, unfortunately for Wolfowitz, there *was* a question about the feelings of the Iraqi people. One fortuitously timed poll was conducted in February 2004, right before the outbreak of hostilities in Fallujah and Najaf that marked the beginning of organized resistance to the occupation, and before the Abu Ghraib revelations.[6] The results showed that support for the invasion and occupation was then mixed. When asked about whether the invasion by US-led forces was right or wrong, 48 percent answered absolutely or somewhat right, and 39 percent answered absolutely or somewhat wrong.[7] The most intriguing question asked whether the invasion liberated or humiliated Iraq. Of all Iraqis polled, 42 percent said liberated and 41 percent said humiliated.[8] In posing this as a binary choice, the pollsters did not allow for what may be both the best answer and the answer that would have been chosen by most Iraqis: that the invasion *both* liberated *and* humiliated Iraq. One of the purposes of this chapter is to explore how this might be so of a people that is forced to be free.

II. Mill's Mistake

Consider an extended passage from an 1859 magazine article that startles our contemporary sensibilities, John Stuart Mill's "A Few Words on Non-Intervention." The main thrust of the piece is to argue against intervention in the civil wars and revolutions of civilized nations, but barbarians are another matter:

> To suppose that the same international customs, and the same rules of international morality, can obtain between one civilized nation and another, and between civilized nations and barbarians, is a grave error . . .

In the first place, the rules of ordinary international morality imply reciprocity. But barbarians will not reciprocate. They cannot be depended on for observing any rules. Their minds are not capable of so great an effort, nor their will sufficiently under the influence of distant motives.

In the next place, nations which are still barbarous have not got beyond the period which it is likely to be for their benefit that they should be conquered and held in subjection by foreigners. Independence and nationality, so essential to the due growth and development of a people further advanced in improvement, are generally impediments to theirs . . .

To characterize any conduct whatever towards a barbarous people as a violation of the law of nations, only shows that he who so speaks has never considered the subject. A violation of great principles of morality it may easily be; but barbarians have no rights as a *nation*, except a right to such treatment as may, at the earliest possible period, fit them for becoming one. The only moral laws for the relation between a civilized and a barbarous government, are the universal rules of morality between man and man.[9]

Mill wrote this the very same year that he published *On Liberty*, which remains just about the most uncompromising rejection of paternalism ever written. *On Liberty* argues for toleration of Mormon polygamy in the Utah Territory, although Mill views the practice as a "direct infraction" of the principle of liberty, "a mere riveting of the chains of one half of the community," and a "retrograde step in civilisation." Still, Mill holds, "I am not aware that any community has a right to force another to be civilised."[10]

There is a ready, uncharitable way to explain these texts: in the first, Mill is flacking for the East India Company. His family and his country had no financial stake in Salt Lake City. Explanations such as this, however, explain away the need to take a writer's thought seriously. Our concern is with reasons, not motives. There are several ways to reconcile the two passages, although none is entirely satisfactory. Most likely, despite their uncivilized practice of polygamy, Mill simply does not consider the Mormons to be an example of "those backward states of society in which the race itself may be considered in its nonage."[11]

Mill's considered view on the matter of intervention in the internal affairs of barbarous nations is not entirely transparent. Our main interest, however, is in the text of "A Few Words on Non-Intervention" that is so jarring to our ears. What, precisely, is Mill's mistake? Instead of *ad hominem* dismissal, let us engage in perhaps overly charitable reconstruction, and, for every appearance of the quaint (and insulting) term "barbarous," substitute "tyrannized," and similarly substitute "democratic" for "civilized." Now the view (which I confess may no longer be Mill's) is much less startling: do not think that the law of nations that applies between democracies also applies between democracies and tyrannies. Tyrannies have no rights as nations, and so no state or government interposes in our moral relations with the persons who live under tyranny. Our duties towards them are direct, governed by "the universal rules of morality between man and man."

What resists this easy translation are the references to "barbarians." In places, we can substitute "tyrants," and the meaning is clear enough. But in places Mill is referring to the individuals who populate a barbarous nation, not its leaders, and to substitute "tyrannized persons" simply will not do. Does a tyrannized person have a mind that is distinctively defective in the way that Mill supposes the barbarian's mind is? Here is Mill's unsalvageable mistake: he thinks that barbarous nations are barbarous because they are composed of barbarians, and barbarians are individuals whose minds are incapable of the great effort of reciprocity and whose wills are insufficiently governed by distant motives. Now, Mill is not claiming genetic inferiority here. Barbarians in Mill are products of culture, not nature, but the ill effects of barbarous cultures operate through the shaping of the mind of the barbarian. Mill's account, even after our politically correct updating, remains insulting, because it supposes that persons who live under tyrants are likely to have tyrannized minds and wills that lack the capacity to think the thoughts and will the ends that persons who live in democracies think and will.[12] This is a sweeping factual claim that needs to be backed up by evidence. It may, for some persons in some tyrannies, be true, but it is not a conclusion Mill or we get for free.

Here, then, is the point of our Millian digression: Mill believes that we may paternalize barbarous nations because we may paternalize barbarians. To force a people to be free is to paternalize a people. Does paternalizing a people entail paternalizing the persons who are members of that people? If so, then justifying the paternalizing of a people depends on justifying the paternalizing of the persons who are members of that people, and the criteria for the justified paternalism of persons are stringent. If those persons are not proper targets of paternalism, then the people made up of these persons is not a proper target either. Yet, if it is possible to paternalize a people without paternalizing its constituent members, then the argument for paternalizing a people does not need to meet the objection of individual persons that they are not proper targets of paternalism. It is humiliating to be paternalized (even, as I will soon argue, when the paternalism is justified). But if we can drive a wedge between paternalizing a people and paternalizing persons, perhaps feelings of humiliation are, in one respect, unfounded.

III. Is Forced Freedom Impossible?

Consider three ways in which it might be *impossible* to force a people to be free.

Forcing a People to Be FREE

The claim is that forcing a people to be free is a conceptual impossibility because if a people is forced, it cannot be free; if free, it cannot be forced. Now, this is true synchronically, unless we entertain a paradoxical understanding of forced freedom that is often attributed to Rousseau. Rousseau infamously writes, "[W]hoever refuses to obey the general will shall be constrained to do so by the entire body; which means only that he will be forced to be free."[13] There is some textual evidence in the *Geneva Manuscript* that suggests Rousseau meant nothing quite as frightening as this sounds, but in any case, I have no use here for accounts of higher freedom.[14] What I mean by freedom is independence, the power of a moral agent to both set and pursue one's own ends without being subject to the domination of another.[15] But there is nothing incoherent about forced freedom understood diachronically. It is not impossible to force a people in time t, so that it is a free people in time $t + 1$, unless one holds to a pedigreed conception of freedom under which any force in the history of a people renders it incapable of freedom in the future. On such a view, there are no free people, because there has never been a political society of any consequence that was freely constituted.

Forcing a People to Be Free

The second claim of impossibility is empirical, not conceptual: there is no known causal mechanism of regime change that has outside force as one of its inputs and a free people as an output. Attempts to force a people to be free are futile. When Mill writes about civilized as opposed to barbarian peoples, this is the view that he endorses:

> The only test possessing any real value, of a people's having become fit for popular institutions, is that they, or a sufficient portion of them to prevail in the contest, are willing to brave labour and danger for their liberation.
>
> I know all that may be said. I know it may be urged that the virtues of freemen cannot be learnt in the school of slavery, and that if a people are not fit for freedom, to have any chance of becoming so they must first be free. And this would be conclusive, if the intervention recommended would really give them freedom.
>
> But the evil is, that if they have not sufficient love of liberty to be able to wrest it from merely domestic oppressors, the liberty which is bestowed on them by other hands than their own, will have nothing real, nothing permanent. No people ever was and remained free, but because it was determined to be so; because neither its rulers nor any other party in the nation could compel it to be otherwise . . .
>
> When a people has had the misfortune to be ruled by a government under which the feelings and the virtues needful for maintaining freedom could not develop themselves, it is during an arduous struggle to become free by their own efforts that these feelings and virtues have the best chance of springing up.[16]

This view is less appealing than might first appear. First, note that Mill conflates establishing a free people through force and maintaining a free people through force. It may be historically accurate that no people ever remained free, "but because it was determined to be so," but it does not follow that no people ever remained free that had its freedom "bestowed on them by other hands than their own."

Second, Mill is not simply saying that if you are not willing to face some risk of dying for freedom then you are not fit for it. If that were the claim, then once a people has shown that its members are "willing to brave labour and danger for their liberation," why require that they brave it alone? A freedom-loving uprising of courageous but hapless Don Quixotes would then merit outside support, a conclusion Mill rejects. So either Mill's view assumes, falsely, that a brave majority always is strong enough to prevail.[17] Or he holds that the inability to wrest freedom from merely domestic oppressors shows insufficient love of liberty. This, to put it harshly but not inaccurately, implies that if you are not sufficiently willing and skillful to *kill* for your freedom, then you are not fit for it. But it is just a contingent matter of good luck that a popular majority capable of living free lives in peace also has the strength, expertise, and resources to be able to overthrow various kinds of tyranny and oppression. That such instruments of causal power are intimately connected with a deep desire for freedom and the capacity to carry forward with freedom just seems to be empirically false. One can know how to operate a printing press without knowing how to operate a rocket-propelled grenade launcher.

How is Gandhi's successful campaign of nonviolent resistance in India to be analyzed under this reading of Mill? First, let us bracket the fact that the British were outside occupiers, since Mill has a different account of such struggles, and suppose, counterfactually, that the British Raj was a "domestic oppressor." I think the Millian stance would have to be something like this. It is admirable that the Indians showed willingness to brave considerable "labour and danger," and fortunate in two senses for them that this nonviolent bravery was sufficient: fortunate in that they have won their freedom and fortunate in having the good moral luck of not having the extent of their love for freedom put to a more stringent test. Had the British (again, assumed to be a domestic oppressor) crushed the nonviolent movement, and had the Indians then refused to escalate into violence, that would have shown insufficient fitness for freedom, and no outside power would have been permitted to intervene.

I see little reason to accept Mill's (and, later, Arendt's and Walzer's) tendency to identify the violent struggle of revolution and civil war with real political voice. Rather, internal violence, though too often enough morally permitted or even required, is the utter failure of politics. The sound of gunfire is never the voice of the people. I do mean to make the counterintuitive claim that the successful violent overthrow of a tyrant, though a moral success, is a failure of politics, if politics is understood in its normative sense as the workings of collective agency. Indeed, as the next section suggests, politics in this normative sense is not possible under conditions of tyranny. If this is correct, then even when both are morally justified, neither internal revolution nor external intervention is an expression of the general will of the people.

The strongest retort to the objection that forced freedom necessarily is doomed to failure, however, is that there have been two spectacular successes: Germany and Japan. Many keys have been stroked arguing that the highly developed political cultures of the prewar Axis powers render those two cases quite unlike any contemporary attempt at regime change. I do not deny the point. My claim is much more modest: the fact of two successes somewhere under some conditions shows that forced freedom is not impossible somewhere else. (It must be said, as well, that differences in prior political culture are not the only moving explanatory parts. I will refrain from saying much about comparing the effort, skill, and commitment brought to bear in Germany and Japan with the situation in Iraq, except to point out the difference in preparation. The war in Europe was over in April 1945. April also was the month that General George Marshall appointed General John Hilldring to begin training the thousands of military administrators who would govern occupied Germany—but the year was 1943.) Since we know that forcing a people to be free is possible, at least under some conditions, we must address the permissibility question. But first, one last try at rendering forced freedom impossible.

Forcing a PEOPLE to Be Free

On this view, one cannot force *a people* to be free because an unfree people is a contradiction: if a people, it already is free; if forced, it cannot have been a people. Now, this view seems to employ an extravagantly demanding conception of a people. It implies that an occupied population ceases to be a people, so that there was no French people in occupied France in World War II. For that matter, it implies that there was no French people under Louis XIV, because the French people under an absolute monarchy hardly was free.

Although extravagant, there is something to the claim, which I will soon explore. For a moment, however, simply suppose the claim is correct. If we are then to make sense of our original question, it must be recast as a question about *forcing individual persons to become a free people.* Now, even if it turns out that a people can be unfree without contradiction, this formulation of the question is independently interesting, and has the advantage of being answerable. Surely it is conceptually possible to force individuals to become a free people, so we can ask under what conditions is it morally permissible to do so. What we thought was one question is actually several:

> When can and may we force an individual to be a free person?

> When can and may we force individuals to become a free people?

> When can and may we force a people to be free?

The answers will depend, in part, on the correct account of the practice Mill was so opposed to, at least among the civilized: paternalism.

IV. What is Paternalism?

On the standard textbook account of the concept, A paternalizes B when A restricts B's liberty for B's own good. Since an action might be undertaken for a variety of reasons, morally sufficient or insufficient, it is most illuminating to see paternalism as an attribute of reasons for action, rather than an attribute of actions themselves.[18] On this view, to justify paternalism is to show that the paternalistic reason for restricting B's liberty—for B's own good—under the circumstances is sufficient. I focus here on reasons, not motives. Paternalistic motives ordinarily do not enter into judgments of the rightness or wrongness of an action, although they do enter into evaluative judgments of the goodness or badness of the actor. The question of paternalism need not arise if there are sufficient nonpaternalistic reasons for action. So, if preventing harm to C is a sufficient reason for A to restrict B's liberty, the action is justified for nonpaternalistic reasons. It may also be the case that the same restriction of B's liberty is also for the good of B. Indeed, if one holds that B has a moral interest in not doing wrong, then to be prevented from wronging C is always for B's own good.[19] Yet it would be superfluous to persist in asking if an action also is justified on paternalistic grounds (and odd for B to demand such a justification) once the action has been justified on the grounds of harm to others. On the view sketched here, if A is motivated by insufficient paternalistic reasons and not motivated by the sufficient nonpaternalistic reasons that apply, B could complain about A's attitudes, but is not wronged by A's actions.

Paternalism is a presumptive moral wrong in need of justification because the paternalist interferes with an agent's freedom to set and pursue her own ends for a reason that denies or discounts the importance of the agent's self-governance. If A does not claim that B has an impaired will, but merely that B is mistaken about her ends, then A discounts the importance of B's moral agency simply, and so disrespects B. If A claims that B's will is impaired, but is mistaken about this, B has been insulted, and is entitled to be indignant, our characteristic response to being paternalized. It is worth examining exactly why indignation is fitting. By claiming that B is insufficiently capable of choosing or pursuing ends for herself, A is treating B as something less than a full moral agent, a creature with a less dignified status. Unjustified paternalism warrants indignation because it takes a swipe at one's dignity.

Now suppose that A is not mistaken, and B knows that A is not mistaken. A precocious and relatively reflective twelve-year-old girl wants to pierce her tongue just like all her friends, but her parents say no. In a moment of clarity, she acknowledges to herself that she is not a fully mature and competent agent yet, and acknowledges that she still needs her parents to make some decisions for her. This recognition is, in a way, humiliating, because the girl now correctly sees that she is a creature of lower moral status than she had thought. This of course is not to say that she counts for less. Considered as a moral patient, she is no less valuable and her claims on others are no weaker. Considered as a moral agent, however, she is not fully an end-in-herself because others do not always have a reason to respect her ends merely because they are hers. Indignation is not called for, since her parents are not failing to recognize her moral status, and have not done anything to lower her status. The recognition of the truth of her lesser agency nonetheless carries with it a bit of self-inflicted shame. She is, after all, a little less dignified than she thought.

If A paternalizes B when A restricts B's freedom for the reason that it is for B's own good, and if the presumptive wrong in paternalism is that A fails to respect B's capacity for choosing ends, then A's paternalistic action is most likely to be justified when the following three criteria are met: B's freedom already is impaired, the good of B at stake is B's future freedom, and B's retrospective endorsement is likely. The strongest case for paternalism is when the liberty of someone who has an impaired or immature will is restricted in order to develop in her the capacity to have a competent and mature will, and from that competent and mature perspective she will endorse the prior restrictions. I have just described the condition of childhood and the practice of parenting.[20] If we may not paternalize children, whom may we paternalize? Still, as we have seen, even justified paternalism humiliates. So perhaps the Iraqi people were both liberated and humiliated.

V. Paternalizing a People

Is it then possible to paternalize a people without paternalizing the individual persons who are members of that people? Recall Mill's mistake about the barbarians. Mill held that uncivilized political societies are uncivilized because they are made up of uncivilized persons, persons who have barbarous minds incapable of enlightened thought. These societies can be paternalized because individual persons within them can be paternalized. Perhaps these societies cannot be forced to be free, since they are incapable of freedom, but they may be ruled by force, taken under the protection of a civilized society, until the individuals reach political maturity. Can we avoid Mill's mistake and recognize that individual adults who are said to make up a people are perfectly mature, competent moral agents, but still make the case that the people itself lacks the capacity to exercise competent moral agency?

Let us return to the extravagant claim that there cannot be unfree peoples. Surely this is false if by "people" we mean the social fact of common sentiments and shared language, culture, or religion that lead individuals to form bonds of solidarity and identify as members of a people. As a matter of social science, it is plausible to think that when it comes to peoplehood, collective thinking makes it so. On this *anthropological sense* of peoplehood, of course the French under German occupation and under the reign of Louis XIV are a people.

Peoplehood, however, can also be understood as a normative concept. On the normative view, the anthropological markers of common sentiment and shared cultural material are neither necessary nor sufficient. Rather, what makes for normative peoplehood is the capacity for shared agency explored in Chapter 3, "All Foundings Are Forced." A people in the *normative sense* must be capable of willing as a people. A normative people is a set of individuals that (1) has sufficient size, density of interaction among the members of the set, and differentiation from members of other sets (despite gradation, ambiguity, and overlap) to fit our commonsense, non-normative notions of a society and (2) is itself the proximate locus of respect and responsibility, and so is an entity that can make genuine moral claims on others and of which others can make genuine moral claims. Note that the first condition is not demanding in the way of common sentiments, solidarity, or shared identity, and so may be satisfied when the conditions for an anthropological people are not satisfied.

It is no small irony that, on this anthropological sense, Iraq may fail to be one people, since it is deeply divided along religious and linguistic lines in ways that make a common Iraqi cultural identity largely illusory. Indeed, off and on since the US invasion, the moral disaster of civil war has threatened. But an outright civil war in Iraq would not show that anthropological peoplehood is a necessary condition for normative peoplehood. Deep cultural division is not conceptually incompatible with the thinner shared commitments to legitimate and just law that collective political agency requires, and we have examples of divided societies that flourish as unified polities. I also believe, as an empirical matter, that what distinguishes divided societies that violently fragment from those that hold together is not the depth of the cultural divisions, but rather contingent shocks to mechanisms of social order, trust, and cooperation. (Yes, the destruction of a tyrant's mechanism of order without immediate adequate replacement would be such a shock.) But this, I confess, is a rather whiggish view of the possibilities for reasonable pluralism.

If a society succeeded in becoming a normative people by constituting itself as a group agent, then one of the important moral claims it would make against others is a claim of immunity from outside interference in its internal affairs. A competent collective agent would claim the respect owed to any competent agent, who ordinarily has the right to exercise self-governance in ways that are harmful only to oneself. Just as it is disrespectful to overrule a competent natural agent's self-governed choice among ends, even when that choice is mistaken, the claim is that it is disrespectful to overrule a competent collective agent's self-governed choice among the claims of its constituent members, even when that choice is mistaken. As is the natural agent's, the collective agent's entitlement to immunity from interference is limited in both scope and force. Clearly, the actions of a group agent that will wrong or harm those outside the group have no protection under this sort of immunity claim any more than a natural agent who is prevented from wronging or harming another can cry paternalism. Moreover, even when only constituent members are affected, the group agent's complaint of disrespectful interference need not supersede all other moral considerations. In particular, as I argue later, a group that violates the basic human rights and political liberties of some of its members is an impaired or even a failed collective agent. From a properly constituted collective agent, however, the claim that interference disrespects is weighty.

Just as a natural individual can fail to be a moral agent in degree, so too shared agency can fail in degree. I do not need to deny that the French under German occupation were a normative people. Understood as a group agent, however, occupied France was impaired, incapable of effective willing. This can be so, of course, even if every single French individual had a mature and competent will. Here, I side with Hobbes and Kant against Locke: there can be no legitimate political society prior to legitimate political institutions.

In what way are the French under occupation a normative people at all? Both in the occupied north and the unoccupied south, both after Germany's military occupation of the entire country in 1942, as well as before, the Vichy state had quite a bit of continuity with what came before, and Vichy exercised substantial autonomy. Much of the legal system and the civil administration of France continued unchanged. The government, though no longer democratic, was responsive to its (non-Jewish) citizens, and was not a mere puppet of Berlin. France was not Poland.[21] One should not press the analogy to impaired persons too far, in part because it is hard to draw a sharp distinction between natural individuals who are seriously impaired persons and those who are not persons at all. But I am supposing that a natural individual whose capacity for self-governance is seriously impaired, but who nonetheless has remaining domains of meaningful, purposeful action responsive to reasons and desires and has enough psychological continuity among these domains, can still be considered an agent, although an impaired one.[22] If the analogy holds, a normative people whose institutions and practices that make it a group agent are seriously undermined but survive in part and show appreciable continuity with what came before can still be considered a group agent, although an impaired one. Not much turns on establishing the possibility of an impaired or unfree normative people, however, since mere normative person-hood is not a sufficient condition for political legitimacy, which is a more demanding standard. With its reversion to authoritarianism and its willing persecution and deportation of French Jews, Vichy could hardly be considered a free group agent that makes and keeps its citizens free, and so could hardly be considered legitimate. I take no stand on its *legality*, for the legal validity of the legislative vote that accepted the armistice, ter-minated the Third Republic, and installed Pétain does not settle the matter of legitimacy one way or the other.

So, here is the truth in the extravagant claim: an aggregation of indi-viduals that does not meet even minimal threshold conditions does not count as a shared agent at all, and so does not count as a normative people at all. Since the conditions for normative peoplehood and anthropolog-ical peoplehood may be different, a people in the anthropological sense may fail completely to count as a normative people. The extravagant claim remains extravagant, however, because it does not admit that an aggre-gation of individuals can meet the minimal threshold conditions for shared agency and so for normative peoplehood, but fail to meet the more demanding conditions for competent and effective shared agency. A col-lective agent can fail the test of sufficient freedom, either because the natural persons that make it up are not sufficiently free, or because their individual capacities for considering, willing, and doing have not com-bined in the ways needed to form a collective agent that is sufficiently free. So not all normative peoples are already free peoples.

The question that began this section can now be answered. It is pos-sible to paternalize a people without paternalizing the individual persons who are members of that people, and the conditions that would justify such paternalism can be offered. A set of individuals who make up a society, by having some measure of group agency, can succeed in being a normative people that is itself an entity entitled to some measure of re-spect, but still fail to be a competent group agent. As an agent with inde-pendent (but not intrinsic) moral standing, a normative people is the sort of entity that can possibly be paternalized, because it has a will that can be forced for the reason that such force is for its own good. That this will already is impaired and that the good in question is the people's future freedom would both count toward the justification of such pater-nalism. This justification would not extend to restrictions on the liberty of individual members of the normative people who are themselves capable of competent willing. But though such restrictions of liberty need justification, a justification of *paternalism* is not needed, since the reason for the restriction on the liberty of the individual agent is not for the individual's own good, but for the good of the collective agent. This might seem to be an excessively formalistic answer, for though the collective agent is an entity with independent moral standing, such standing ultimately comes from the standing of the natural agents that constitute it. Recall, however, that one of the defining attributes of a genuine collective agent is that the distribution of moral claims from and to its constituent members is no mere pass-through. Although a collective agent has interests and a will only because its constituent members have interests and wills, it is not the case that anything done for the sake of the collective agent is done for the sake of each constituent member. The short answer why an individual forced to constitute a free people need not be paternalized is that such force need not be for the individual's own sake, but for the sake of others. The nonpaternalistic justification for such force is offered later, in Section VIII.

VI. Why is Free Group Agency So Morally Important?

We have explored the conditions for achieving free group agency, but have not yet examined why this achievement is so important. What, one might wonder, is the great moral significance of becoming a normative people? This is a very large question indeed, and here I shall attempt only to present a typology of answers, some more prosaic and some more lofty, that have some initial plausibility. These answers are not mutually exclusive, so insofar as acting together is morally important, its importance may be overdetermined.

First, the achievement of free collective agency could realize a good necessary for survival or basic functioning. So, perhaps prudence universally demands that we end the state of nature's war of all against all. Or free collective agency could realize a contingent good whose importance depends on the ends that persons pursue. The aspiration to flourish as a distinct linguistic community may be an end no more necessary than the aspiration to climb Everest, but the right sort of social cooperation is necessary for success in both. Or the achievement of free collective agency could fulfill a moral duty. So, argues Kant, we have a duty to engage in collective self-rule once we have disputes about what our rights are.

Second, these duties or goods could be connected to collective agency instrumentally, in that collective action is the means to fulfilling a preexisting duty or realizing a preexisting good. Life, liberty, and happiness, independently valued ends, might be best achievable if we act together. Or the duties and goods could be connected to collective agency constitutively, in that they are conceptually possible only under collective agency. This is tautologically true if acting together is a great good in itself. More subtly, we may have a duty to enter into a political relation that gives us duties to each other that we would not and could not otherwise have.

Third, the requirement that group agency be *free*, in that the conditions for genuine collective agency outlined earlier are met, could be a requirement in two senses. Freedom could be necessary because only free group agency, not any other sort of social coordination, does the work of realizing the aforementioned necessary or contingent, instrumental or constitutive goods or duties. For example, perhaps it is the case that warships staffed with volunteer sailors who choose their own officers outsail and outfight ships of impressed seamen whose coordination is extracted by threat of flogging. So, if a seaman is to go to sea, then his interest in survival is best instrumentally realized by joining a free crew of free sailors. Or freedom could be an independent normative requirement, in that the only morally permissible forms of social coordination are free ones, whether or not forced coordination instrumentally or constitutively realizes goods or satisfies other duties. Perhaps impressed sailors survive just as often as free ones, but coordination by flogging is morally impermissible.

To summarize, group agency may have importance because it realizes a necessary good, a contingent good, or fulfills a duty. Group agency may be instrumental to these goods or duties or constitute them. And group agency must be free either because only free group agency, not any other form of social coordination, realizes these goods or duties, or because freedom is an independent normative constraint. These distinctions yield twelve possible combinations. Not all are of interest, but the standard arguments for the importance of social cooperation are usefully differentiated by locating them on the resulting grid. Note too that there are many ways to find moral importance in free group agency that do not depend at all on communitarian, collectivist, or participatory democratic premises that see deciding and doing things together as somehow intrinsically more valuable than deciding and doing things individually.

VII. Can Subsets of an Unfree People Be Free?

I argued earlier that on no plausible normative account of group agency, and therefore of legitimacy, does a tyrannical regime that recognizes no constraints on the arbitrary will of the tyrant and that systematically violates basic human rights personify the people it rules. But might a tyrannical regime personify a subset of the population it rules, or might subsets constitute their own shared agent? First, consider the case of a separatist or revolutionary movement. Surely, once members of such a movement are the targets of massive human rights violations, they do not constitute a shared agent with their persecutors, even if the initial rebellion was unjustified. It would be utterly perverse to think that a regime that engages in mass atrocities against groups of subjects personifies those subjects. The victims of atrocity are not the authors of their own victimization. It does not follow, however, that such secessionists or revolutionaries have succeeded in constituting a new shared political agent. Political legitimacy does not follow some law of conservation under which it can neither be created nor destroyed, but only changed from form to form. The social solidarity that both makes large-scale political dissent possible and makes group-based suppression instrumentally rational may underwrite anthropological peoplehood, but there is no normative peoplehood without the institutions and procedures necessary for the formation of large-scale shared agency.

Second, consider the case of a favored group that is not subject to massive atrocity. One might think that such subjects constitute a smaller shared political agent personified by the regime. Under sufficiently repressive regimes, however, where all political dissent is stifled and where one's basic well-being is unprotected and insecure, this is not so even of those who are faring well. No one who lives in fear and must curry favor to avoid the arbitrary whims of an unconstrained, absolute ruler is free enough to constitute a shared agent. A regime that considers everything about you violable and has the absolute power to violate you does not represent or personify you, even if in fact you are not violated. Well-treated cattle do not share agency with their rancher.

Finally, could a ruling class, party, or bureaucracy constitute a group agent? Perhaps. Officials in a tyrannical regime may have met the necessary and sufficient conditions for constituting a shared agent of its kind, an organized crime syndicate, and so would be capable of unified agency that makes its individual members responsible authors of the regime's actions. But such a regime does not personify the people it rules.

In a tyranny, the tyrant does not personify the people, and there is no other candidate. Although I will subscribe to a part of Kant's political philosophy in the next section, I do not subscribe to his view that the legislative head of state must never be resisted because only the legislature can speak for the general will.[23] It may be the case that, although no body other than a current head of state can possibly speak for the general will, neither can the current head of state. The general will in some circumstance may simply not exist; it may never have existed or it may have gone out of existence. It does not follow from there being a duty to leave the state of nature that it is impossible to be returned to the state of nature, or that one must act as if it is impossible. Indeed, in a passage that generally denies the legitimacy of revolution in order to reform a despotism, Kant implies that the general will can dissolve through natural causes: "Thus political wisdom, in the condition in which things are at present, will make reforms in keeping with the ideal of public right its duty; but it will use revolutions, where nature of itself has brought them about, not to gloss over an even greater oppression, but as a call of nature to bring about by fundamental reforms a lawful constitution based on principles of freedom, the only kind that endures."[24]

If the tyrant does not speak for the people, the people is mute, and incapable of competent, unified moral agency—incapable of competent willing. Sufficiently determined pollsters or social scientists conceivably could measure public opinion in a tyrannized society, but a poll merely aggregates: it cannot unify. Poll results no more speak for the will of a people than a listing of a person's desires speaks for the will of a person.

So Mill almost has it right about barbarous peoples. He is just wrong about the barbarians. A people that is not capable of shared agency simply is an aggregation of individuals who exist in a state of nature with each other and with other peoples. So, he is right that the "only moral laws" for those relations "are the universal rules of morality between man and man." Yet without further argument, such men are presumed to be competent moral agents.

Presumptively competent individual agents may fail to form a competent group agent due to a number of causes—physical danger, language barriers, lack of necessary infrastructure—that do not call into question their individual competence as agents. But might some causes of their failure to form a group agent count against their individual competence as well? If so, then a barbarous people could be evidence of barbarians, and I have been uncharitable to Mill. How might this be so? On a thick view of competent moral agency, failure to recognize one's interest in overcoming coordination problems to form a group agent (when indeed one has such an interest) may count as a form of irrationality, and failure to be properly motivated by such an interest may count as weakness of will. On an even thicker moralized view of competent individual agency, failure to recognize the moral law or to be properly motivated by the moral law may count as irrationality and so be a failure of competent agency. I have in mind a thinner view of irrationality here, under which prudential and moral mistakes are not *per se* impairments of agency.

We now can give a partial answer to the question of whether setting a people free is a reason for coercion that meets the criteria of justified paternalism. (This labored formulation reminds us that paternalism, as used here, is an attribute of reasons for action, not of actions themselves.) A society whose members are deprived of the most basic rights and freedoms might not count as a normative people at all. If what I have called the extravagant view is supported by the morally relevant political facts, there is no normative people to paternalize—there is no shared agent that is the locus of respect and responsibility—so the complaint of unjustifiably paternalizing a people does not arise. The invaders are subject only to the "universal rules of morality," standing in relation to each person as one stands to individuals in a state of nature. Alternatively, if such a society is to be counted as a normative people, it is a seriously impaired people, incapable of competent and effective shared agency and self-governance. Insofar as such a people has a will that is subject to being coerced by external military intervention, it is a will whose freedom is not very valuable, and a will that, by hypothesis, is overborne by the intervenor for the sake of its own future freedom. Although such a people is capable of being forced for paternalistic reasons, such reasons under the circumstances overcome the ordinary presumption against paternalism. Of course, much more is needed to justify a military invasion than showing that objections to paternalism can be met.

VIII. Forcing Individuals to Be a Free People

Individuals could concede that the people of which they are members has no ground to complain about being paternalized, but this hardly robs individuals of all moral complaint. Each can complain that as a mature, competent individual agent it is up to each to decide whether to accept the grave risks of violence, destruction, and upheaval that an invasion and occupation would bring. Even if the risks to personal safety and restrictions on personal freedom that military intervention imposes are less onerous than life under tyranny, ordinarily it is no defense against the charge of wrongdoing that one has replaced a worse wrongdoer. The conditions for justified paternalism, by and large, are not met in the individual case. So we still have not established that it is morally permissible to force individuals to become a free people.

The best response is to deny that the reason individuals are forced is for their own sake, and so deny that the invasion paternalizes individuals. True, each is being forced to constitute a free people, but this is being done for the sake of one's neighbors, or one's children, or one's neighbors' children. To see why this is a plausible nonpaternalistic account of the reasons for intervention, we turn to Kant.

Unlike his social contract predecessors, who saw leaving the state of nature as the rational or prudent thing to do, Kant held that it was also a duty to do so. Once we interact in a way that might lead to disputes about our rights, we each have a duty to each other to enter into a civil condition, so that we are not judges in our own case. "When you cannot avoid living side by side with all others, you ought to leave the state of nature and proceed with them into a rightful condition."[25] Only in that way do we treat each other with the respect that we are owed. Furthermore, "each may impel the other by force to leave this state and enter into a rightful condition."[26] To realize my rights and yours, I may, and perhaps must, coerce you into meeting the conditions for shared agency.

For Kant, once a right has been established, there is no further question of whether the coercive enforcement of that right is justified. Rather, to have a right just is to have the authority to force compliance, and, correlatively, to have a strict duty of justice simply is to be subject to co-ercive enforcement.[27] Ordinarily, when one is justified in using force—say, in self-defense—one also is justified in enlisting the forceful aid of others. I do not have to stand by and watch you defend yourself against wrongful attackers. (Whether I have a duty to defend you or not depends, in part, on the risks and burdens I face.) On a vastly different scale, if you are justified in forcing your neighbors in a state of nature to do their duty and enter into a rightful condition with you, I do not have to stand by and let you force them alone. Perhaps, in the self-defense case, you may refuse my help and I must respect your refusal. If that is so, then if there is unanimous agreement among those in a wrongful state of nature that they want to stay that way, or that they do not want outside help in forcing each other into a rightful condition, then perhaps they too may refuse external help and outsiders must respect that refusal. (I say perhaps because the analogy to refusing help in the self-defense case is not perfect. The duty to leave the state of nature may not be reciprocally waivable.) As a formal matter, however, just one person wrongfully kept in a state of na-ture would have the authority to invite the world's help in forcing her neighbors into a rightful condition, and, also as a formal matter, the in-tervenor would then have a nonpaternalistic reason to force individuals to be free. First-order moral considerations surely would tell against this being an all-things-considered sufficient reason for military intervention in such an unpromising case, but the example demonstrates the point: individuals may sometimes be forced to do their duty, and when that is so, they are not forced for their own sake, but for the sake of those to whom the duty is owed.

Kant admittedly is silent on whether we are permitted to force distant others who do not have a duty to enter into a civil relation with us to enter into one with each other, but it is precisely this extension of the view that would have to be made in order to justify forcing natural persons to con-stitute a free people. If this extension can be made, then the reply to the individual who complains about being paternalistically forced to consti-tute a free people is that, though indeed forced, he is not paternalized. Rather, he is being forced to comply with his natural duty to his fellow countrymen.

Now, Kant clearly repudiates forced colonization, which might suggest that he would reject this extension:

Lastly, it can still be asked whether, when neither nature nor chance but just our own will brings us into the neighborhood of a people that holds out no prospect of a civil union with it, we should not be authorized to found colonies, by force if need be, in order to establish a civil union with them and bring these men (savages) into a rightful condition (as with the American Indians, the Hottentots, and the inhabitants of New Holland). . . . But it is easy to see through this veil of injustice (Jesuitism), which would sanction any means to good ends. Such a way of acquiring land is therefore to be repudiated.[28]

But Kant here does not address colonization in order to force savages to enter into a rightful condition with *each other;* rather, he rejects colonization to force savages to enter into a civil union with *us.* In any case, the thrust of the passage is to put limits on the acquisition of land, rather than limits on the use of force.[29]

Because Kant's treatment of private right in a state of nature largely concerns the acquisition and transfer of external objects, one might be tempted to think that the sole purpose of public right is to adjudicate conflicts in the acquisition and transfer of property. If that were so, then a Kantian defense of a military intervention would depend, strangely enough, on whether the target regime has adequate civil courts to adjudicate property disputes. This is an excessively narrow reading of why Kant holds that we must leave the state of nature, however, and therefore an insufficiently demanding account of what it takes to enter (and I would say remain in) a rightful condition. *"There is only one innate right,"* for Kant: *"Freedom* (independence from being constrained by another's choice), insofar as it can coexist with the freedom of every other in accordance with a universal law, is the only original right belonging to every man by virtue of his humanity."[30] To be secure in one's possessions is important in Kant because control over things secures our freedom. But the civil condition secures us more generally against the "maxim of violence" that follows from the right of each in a state of nature to do what seems right and good.[31] Threats to our freedom can arise from many sources, including "the inclination of men generally to lord it over others as their master."[32] The provisional rights that a civil condition makes actual are not only rights to things, but rights to persons in the household, the limits of which mark off the correlative rights of wives, children, and servants *against* mistreatment by their master. Such dependent persons, or passive citizens, never lose their natural liberty and equality. "On the contrary, it is only in conformity with the conditions of freedom and equality that this people can become a state and enter into a civil constitution."[33]

The necessary conditions for the formation of a general united will among the active citizens are considerably more stringent:

> In terms of rights, the attributes of a citizen, inseparable from his essence (as a citizen), are: lawful *freedom,* the attribute of obeying no other law than that to which he has given his consent; civil *equality,* that of not recognizing among the *people* any superior with the moral capacity to bind him as a matter of Right in a way that he could not in turn bind the other; and third, the attribute of civil *independence,* of owing his existence and preservation to his own rights and powers as a member of the commonwealth, not to the choice of another among the people. From his independence follows his civil personality, his attribute of not needing to be represented by another where rights are concerned.[34]

So a society in which large numbers of persons are denied their natural liberty and equality and in which perhaps no one possesses the three attributes of a citizen arguably remains a Kantian state of nature, even if there are mechanisms for the orderly transfer of property.[35]

Lest I be accused of conscripting Kant into a cause he would not recognize, let me be clear about my claim and its limits. My own view is that there is a nonpaternalistic reason to force individuals who live side by side to become a free people: they each have a duty to leave the state of nature and enter into a civil relation with each other. If such a reason is sufficient to justify the force involved, then it does not matter that entering into a civil relation is also for the good of each. If there are sufficient nonpaternalistic reasons for using force, it is otiose to inquire about the sufficiency of the paternalistic reasons. Kant does not address whether there is such a permission, let alone a duty, for any outsider to force others into a rightful condition. One might think that, since Kant insists that the legitimacy of existing authority not be questioned and that forced colonialism is repugnant, he cannot be enlisted in support of such a view: Kant would either deny that people living under tyrannical rule can be judged to not be in a rightful condition or deny that outsiders have any right to force them into a rightful condition. I have argued, however, that Kant puts fairly demanding conditions on what it takes to enter into a rightful condition, and that the case of the colonial land grab that he repudiates can be differentiated from our case: his savages have no duty to enter into a rightful condition with colonists before the colonists' arrival, but the savages do have a prior duty to enter into a rightful condition with each other. So my claim that there could be sufficient nonpaternalistic reasons to force individuals to become a free people is not, as far as I can tell, inconsistent with Kant's political philosophy.

IX. Is Intervention a Duty?

Permission to intervene is one thing, a duty to intervene another. Since there are limits on the sacrifices morality requires us to make for each other, and since military intervention almost always is costly in blood and treasure, intervention often may be a sacrifice too great for morality to require. Surely Lord Byron had no duty to give his life for Greek independence. When the would-be intervenor is a group agent, we must be careful in the aggregation and distribution of burdens across its members to assess sacrifice correctly. Monetary cost can be distributed widely, but death and injury are concentrated. The technical calculations of generals and the political calculations of elected officials about "acceptable" casualty rates often involve morally unacceptable aggregation across lives that fails to treat individuals with respect. Each battlefield death must be justifiable to the soldier who is to die, and that is no easy matter. The justification goes something like this: from some morally appropriate *ex ante* point of view, the risk of death that you face is reasonably proportionate to the moral importance of the ends at stake, fairly distributed, and decided under institutions or practices or procedures that are connected to you in ways that respect your equal freedom. The argument for the correct point of view is crucial: if too *ex ante* and general, the separateness of persons is threatened and too much individual sacrifice is permitted; if too *ex post* and particular, nearly all have vetoes and not enough individual sacrifice is permitted. Justifying sacrifice for the end of repelling an existential threat to one's own normative people is easier than justifying sacrifice for the end of establishing the normative peoplehood of others. Why? Recall that to be both a free enough author and a free enough subject of the collective agent for this purpose in this way, one either has to consent, or to voluntarily benefit from the cooperation of others, or to face a practical necessity. Dangerous military service is a practical necessity primarily in defense of one's own people, and the other conditions are less likely to be met in the case of intervention as well. So group agents might be prohibited from requiring its members to fight in otherwise permissible interventions. A volunteer force fares better in this regard than a conscript army, but there are substantive limits to the risks that can be imposed even on recruits, just as there are limits to the risks that can be imposed on voluntary employees.

Let us then isolate the question of whether there is any sort of presumptive duty upon outside powers to force others into a civil condition with each other from the question of how much sacrifice is beyond the call of duty. Suppose the fantasy of the gunboat diplomat came true, and some intervenor had the absolute power to force others into a civil condition by making a nearly costless but credible threat that puts none of the intervenor's soldiers at the slightest risk. If there is any sort of duty of rescue among unconnected strangers of the pull-the-drowning-baby-out-of-the-puddle variety, then there is a duty of intervention in this case too. But such pure cases are implausible.

X. How Free is Free Enough?

I have said a lot about the criteria for entrance, but nothing about the criteria for exit. How free does a people have to be before the intervenor must withdraw?[36] An obvious worry about a claim that intervenors may or must stay until a well-functioning democracy has been established is that there are precious few well-functioning democracies around the globe. Does the argument for democratic institution-building underwrite a frighteningly broad permission to engage in never-ending democratic jihad wherever there are defects in collective will formation?

The worry is misplaced, and would be misplaced even if it turned out that *no* country in the world meets the test of legitimacy. This is because, even if there are no governments that are morally immune from intervention by virtue of respect accorded to them in light of the respect due to the subjects they represent, first-order moral considerations will ordinarily forbid intervention because intervention will do more harm than good, destroy more than build, and inflict misery and danger on innocents that cannot be justified to them.

There are second-order considerations that tell against democratic jihad as well. An advantage of the view presented here is that there is an important asymmetry between conditions for entrance and conditions for exit. Suppose that there were some form of theocracy in which the conditions of normative peoplehood and of political legitimacy, though far from ideal, surpass the threshold that immunizes that regime from outside intervention. Or suppose that there were some form of rule by an autocrat that met the threshold conditions.

There are two separate thresholds at play: minimal normative peoplehood and minimal political legitimacy. A collectivity can count as an impaired normative people but fail to have political legitimacy. Here I am assuming that the theocracy and the autocracy meet both tests. Both forms of government would have to minimally satisfy both the human rights prong and the representativeness prong of the test for political legitimacy. In the case of the theocracy, this would require, among other matters, that women be granted more personal freedom than is commonly the case in societies ruled by Islamic law today, and that nonconforming religious beliefs and practices, though politically disfavored, be tolerated. In the case of the autocracy, the ruler would need to be not only responsive to the interests of his subjects but also, in some measure, responsive to their wills, as Louis XVI appeared to be when he called for the *Cahiers de Doléances* in 1789. I have in mind forms of rule that meet Rawls's notion of a decent consultation hierarchy, rather than what he calls benevolent despotism.[37]

Further suppose that constituting a normative people along the lines of a theocracy or an autocracy is the preferred option among an occupied population, and would also be both quicker and less costly in blood and treasure to bring about.[38] It still does not follow that the intervenor must, or even may, aim at theocracy or autocracy. By assumption, both of these forms of rule, if established, would be owed respect and so be immune from intervention. But until a normative people is constituted, there is no competent will of the people that is owed such respect. The fact that most want a theocracy or an autocracy is simply that: a social scientific fact that by itself has no legitimate authority at all. Strange as it may sound to ears that conflate cultural sensitivity with political respect, until individuals are constituted in the normative sense as a free people, nothing is owed to the people in the anthropological sense *qua* people.

Much, of course, is owed to individuals. There are limits to how much each can be asked to sacrifice for the freedom of his neighbor. Just as first-order moral considerations and the probabilities of success may tell against intervention in the first place, first-order moral considerations and the probabilities of success may tell against a more ambitious plan for regime change. Although the anthropological facts have no intrinsic normative force, they of course matter instrumentally. Though Mill is wrong about impossibility, surely he is right to worry that free institutions externally imposed are less likely to take root. So the changer of regimes must take into account blood, treasure, and odds. And surely there is a diverse set of political institutions to choose from that are free enough and just enough. Over that range, respect for individual self-governance would take precedence over the intervenor's views about ideal collective self-governance—though how disagreement among individuals is to be resolved necessarily is underspecified in the absence of legitimate decision rules for resolving disagreements. But these all are what I have called first-order moral considerations. Until properly constituted as a shared agent, occupied persons simply are individuals owed respect as individuals. Therefore—here is the crucial point—this range of free enough and just enough political arrangements is likely to be narrower and more demanding than the range of constitutions and institutions that, once in place, are morally immune from intervention. Hence the asymmetry of criteria for going in and getting out.

The implication is striking: an occupying force may, and perhaps must, prevent the formation of some forms of government that it would not have been permitted to overthrow, had they existed. I am not proposing that powers that have not yet intervened must forcefully stop the formation of legitimate but less-than-just institutions around the world. That indeed would be a counsel for global democratic jihad. Rather, once a power has chosen to intervene with force, and thereby has assumed responsibility for the fate of an occupied population, it acquires a presumptive obligation to forge not merely legitimate but also just institutions. This presumption can be rebutted on various grounds: the higher standard may be impossible to reach under the circumstances, or require too much sacrifice by the intervenor, or impose too many burdens on the population. It is a mistake, however, to think that because fairly low levels of sacrifice by a would-be intervenor are enough to make intervention merely optional, the same low level of sacrifice is enough to permit withdrawal. Even though it may be optional for an intervenor to take a population under its protection, it is not equally optional to withdraw that protection.

So we have reached the surprising result that, in Iraq, US forces were permitted to, and perhaps were required to, prevent the formation of a minimally legitimate government in order to hold out for more extensive political freedoms and human rights protections, even if that is not what most Iraqis wanted. Although only the hardhearted can fail to be moved by the purple-fingered voters who braved political violence to participate in peaceful elections in Iraq, the adoption of a constitution by referendum and the election of a parliament do not yet constitute a minimally legitimate government. They do not because a government is legitimate only when it can and does act to secure and protect a minimally adequate list of rights and freedoms on behalf of its free (enough) constituent individuals, and surely a government unable or unwilling to prevent widespread sectarian warfare has not met these conditions. Although protection of the basic rights and freedoms of Iraqis is of the utmost moral urgency, if my argument about the asymmetry of entry and exit is correct, the provision of this protection *by a minimally legitimate Iraqi government* may be considerably less urgent. The onset of legitimate government is not an unalloyed good, for one should not be indifferent between the establishment of a minimally legitimate government and a just and democratic government. Admittedly, a principle that, for the sake of bringing about self-governance, prescribes an *indefinite* protectorate would be self-undermining in cases where legitimate but unjust self-governance is possible.[39] Rawls says that the end of a just war is a just peace.[40] Similarly, intervention must have an end, with the temporal end driven by its purpose. In purely humanitarian interventions, the end is protecting basic human rights, and this may require, without contradiction, indefinite occupation if self-rule that protects human rights is impossible. But an intervention that aims at forcing a people to be free has misfired if it finds itself permanently preventing possible legitimate self-governance. As with so many questions in nonideal theory, reasonable people may make different judgments about how long an intervenor may hold out for not merely legitimate but just self-rule before the intervention becomes self-undermining. These, I hasten to add, are theoretical considerations.

I make no claims about the actual capacity of the forces that occupied Iraq to have brought about any positive political change whatsoever under the circumstances.

All foundings are forced. If we, collectively, are free, it is because we too have been forced to be free. In a state of nature, there are no legitimate procedures that can bootstrap us into legitimate government, although rhetoric that makes believe that there is such a procedure is a useful lubricant for achieving legitimate government. When some of us force others of us to be free, the victors look back with pride, the defeated beget political orphans, and so the next generation can tell a just-so story about freedom's origins that is often useful, largely harmless, and nearly always false. But when they, the foreigners, force us to be free, shame replaces pride, and the just-so story is harder to tell. This is why the just-so stories about homegrown freedom are not entirely harmless—they set up founding expectations elsewhere that are normatively too demanding. The truth is different: sometimes a people must be humiliated before it can be free.

PART III

Inhumanity, Despotism, and Wantonism

CHAPTER 5

The Three Tyrannies

Chapters 3 and 4 introduced a normative conception of legitimacy that I have called the free group agency view. On this account, a political authority legitimately governs subjects only if the authority's governance realizes and protects the freedom of those subjects over time. This is so only when the authority is a free enough group agent constituted by free enough subjects conscripted as members of that group agent. Articulating both internal and external notions of freedom, we say that an authority legitimately governs subjects only if the authority is a sufficiently self-governing and independent group agent constituted by sufficiently self-governing and independent subjects. To be sufficiently self-governing, an individual agent must have adequate capacities of considering, willing, and doing. To be sufficiently independent, an individual agent must enjoy those basic rights and liberties that protect against being dominated. For the *group* agent to be sufficiently self-governing, it must be able to combine the considerations, choices, and acts of its independent and self-governing members in such a way as to constitute a group agent that itself has adequate capacities of considering, willing, and doing. For the group agent to be sufficiently independent, it must make and keep its conscripted members free of individual domination, and itself be undominated by external forces. When these conditions hold, subjects are coauthors of the authority that governs them, and therefore are not merely ruled subjects, but self-governing citizens.

Chapters 5, 6, and 7 trace out the implications of the free group agency view for the legitimacy of political institutions and practices in democracies. First, I will argue that three principles of legitimacy—the liberty, equality, and agency principles—follow from the free group agency account. Then I will show that each of these three principles has surprising and partially revisionary implications for some of our standard understandings of legitimate political institutions and practices in a democracy. The liberty principle, as I understand it, allows, and perhaps requires, various counter-majoritarian institutions such as a substantive bill of rights, judicial review, and even unamendable constitutional provisions, in stark contrast with the view that counter-majoritarian institutions undermine the legitimacy of democratic governments. The equality principle, as I interpret it, revises widely accepted accounts of representation and legislative ethics. Citizens are entitled to equal normative power in selecting who governs, but not necessarily equal causal power in selecting who governs, and not necessarily equal power of either sort over the substance of law and policy. If this is so, then conventional understandings about the moral force of electoral mandates and campaign promises are upended. The agency principle introduces a previously unnoticed way in which the legitimacy of governments can be endangered: a political group agent that is seriously defective in its capacities of considering, willing, and doing can fail to exercise normative power over citizens even when its laws and policies otherwise satisfy the liberty and equality principles. A government that cannot govern itself cannot legitimately govern others.

I. Ideals and Thresholds

All along, I have peppered the formulations of the free group agency view with weasel words like "adequate," "sufficient," and "enough." Why? To acknowledge that the independence and self-governance we require to be genuinely free though enchained are not fully attainable in any empirical polity. If the free group agency conception of legitimacy is roughly right, but full freedom is beyond our actual grasp, what follows? Must we concede to the philosophical anarchist that the conditions for genuine legitimacy are impossible in our world? No, I believe that we can deflect this skeptical conclusion if we locate the idea of legitimacy on the correct side of a number of interconnected distinctions about what sort of property legitimacy is. First, we should take questions of legitimacy to be primarily practical queries about what to do, rather than theoretical queries about what to believe. Second, we should understand legitimacy to be a relational property that characterizes the normative connections among rulers, enforcers, subjects, and intervenors, rather than a monadic property, an attribute that something can have on its own, the way that a particle has the property of mass. Third, and relatedly, we should acknowledge that, depending on which practical question is asked about which of these normative relationships, legitimacy is to be understood either as an ideal that guides or as a minimal threshold that binds. Above some adequate threshold on the conditions for legitimacy, we are simultaneously to act *as if* the ideal has been met, while aspiring to approach closer to it. Below some threshold of adequacy, it would be perverse to continue to act as if the authority in question were legitimate, and so we may or even must resist illegitimate rule and seek to establish or reestablish legitimate governance.[1]

To be clear, the ideal in question is the ideal of legitimate government, not of just or of good government. Though certain aspects of justice and goodness are preconditions for free group agency, and though the demands of legitimacy, justice, and goodness may in extension track each other over some range, justice and goodness are distinguishable normative ideas. It is not my view that, when actual governments are above the threshold of legitimacy but fall short of the ideal, this is so only because they are insufficiently just or good. Legitimacy is not simply justice-lite.

Notice that the skeptical challenge to the possibility of a genuinely legitimate government is deflected in much the same way that the skeptical challenge to the possibility of genuinely autonomous moral agency is deflected. To have a will responsive to reasons only, and not to causes, is an idealization that no empirical natural agent can meet. Looking at ourselves from the third-person point of view of the behavioral and social sciences, we are not perfectly reason-responsive agents, but rather, are to varying degrees irrational and impaired, always caused, and sometimes merely caused. A moral empiricist might then conclude that some measure of irrationality and impairment justifies some measure of paternalistic interference for our own good. We might object, however, that we do not treat each other with proper respect if we view each other's choices as coercively correctible in proportion to their defects in reasoning. In contrast, a two-level approach to paternalism would direct us to respect each other from the second-personal, relational point of view *as if* we are fully capable of self-governance over some range of actual imperfect rationality, until it is perverse to continue to do so.[2] When we view ourselves from the first-person point of view of an agent, the matter is complicated: to act, we must conceive of ourselves as already capable of genuine action, but genuine actors must be guided by an ideal of reason-responsiveness, and so both acknowledge the gap between the actual and the ideal, and strive to narrow it. The way Christine Korsgaard puts it, constitutive standards that define an activity are at the same time normative standards that guide that activity.[3]

Similarly, the social contract and the general will are idealizations that no empirical political society can possibly meet. Looking at our legal and political institutions from the third-person point of view of the behavioral and social sciences, we do not constitute perfectly reason-responsive group agents that make and keep us free, but rather, our group agency is to varying degrees defective, and to varying degrees our institutions fail to make and keep us free. Nonetheless, when, from the second-person perspective, we view our normative relationships with the group agent that governs us, we are to respect our political institutions *as if* they are fully capable of collective self-governance over some range of actual impairment and actual domination, until it is perverse to continue to do so.[4] Rawls's natural duty of civility, which requires of us "not to invoke the faults of social arrangements as a too ready excuse for not complying with them," can be understood as following from this idea of treating our political arrangements over some range of faultiness as if they are ideal, though empirically they cannot be so.[5] From the first-person, perhaps plural, point of view of a political authority, again the matter is complicated. To exercise normative and not merely causal power over others, the authority must take itself to be genuinely legitimate, but genuinely legitimate authorities must be guided by an ideal of free group agency, and so both acknowledge and strive to narrow the gap between the actual and the ideal.

II. Democratic Ideals and Thresholds

So far, the exposition of free group agency has developed without much mention of democracy. Our discussions of how political legitimacy went missing before the invasion in Iraq and could have been found after the revolution in Libya neither presupposed nor concluded that a legitimate government must be some sort of democratic government. In *The Law of Peoples,* Rawls pictures what he calls a decent hierarchical society that, though not reasonably just, ought to be tolerated by liberal societies as a member in good standing of the Society of Peoples. The conditions for Rawlsian decency are more demanding than often supposed, but they do not demand democracy. The legal system of a decent society secures the human rights of its members, including freedom of religion and thought, is guided by a common good idea of justice, represents its members through associational groups, and imposes *bona fide* moral duties and obligations on its inhabitants.[6] Although decency is the term Rawls coins to mark illiberal and undemocratic governments that nonetheless have normative power over their subjects and normative immunity from intervention, clearly he is articulating an idea of legitimacy.[7] In Chapter 4, I endorse at least the outlines of Rawls's account, agreeing that there could be an autocracy or a theocracy that met the threshold criteria of political legitimacy, and that therefore would be morally immune from forceful intervention aimed at democratic regime change. If decent consultation hierarchies meet the criteria of legitimacy, then, *a fortiori,* all democracies—even imperfectly representative and imperfectly liberal ones—would meet the criteria, so long as people were represented at least as well as in decent consultation hierarchies and their human rights were at least as secure. It appears, then, that the free group agency account does not constrain, and therefore has little to say about, governance in a democracy.

This conclusion, however, does not reflect the varying relational and practical perspectives from which we make judgments of legitimacy. *The Law of Peoples* is constructed from the point of view of the foreign policy of a reasonably just liberal people, and the practical question it asks is whether liberal societies must tolerate the merely decent ones.[8] To answer that question, we need to specify a threshold above which a government is immune from outside intervention. But recall that the discussion of "How Free Is Free Enough?" in Chapter 4 sets a higher threshold for when an intervenor is permitted to depart the target country. This is not an inconsistency, but a different answer to a different question about parties who now stand in a different normative relationship. No single threshold will deliver the answers to all of our prescriptive questions, because whether we are to treat a government as falling short of legitimacy's threshold or as if it approximates the ideal will depend on the prescriptive question asked by an actor from some relational perspective.

One upshot of this way of thinking is that legitimacy pins moral agents to a normative ratchet: to advance towards the ideal is a worthy moral aspiration, but not always strictly required; to retreat from the ideal, in contrast, ordinarily is a strictly forbidden moral wrong. So knowing only the level of realization of the ideal of free group agency is not enough to determine our moral prescriptions. We need to know as well the direction and the rates of change. The achievement of Rawlsian decency might be sufficient to preclude forceful intervention but insufficient to permit the withdrawal of the intervenor. And surely the citizens and officials of a liberal democracy that is descending into mere decency are not to act as if legitimate government is not under threat. A legislator in a defective democracy might not have a strict duty to enact measures to increase voter participation from 50 percent to 80 percent, but might have a strict duty to oppose measures to decrease voter participation from 80 percent to 50 percent. The question, "Is an electoral system that has 50 percent voter participation legitimate?" is not well-posed, and so has no determinate answer. If you are puzzled by this asymmetry, and think that I suffer from the irrationalities of status quo bias or loss aversion, you might be in the grip of a moral picture in which prescription necessarily follows from evaluation, and evaluation is a matter of weighing and adding up measures of valuable monadic attributes, properties of the thing itself. But I have claimed that legitimacy is relational and practical, not monadic and theoretical. When we consider the primary question of morality to be prescriptions about what we should do, rather than evaluations of states of affairs, then it is entirely possible that evaluations do not wholly determine prescriptions.

The proposal that we think of the idea of legitimacy within a two-level framework of regulative ideals and constraining thresholds should not be conflated with a suggestion that legitimacy is a continuous variable, an attribute that an authority can possess to a greater or lesser degree. Indeed, I think that it is more perspicuous to think of legitimacy as a binary property, something that an authority either dispositively has or fails to have with respect to some subject in some context, and that this binariness not only is consistent with but follows from a two-level account. Legitimacy, as I understand it, is a normative power, and normative powers, like rights, liberties, and duties, are meant to be action-guiding, telling us what we must, may, or must not do. The *grounds* for having a specified normative power can be stronger or weaker, but the threshold for possessing that normative power, so specified, either has been cleared or it has not. To be sure, the range and domain of normative powers will vary. A ruler might have the normative power to change the normative circumstances of him but not of her, over this issue or action but not over that, with any number of restrictions on scope or jurisdiction. A normative power might be shared, so that we together, but not either of us alone, have legitimate authority. But once specified, a ruler either has a normative power that correlates with a subject's normative liability, or the ruler does not. To think of the legitimacy relation as something that admits of degrees is to deprive the concept of its action-guidedness, of its prescriptive force. Illegitimacy is the strongest complaint we have in the contemporary vocabulary of political morality, and the judgments of the subjects of authority about the legitimacy of their rulers are of first importance, telling us when we are normatively liable and when we can justifiably resist. Normative power is binary, legitimacy is normative power, so legitimacy is binary.

How then are we to understand empirical authorities that fall short of the ideal of legitimacy? If legitimacy is a binary attribute, then authorities either are or are not legitimate. If they are legitimate because we are to act as if they are, what work is done by judging them to fall short of the ideal? And if they are not legitimate because they fall short of the ideal, as all empirical authorities do, then why aren't the philosophical anarchists right after all? The answer is that this indeterminacy is a feature, not a bug, of a two-level theory of legitimacy. Above the minimal threshold, and below the ideal, we live in a range of irreducible judgment about the claims of authority over us. The power-liability account tells us that legitimate authorities have the normative power to change our normative situation, but does not tell us when the entailed change is a moral duty to comply or merely a moral liability to the consequences of our noncompliance. You might find such indeterminacy in turns maddening or frightening, but such indeterminacy is consistent with the classic Rawlsian account of civil disobedience, which also is a matter of judgment that cannot be domesticated by rules. Civil disobedience in a constitutional regime, says Rawls, reveals both the autonomy and responsibility of citizens: autonomy, in that each is ultimately free to judge the claims of authority; responsibility, in that each is accountable to her fellow citizens for that judgment. "Equals accepting and applying reasonable principles need have no established superior. To the question, who is to decide? The answer is: all are to decide, everyone taking counsel with himself, and with reasonableness, comity, and good fortune, it often works out well enough."[9]

III. Democratic Puzzles

Some of our deepest convictions about democracies create puzzles in our assessment of their legitimacy. Majority rule appears to be a procedural requirement on any plausible account of equal political freedom. What argument can be made for *minority* rule? Alas, majorities can enact laws that deprive citizens of equal political freedom, and other basic freedoms as well, but counter-majoritarian constraints on such laws interfere with majority rule, and so appear to lack the legitimacy that democratic procedures provide. The procedural demands on legitimacy and the substantive demands on legitimacy apparently can conflict, with no obvious ground of resolution. As Judith Shklar pithily put it, "liberalism is monogamously, faithfully, and permanently married to democracy—but it is a marriage of convenience."[10] Those who support constraints on majority rule may do so in the name of human rights or justice or liberalism, but in so doing, must they not concede that human rights or justice or liberalism have normative priority over democracy? Or they may claim, with Ronald Dworkin, that *true* democracy is more demanding than simple majority rule and has constitutive or instrumental preconditions.[11] But Dworkin's move doesn't settle how or who is to decide what those preconditions are, other than by majority rule. So even if genuine democracy is a thicker and more demanding notion than majority rule, goes the objection, the public rendering of what genuine democracy is can be determined legitimately only by some democratic procedure. To insist on substantive constraints on *that* procedure for its results to be genuinely democratic is to threaten infinite regress. There is no *deus ex machina* to impose such constraints *ab ovo*, and if there were, surely such constraints would lack legitimate authority over a democratic people.

Alternatively, consider that somehow a system of majority rule appeared with all of the requisite counter-majoritarian constraints necessary to make its legislative procedures genuinely democratic already in place. If a majority, following those procedures, voted to do away with constraints on majority rule, in what way could *that* result be considered undemocratic? Or if, by stipulation, the counter-majoritarian constraints were irrevocable, how could such an unchosen, unwanted, and permanent arrangement be considered democratic? The crème brûlée argument against normative proceduralism presented in Chapter 1 shows that the criteria for legitimate authority can, without contradiction, be in part substantive. Therefore, a government that followed the best procedures for establishing legitimate rule might still fail to do so by not protecting basic rights and liberties: Philippe du Plessis-Mornay's tyranny by practice is a thing. But we have not yet shown how to legitimately require governments to protect basic rights and liberties against the choices of democratic majorities: Mornay's tyranny without title is also a thing.

Our puzzlement recurs when we ask if the decision procedure of majority rule meets the standards for genuine group agency. The acts of a self-governing group agent are responsive to group choices that are responsive to the reasons of the group, which in turn are responsive to the reasons of the self-governing individual agents that constitute it. But actual electorates in actual democracies are very poor approximations of group agents. Even if every voter were informed, reflective, and disciplined enough to be individually self-governing, the aggregation of the choices of voters falls short on the three ways that group agents are constituted. Majority rule does not even pretend to coherently mesh the aims and plans of voters. It also often does a poor job of creating unity out of multitude through representation, since majoritarian representative bodies rarely achieve the requisite internal unity. Constitution by procedure, the most promising route, succeeds in creating a group agent only when procedures combine the reasons of its constituent members in reasonable ways, which majority rule achieves only by accident, since standard electoral practices and procedures do not create the functional capacities of reason-responsive reflection and deliberation. True, group agents can be constituted by procedure, but not by *any* procedure.

Alas, as the great democratic theorists Burke, Madison, and Mill understood (in somewhat different ways), reason-responsive reflection and deliberation are often purchased by the coin of popular participation and responsiveness. In a republic of any scale, majoritarian procedures that treat the political choices of each citizen equally cannot reliably make reasoned collective choices, and deliberative procedures that seek reason-responsive choices, or at least coherent and consistent choices, cannot treat the political choices of each citizen equally. To realize the general reason of the whole that Burke sought, to control the violence of faction Madison feared, or to enact government by talking as Mill envisioned, democratic institutions and practices must prise a gap between the aggregated preferences of citizens and public action.[12]

The free group agency conception of legitimacy, then, seems to trip over itself. Legitimate government requires an independent and self-governing group agent constituted by independent and self-governing citizens. But to make and keep individual citizens free, there must be constitutional constraints on the normative powers of the group agent, apparently limiting its independence. To make and keep the group agent self-governing, there must be institutional checks on the normative powers of citizens to enact their political preferences, apparently limiting their independence. If citizens are to be respected as self-governing equals, they must have the normative power to make their own mistakes, including mistakes about what freedom demands.

Can we solve this three-way puzzle of conflicting principles by invoking the two-level theory of thresholds and ideals? In part. With respect to binding thresholds, there can be a set of realizable political institutions that are minimally adequate on each of the three dimensions, but there is no easy solution with respect to action-guiding ideals. The ideals of liberty, political equality, and group agency not only can conflict, but, over the range occupied by most of the world's imperfect constitutional democracies, do conflict, acutely and contentiously. Vulnerable minorities accuse the majority of their co-citizens of indifference to their rights and liberties. Majorities of voters accuse elected officials of ignoring their preferences and interests. Elected officials accuse the courts of usurping their powers of judgment. So how are the ideals of legitimacy able to guide our actions when they guide us in three different directions?

The key to resolving the puzzle is to recognize that the three principles of legitimacy apply to three distinguishable dimensions of public governance: the liberty principle puts constraints on *what* to decide, the equality principle tells us *who* is to decide, and the agency principle shows us *how* to decide. The argument for the three principles begins by illustrating, through fanciful hypothetical examples, how their extreme violation is utterly incompatible with the free group agency conception of legitimacy, and therefore commits three kinds of tyranny. I will then explore various defects in democratic governance, and show how the three principles of legitimacy, understood as ideals, guide our democratic practices and institutions with fewer conflicts than would be the case if the three principles had equal force in all dimensions.

IV. Three Ways for Legitimate Law to Misfire

In the country of Majoritaria, there is scrupulously universal and equal suffrage, and all citizens participate directly in enacting legislation. Legislative procedures enable exhaustive and reflective deliberation. No citizen has any reasonable complaint about not being heard. Under such conditions, citizens gather in the Assembly of All to consider a proposed Organ Harvest Act, under which public health officials are to be empowered to forcibly (and, invariably, fatally) remove organs for transplantation from anyone whenever the lives of five or more can thereby be saved. The debate begins on a matter of procedure:

> *Demi:* I propose that we decide whether to institute forced organ harvesting by majority rule.
>
> *Libby:* Majorities do not have legitimate authority to decide whether to institute forced organ harvesting.
>
> *Demi:* I propose that we decide whether majorities have legitimate authority to decide to institute forced organ harvesting by majority rule.
>
> *Libby:* Majorities do not have legitimate authority to decide whether majorities have legitimate authority to decide to institute forced organ harvesting by majority rule.

Demi and Libby have reached a turtles-all-the-way-down impasse: there is no mutually agreeable procedure by which they can resolve their procedural disagreement. Demi will argue that majority rule is in fact how decisions are made in Majoritaria, but Libby will retort that, without substantive protections that prevent atrocities like the Organ Harvest Act, the existing method lacks normative force. If a majority of citizens vote for the Organ Harvest Act, it will in fact become black-letter law in Majoritaria, but Demi will not have answered Libby's complaint. Death by forced organ harvesting is a most vivid instance of violating the bodily integrity of some for the use of others, and so a case of freedom-destroying domination. Whatever the merits of the majoritarian procedure that yields the Organ Harvest Act, the resulting statute has no normative force. Rather, the legislation is *inhumane,* rendering Majoritaria a *tyranny by practice.*

Across the river, in Reginaland, Frederica the Greatest reigns with absolute power and absolute justice, as did her forebears from time out of mind. After exhaustive and brilliant analysis, she unilaterally decrees perfectly wise and fair laws. The land is free of deprivation and treatable illness, all economic inequalities are for the benefit of the least advantaged, cultural life flourishes, the arts and the sciences thrive. Her impartial judges interpret and apply her laws wisely, and her police and army stand by to impose her will by force, but they have little to do, because the natives are restful. Freedom of religion and expression is unfettered, and subjects regularly debate political matters without fear. But Frederica doesn't bother to listen—she simply legislates in accord with her infallible best judgment (seeking advice from time to time from the august faculty of the Frederica School of Government). Although Reginaland has no legislature, two of Frederica's subjects discuss the matter at their debating club:

> *Rex:* Frederica the Greatest has written perfectly just laws. What more do you want?
>
> *Lex:* To be an author of those laws, not merely their subject.
>
> *Rex:* Even if the laws you author leave you less free?
>
> *Lex:* I cannot be free if I have no choice in who governs me.
>
> *Rex:* I agree that you are most free when you choose who governs you, but it does not follow that *we* are most free when *we* choose who governs *us.* That is a fallacy of composition.
>
> *Lex:* No, it does not follow, but collective self-governance might possibly make and keep us free. Without collective self-governance, freedom is impossible.

Now, there is of course a contradiction in the description of Reginaland: it cannot be perfectly just if the queen's subjects have no say at all in how they are governed. They are being denied an important, perhaps the most important, political freedom. But if, by hypothesis, Reginaland's laws in every other respect track justice, what is their normative status? Has Queen Frederica succeeded in enacting legitimate law that changes the normative situation of her subjects, or is she merely a source of useful threat? Her subjects have a damning complaint, whether or not it is voiced: by being deprived of any share in collective self-governance, let alone a fair share or a (non-zero) equal share, they are dominated, and so, despite the liberality of her commands, deeply unfree. Queen Regina is a *despot*, rendering Reginaland a *tyranny without title*.

On the other side of the mountain lies Randomark, a constitutional democracy that has universal equal political participation and a demanding Bill of Rights that protects its citizens from substantive injustice. In Randomark, every citizen's proposal for new legislation is treated equally by gathering up all proposals for legislation at regular intervals and selecting one at random. The proposal becomes law unless it is found by Randomark's Supreme Court to be in violation of the country's constitution.

This week, millions of citizens submitted proposals for legislation, and in a scrupulously honest, equally weighted lottery that instantiates the essential political equality of each Randomarkian, the winner is the Circle Simplification Act. In order to make geometry easier for schoolchildren, the law fixes π at exactly 3.2. The author no doubt was inspired by legislation passed by the Indiana State House, "A Bill for an act introducing a new mathematical truth and offered as a contribution to education to be used only by the State of Indiana free of cost by paying any royalties whatever on the same, provided it is accepted and adopted by the official action of the Legislature of 1897," in which it is stipulated that "the ratio of the diameter and circumference is as five-fourths to four."[13]

The Circle Simplification Act is bizarre in three ways. First, it is demonstrably false. Second, even if it were true, truth in mathematics is not determined by legislation. Third, even for matters that are properly decided by legislation, lawmaking by random lottery is a preposterously irrational procedure. What, if anything, is the normative significance of this third flaw?

The good citizens of Randomark think that legislation by random lottery instantiates equality among citizens. They are not categorically mistaken about randomization, because under some circumstances, decision-making by lottery indeed is the best way to recognize equal claims. Choosing *who* is to exercise normative power by lottery, as we do in selecting juries and as the ancient Athenians did in selecting most officeholders, under the right background conditions recognizes the equality of persons. Similarly, if there is an indivisible good and there are no reasons whatsoever to distinguish one claimant from another, allocation by lottery may indeed be the fairest procedure. But choosing among competing legislative proposals manifestly is not such a case. The reason is not merely the obvious suboptimality of such a decision procedure, but its failure to exercise competent group agency at all. A legitimate government is a free group agent constituted by free natural agents, or, with more nuance, an independent and self-governing group agent constituted by independent and self-governing natural agents. To be a self-governing agent, an agent must exercise the three capacities of considering, willing, and doing to an adequate degree. For a group agent to be collectively self-governing, it must combine the individual self-governing wills of its constituent members in some adequate way. Recall the existence proof of group agency by procedure: when a group agent combines the considerations of individual agents in a reasonable way to make a decision that no single agent would make. Legislation by random lottery fails to consider reasons for action at all, and so fails to be the action of a self-governing group agent at all. Two of the country's subjects of random governance discuss Randomark's peculiar institution:

> *Randy:* I propose that we decide the value of π by equally weighted random lottery.
>
> *Raisa:* An equally weighted random lottery is not a legitimate method for deciding the value of π.
>
> *Randy:* I propose that we decide whether lotteries are a legitimate method for deciding the value of π by gathering up proposals for methods of determining π and choosing the winner by equally weighted random lottery.
>
> *Raisa:* A lottery is not a legitimate method for deciding whether lotteries are a legitimate method for deciding the value of π.

Turtles all the way down again. Less preposterously, Randy might have taken the line of argument Demi of Majoritaria pursued earlier, and sought to authorize Randomark's legislation-by-lottery scheme by majority rule. But Raisa's retort would parallel Libby's: majority rule cannot give normative force to irrational decision procedures any more than it can give normative force to inhumane decisions. Randomark is a *group wanton*, not a group agent, and so a *tyranny of unreason.*

Notice that Majoritaria, Reginaland, and Randomark fail in three distinct dimensions of public governance. By not providing substantive protections against violations of basic rights and liberties, Majoritaria is prone to failure on *what* to decide. By depriving subjects of self-governance, Reginaland fails on *who* decides. By adopting procedures unresponsive to the relevant reasons for action, Randomark fails on *how* to decide. These three dimensions are controlled by three distinct principles. *What* to decide is subject to a *liberty* principle, under which all citizens are entitled to external freedom from domination by the unilateral will of others. *Who* decides is subject to an *equality* principle, under which each citizen is to have equal say in selecting who bears decision-making powers. *How* to decide is subject to an *agency* principle—I barely resist the temptation to name it the more stirring but less legible *fraternity* principle—under which decision-making powers are to be exercised by decision-makers who constitute an independent and self-governing group agent that counts all citizens as independent and self-governing members. The liberty principle is outcome-sensitive: there is no pure procedure that guarantees the substantive freedom of citizens, and citizens who are not substantively free cannot form a free group agent. The equality principle comes the closest to enacting a pure procedure: those who are empowered to decide for others, if they are not to dominate those others, must be chosen in a way that is sensitive to the choices of those others, but not directly sensitive to the predicted substantive outcomes of those choices. The agency principle is both choice-sensitive and outcome-sensitive: it is what Rawls calls an imperfect procedure. If independent, self-governing group agency is the joining of the wills of independent, self-governing natural agents in ways that realize and sustain their independence and self-governance, then the group's decisions must be responsive to reasons that, in some sense, are reasons for the members of the group. This is most easily seen in simple group agents constituted by shared aims and plans, but it remains a condition for successful group agency constituted by representation or procedure as well.

A government that seriously fails to satisfy the liberty principle in what to decide is inhumane, a tyranny by practice. A government that seriously fails to satisfy the equality principle for who decides is despotic, a tyranny without title. A government that seriously fails to satisfy the agency principle for how to decide is wanton, a tyranny of unreason. Adding this elaboration, the free group agency account now reads like so:

Free Group Agency

1. A government legitimately governs its citizens only if it adequately realizes and protects their independence and self-governance.
2. The independence and self-governance of citizens are realized and protected only if their government is an independent and self-governing group agent constituted by such citizens.
3. A government is a self-governing group agent only if it has adequate capacities of considering, willing, and doing.
4. Citizens are independent only if they are not dominated by inhumanity, despotism, or wantonism.
5. Citizens are not dominated by inhumanity only if each has a fully adequate set of basic rights and liberties consistent with an equal set for all *(the liberty principle)*.
6. Citizens are not dominated by despotism only if they have adequate and equal normative power to choose who exercises the normative powers of governance on their behalf *(the equality principle)*.
7. Citizens are not dominated by wantonism only if their government is a self-governing group agent responsive to the reasons that apply to its citizens *(the agency principle)*.
   Therefore:
8. A government legitimately governs its citizens only if it complies with the liberty, equality, and agency principles.

V. Do Constitutional Constraints on Majority Rule Threaten Legitimacy?

The crème brûlée argument against proceduralism—that the proof of the pudding is in the eating—claims that the criteria for legitimate authority can be in part substantive, and that we have places to stand from which to judge that such substantive criteria have not been met. No procedure for enacting law and policy by itself can guarantee the protection of basic rights and liberties, and so guarantee legitimate law. The Assembly of Majoritaria does not have the normative power to enact the Organ Harvest Act, and so when it exercises its causal power to do so, it acts illegitimately, and not merely unjustly. But I have not yet shown how institutions that protect basic rights and liberties by constraining electoral majorities can have normative power, and so can act legitimately. Queen Frederica the Greatest protects the basic rights and liberties of her subjects, but she nonetheless is an illegitimate despot. Perhaps the disconcerting truth about legitimacy is that, when electoral majorities make serious mistakes about basic rights and liberties, the dual demands of the liberty principle over what to decide and the equality principle over who is to decide render legitimate governance impossible.

Before the proceduralist in you screams that no theory of legitimacy leading us down such a *cul-de-sac* can be correct, recall that we always have a place to stand to make such judgments from the third-person, second-person, or *ex post* first-person points of view, and those judgments guide us in the design of institutions *ex ante*. Nor does it follow that these judgments require us to take our chances with electoral majorities. We cannot exclude the possibility that the morally best path is to causally empower counter-majoritarian institutions to constrain the causal power of electoral majorities when they act inhumanely, and so without normative power, even though when such counter-majoritarian institutions exercise those causal powers, they act despotically, and so without normative power too. As we saw in the Libya case, there is no Law of the Conservation of the General Will that guarantees the existence of legitimate authority under all circumstances. Unless the most edgy reading of Hobbes is true, a legitimacy-free zone is not a morality-free zone, and if we must choose, humane illegitimacy is morally preferable to inhumane illegitimacy.

To be clear, I am not conceding that the liberty principle and the equality principle can conflict in ways that make legitimate government impossible. I am merely saying that it would not be an embarrassment to substantive accounts of legitimacy if such dystopic conflicts could occur. My own view is that the equality principle, properly interpreted, allows quite a bit of room for constraints on majority rule in the service of basic rights and liberties. Even when citizens have no normative power to choose the laws that govern them, if they have equal normative power to choose *who* governs them, they can be governed legitimately. The task ahead is to show that this is so.

The Lithian Stone

Imbedded in the commons of the city-state of Lithia is a carved granite tablet. There are several myths about the origins of the stone. Some believe that the ancestors of the Lithians left it for their descendants. The more fanciful believe it to be a projectile from outer space, the gift of a superior alien civilization. Whatever its origins, the words on the ancient tablet have been law in Lithia for as long as anyone can remember. Carved on its face are three commandments:

> THOU SHALT NOT HARVEST THE BODY PARTS OF ONE TO SAVE FIVE.
>
> THOU SHALT NOT SUFFER A BENEVOLENT DESPOT.
>
> THOU SHALT NOT ENACT LEGISLATION BY RANDOM LOTTERY.

Carved on its reverse is a fourth:

> THOU SHALT NOT REPEAL ANY OF THESE COMMANDMENTS.

Lithia has no record of any moment of constitutional ratification. Nor is there a history of past endorsement or a current practice of periodic recommitment by the people of Lithia. Indeed, it is part of Lithian legal tradition that the commandments always had and always will have the normative power to bind Lithians, whether they recognize the authority of the tablet or not. To be sure, some Lithians question the legal status of the tablet because of the oddness of vesting a mysterious stone with such binding force. Many of the elected representatives to the city's legislative assembly object on principle to the unamendability provision, and the assembly once voted to repeal the fourth commandment, THOU SHALT NOT REPEAL ANY OF THESE COMMANDMENTS, on the ground that such a restriction is incompatible with democratic government. Despite this criticism, the judges of the high court of Lithia defended the Lithian commandments against legislative challenge by ruling the repeal unconstitutional, and the assembly, not willing to provoke a crisis over a principle without immediate consequence, had not pressed the matter.

Recently, however, a pragmatic reason to revisit the normative force of the commandments has arisen. Transplant surgeons at the Lithian Institutes of Health complained to the legislative assembly that the prohibition on involuntary organ harvesting was costing lives. If forced transplantation were authorized, five Lithian lives could be saved for one life lost, at a net gain of four lives, and this would lengthen life expectancy in Lithia. Ordinarily a quiet country without much political controversy, Lithia is now electric with discussions of political philosophy and constitutional theory. The cafés and pubs around the commons are staying open to accommodate late night deliberation. Protest movements for and against organ harvesting and for and against the authority of the tablets have camped out on the green (though all keep a respectful distance from the tablet itself, which is illuminated at night and tended by a single constable standing at attention in Neolithic livery). The more thoughtful Lithians are morally appalled by the organ harvesting proposal, considering it to be an inhumane violation of basic rights, but many are sympathetic to the view that governments derive their just powers from, and only from, the consent of the governed, and so question the legitimate authority of the tablet. One especially clever young woman has pointed out that the commandments are internally inconsistent: to be subject to an unchosen and unamendable constitution is to be subject to the rule of a despot. To escape tyranny by practice and tyranny of unreason, the tablet imposes tyranny without title. Others argue that one cannot be dominated by a stone. Who has the better argument?

Dominated by a Stone?

I have not carved Lithia's stone merely to amuse (or annoy). Lithia isolates the question of the legitimacy of unchosen constitutional constraints on majority rule from other important but different questions with which it might be conflated. Our question is not whether courts should have the last word on saying what those constitutional constraints are, or how constraints in a constitution should be interpreted, or how constraints in the Constitution of the United States should be interpreted. Nor is the hardness of our question softened by the thought that constitutional constraints on majority rule are made sufficiently democratic by popular procedures of enactment such as ratification and amendment. Lithia's unchosen commandments might as well have fallen from the heavens. If

Lithia's imaginary constitution is legitimate, then, *a fortiori,* so are actual constitutions adopted by actual procedures that claim some sort of connection to the choices of the people.

Well then, are the people of Lithia dominated by a despotic stone? The natural world cannot dominate. Nature can deprive one of options, and thereby harm, but nature has no will, so cannot coerce. A rockslide can block one's path, but rocks do not thereby deprive the walker of freedom understood as independence. Nor can the Lithian stone. But surely, you say, this is just semantic quibbling. The tablet merely is the medium of some author's will, the way a note slipped to a teller is the medium of the will of a bank robber. No, the bank robber's note does not coerce, but the bank robber does. The stone upon which the Lithian commandments are carved does not coerce, but the intentional agents who erected the stone might, reaching forward across the centuries to bind today's Lithians.

True enough, but the original authors of the Lithian stone do not coerce either, because they do not have *causal* power over current Lithians. Lithia's current legislative, executive, and judicial officers exercise such causal power, not the stone's original authors. Whether this imposition by the current officers of Lithia is the infliction of wrongful domination or the exercise of legitimate *normative* power depends, in part, on whether the equality principle is satisfied in the selection of these officers, not on whether the equality principle was satisfied in the selection of the commandments' original authors. Indeed, the Lithian stone's original authors could not have been selected by its original subjects wielding equal normative powers because, to sing our refrain, all foundings are forced. Nor could the commandments' original authors have been selected by its current subjects because no one can travel back in time. Although it is possible for today's subjects to exercise equal normative power to affirm ancient law, the principles of legitimacy do not require that they have such normative power or exercise it. There is a reason the three ways of becoming a member of a group agent are called "conscription": to live under a lawful condition that protects basic rights and liberties is a practical necessity, so practical necessity conscripts the citizens of Lithia as members of a political group agent governed in accordance with the Lithian commandments, with or without recognition or endorsement. If the election procedures in Lithia provide its citizens equal normative power over choosing who governs, then THOU SHALT NOT SUFFER A BENEVOLENT DESPOT, a practical necessity, is satisfied. If the equality principle is satisfied, then Lithians have no complaint about being subjected by their officers to the unchosen THOU SHALT NOT HARVEST THE BODY PARTS OF ONE TO SAVE FIVE, another practical necessity. If the citizens of Lithia are being reasonable, they will recognize the normative force of the Lithian stone, but their recognition is not required for the stone's legitimacy.

Do not misunderstand. This is no backslide to the command-backed-by-force conception of legitimate authority of Thomas Hobbes and Robert Ladenson I rejected in Chapter 2. Legitimate authority is best conceived as a normative power that entails normative liability. For some authorities—in particular, legal authorities—perhaps physical power is one of the preconditions for having this normative power. Why? If physical power is empirically needed for law's effectiveness, and if law's effectiveness is empirically needed to make and keep persons free, then indeed the possession of physical power might be an empirical precondition for the exercise of legitimate rule by law. This is why the legitimacy claims of the National Transitional Council of Libya cannot be self-enacting, but might be self-fulfilling. The immediate question at hand, however, is not what makes law legitimate, but what makes law coercive. The only law capable of wrongful domination is coercive law (setting aside whether noncoercive law is a coherent notion at all). To make such law legitimate, only that which makes it coercive needs to satisfy the equality condition, and what makes Lithian law coercive are the practices of current Lithians, not the intentions of past stone carvers. On this, we should follow Thoreau: "for it is, after all, with men, and not with parchment that I quarrel."[14]

Nor am I denying that normative groups capable of action can extend over time and survive the replacement of all individual members, or denying that words can constitute speech acts, and therefore are capable of coercing. Such a denial would contradict one of the core arguments of this book. On plausible accounts of moral responsibility for speech, a speaker sometimes is responsible for the wrongs committed by the actions of a listener, even when the listener acts voluntarily: one can wrong by incitement and conspiracy. So the authors of the Lithian commandments are capable of wronging future generations with words as much as with bombs on thousand-year timers. But the Lithian commandments are not bombs. By construction, they protect current-day Lithians from violations of the liberty principle like thousand-year-old armor. So the Lithian commandments do not dominate by inhumanity. At issue is whether they dominate by despotism or by wantonism. But I have argued that genuine consent of the governed is neither possible nor necessary, so it matters not that the authors of the Lithian commandments were not and could not have been freely chosen by today's inhabitants of Lithia. No procedure for authoring legislation could have been freely chosen by them. What does matter is that the Lithian commandments count as a reasonable and rational intention of a free group agent constituted by free natural agents. If Lithia's legislators, judges, and constables are selected in compliance with the equality principle in that every citizen has, in the requisite sense, equal say in choosing who governs, then the Lithian commandments are not despotic. If, as the example stipulates, the Lithian commandments comply with the liberty principle in that they protect basic rights, they are not inhumane. If the decision-making practices and procedures of officials comply with the agency principle in that they are responsive to the reasons that apply to their citizens, and citizens have reason to protect each other from domination, then officials who respect the constraints that the Lithian commandments impose on their choices and actions are not wanton. The conditions for the legitimacy of the Lithian commandments therefore are met.

What Makes the Stone Law?

Consider now the public officials of Lithia, who, let us suppose, have either been elected to office or appointed by those who have been elected in accordance with the equality principle. Do they have good reasons to respect the Lithian commandments? Indeed, the public officials of Lithia have the best of reasons to comply with and enforce the Lithian commandments. The first three provisions prohibit three threshold violations of the three principles of legitimacy, and the fourth provision prohibits revoking these morally necessary prohibitions. No legislator should enact, no judge should uphold, and no executive officer should enforce a threshold violation of legitimacy, and so there are no circumstances under which such officers have reasons to be unburdened of these necessary constraints or have reasons to be empowered to unburden themselves or others of such constraints. What is a practical necessity for the citizens of Lithia is a practical necessity for their officers as well. In addition, unlike the citizens of Lithia, who cannot be conscripted into the obligations of citizenship through consent or fair play, the officers of Lithia can genuinely consent to assume the obligations of office if they are free to refuse to serve. Even if they do not consent, if their positions afford them advantages, such as superior income and power and prestige, that they are free to refuse by not serving, they can acquire the obligations of office through fair play.

To show that the Lithian commandments are laws that have normative power over Lithia's citizens and officers, don't we need to do more than note that they have compelling reasons to comply with the commandments' content? We might think that we need to show that Lithians have what are called content-independent reasons. Otherwise, the fact that the commandments have been commanded adds no moral force to what they have compelling reasons to do anyway, rendering the commandments themselves epiphenomenal. If legitimacy is a kind of normative power, and normative power is the capacity, through one's speech acts, to change the normative circumstances of another, in what way do the commandments change the normative circumstances of Lithians? One cannot demonstrate that one has a general moral duty to obey the law of some legal system merely by pointing out that the law prohibits murder and we have a moral duty not to commit murder, because we have a moral duty not to murder whether or not the law prohibits it. The Lithian commandments might not change anyone's normative circumstances any more than a blog post listing the top ten true propositions of political morality. So we have not yet shown that Lithians have reasons to respect the Lithian commandments simply because they are commandments.

The demand for content-independence, however, is not the best way to articulate the challenge that the stone's inscriptions, though true moral propositions, aren't laws. As a criterion of lawishness, content-independence, full stop, is too strong. Indeed, all substantive accounts of legitimacy must reject strong content-independence. Had the Lithian tablet *required* organ harvesting, *required* benevolent despotism, and *required* legislation by lottery, Lithians would have no content-independent reasons at all to comply. They would be utterly mistaken to think that, on the one hand, the stone commands them to be inhumane, despotic, and wanton, but on the other, the stone is their law, so they have reasons both for and against obedience. If what counts as valid law is a complicated, non-normative social fact, then perhaps these inverted and so perverted commandments are valid law, but surely they are not legitimate law, and so do not have genuine normative power over anyone. The social fact of legal validity might depend on mistaken beliefs about the commandments' legitimacy and mistaken beliefs about content-independent reasons for compliance, but to sing another refrain, holding that "legitimate" simply means "believed to be legitimate" is a conceptual confusion.

Rather than subscribing to strong content-independence, we should cancel our subscription to what Joseph Raz calls the "no difference thesis," and rightly rejects.[15] Though properly carved constitutional constraints will require and prohibit actions that are in the neighborhood of what any reasonable legal system would need to require and prohibit, it isn't necessarily the case that such constraints are morally superfluous, constraining democratic legislatures to do or not do precisely what they already have compelling reason to do or not do. Concrete constitutional constraints make a difference when they fix what is morally indeterminate, and they are not despotic when such concreteness is needed. There is no compelling reason for the US Constitution to specify that the president must have "attained to the Age of thirty five years," rather than thirty-four or thirty-six. But there are good reasons not to have made the standard "the attainment of mature judgment," or not to leave the writing of at least some of the basic rules of democratic competition to the competitors themselves.

More generally and deeply, conventional law makes indeterminate duties determinate and potential powers actual, and these attributes not only protect the Lithian commandments from the charge of despotism, but give the stone the normative power to change the normative circumstances of Lithia's officers and citizens. Prior to law, none of us have moral permission to harvest organs from the unwilling, and all of us have a moral duty to protect the vulnerable from bodily violation if we can do so without undue risk or burden. We do not, however, have the unilateral authority to specify for others what counts as bodily violation and undue risk or burden, or to remedy noncompliance with our specification of such a duty. Prior to law, we are able to legislate for ourselves but not for others, judge for ourselves but not for others, and use force to protect but not to punish.[16] Prior to law, Lithia has no officers at all, let alone officers normatively empowered to specify, adjudicate, enforce, and punish, so though the Lithian commandments track the prior moral duties of Lithians and their officers, they are not normatively superfluous.

The challenge to constitutional constraints is that they are despotic, because they preempt the rightful normative powers of democratic majorities. But for at least some constitutional constraints, democratic majorities never had the rightful normative powers to enact what the constraints preclude. Who is to judge what are the rightful normative powers of democratic majorities? Like Libby in Majoritaria, the citizens and officials of Lithia are to judge, and you and I are to judge their judgments. To sing yet another of our refrains, the proof of the pudding is in the eating.

The Legitimate Reading of the Law

I said earlier that the tale of Lithia is constructed to isolate the question of the legitimacy of unchosen constitutional constraints from questions about how to read a constitution, but in the end, our discussion does give some guidance in the task of constitutional interpretation. Ronald Dworkin famously argues for the moral reading of the law.[17] Whether he is right or not is too large a question to address here, but our argument supports a related but different prescription, that judges engage in the *legitimate reading of the law*, a view that I will quickly and incompletely sketch.

If, as a conceptual matter, legitimacy is the normative power to govern, then it follows that judges do not have the legitimate authority to support and enforce an *illegitimate* reading of the law: to do so would be to exercise raw domination over the law's subjects. True, the office of judge is a role created by legitimate political institutions, so the authority of judges to enact their own views about what goodness and even justice demands is properly circumscribed by the legal procedures and materials that make and keep those political institutions legitimate. Even Dworkin concedes that, though justice requires the fair distribution of income, his interpretive theory cannot find economic entitlements in the US Constitution.[18] But just as ordinary citizens have no place to stand other than in their own shoes when they exercise the autonomy and responsibility of citizenship, so too judges, who cannot escape making judgments about the conditions of their own legitimate authority. This is so on whatever normative conception of legitimacy the judge believes upon reasoned reflection to be correct. Now, a judge who holds a very undemanding normative conception of political legitimacy is spared this crisis of conscience, for she is not likely to think that she is ever called upon to affirm and enforce illegitimate law. If, for example, one's normative conception of legitimacy is that any law enacted in accordance with existing procedures is valid law, and that all valid law is legitimate law, then the question of the legitimacy of valid law does not arise. But if you have stuck with my argument this far, you will agree that no legal code's claim of legitimacy incorrigibly makes it legitimate any more than a religious text's claim to be the word of a god incorrigibly makes it the word of a god. An autonomous and responsible judge cannot avoid making judgments about the legitimacy of the laws she is tasked with interpreting and applying, and in doing so, she must appeal to a normative conception of political legitimacy external to the legal institutions and materials she is judging: no law is self-legitimating. If her normative conception is in part substantive, then she must judge the legitimacy of received laws and received canons of legal interpretation in light of those substantive conditions. If her normative conception is something like the free group agency view, then she must judge constitutional provisions that require forced organ harvesting, autocratic rule, or legislation by random lot to be inhumane, despotic, or wanton, and having done so, she must conclude that she does not have the legitimate authority to affirm and enforce such laws.

What, then, is the judge to do when confronted with the task of interpreting and applying illegitimate law? She could resign. Resignation, though, merely resigns the commission to more obedient and suppler people, and fails to express the gravity of her objection, which is that *no one* is authorized to affirm and enforce such laws.[19] Resignation is the appropriate response to a conflict between personal and professional obligation, or to reasonable disagreement about what the common good or justice requires, but resignation is not the best match for legitimacy-based reasons to object.[20] The judge instead could refuse to carry out her institutional duties and declare the law to be illegitimate on extra-legal grounds. Standing in the court house door does match her action to the reasons for her objection, but a strategy of refusal might risk too much political instability for not enough moral efficacy. Acknowledging that this is a political judgment about which I claim no special insight, it does seem to me that a judge who refuses to exercise her duties of office stands a good chance of being removed from that office, and risks focusing public discussion on her act of official protest and away from the illegitimacy of the laws she protests. What else? The judge can engage in deception, and attempt to subvert the illegitimate law by willfully denying that like cases are alike and different cases are different, by pretextually raising procedural obstacles, or by making false findings of fact. Such actions deeply disrespect existing legal actors and institutions, but there are grave circumstances where such disrespect is warranted. A pre-Civil War judge who, through some subterfuge, could prevent the forcible return of a human being to the slave master's whips and chains surely was morally permitted, if not required, to do so. The deference most Northern judges paid to the supposed moral power of the founding generation's Faustian bargains over slavery today seems morally obtuse.[21]

Our judge has not yet exhausted her alternatives, for she can affirm and enforce a reading of the law that gives it the normative power it claims but does not always have. If the laws are abstract or indeterminate or otherwise call out for interpretation, she must read them in a way that gives them legitimate authority. Other canons of interpretation, such as deference and avoidance, properly constrain her from reading into the law her full-blown views of goodness and justice, and arguably constrain her from taking the *ideal* of legitimacy as her guide. A duty of civility demands of judges as well as citizens that they act *as if* law is legitimate until it is perverse to do so. But if a legal interpretation, construction, or doctrine, otherwise appealing on textual or precedential grounds, delivers a result that falls below the threshold on the normative conception of legitimacy the judge reasonably holds, then the illegitimate reading must give way to a legitimate reading. When a judge does so, she is not being disobedient, deceptive, or self-deceptive, for to make the law legitimate is a constitutive aim of adjudication.

What if the text of the constitution is itself unambiguously illegitimate? The abolitionist Wendell Phillips said of the fugitive slave provision, "There stands the bloody clause—you cannot fret the seal off the bond. The fault is in allowing such a constitution to live another hour."[22] For Phillips, the slave constitution said what it said, and Northern disunion was the only morally acceptable resolution. The legitimate reading of the law provides an alternative. I have claimed that valid law is a complicated social fact, and on that complicated social fact, slavery was as lawful under the US Constitution prior to the Thirteenth Amendment as it was lawful in ancient Rome. So Phillips was correct about legal validity. We argued in Chapter 1, however, that not all valid law is legitimate law, and mere validity is insufficient to endow laws and legal institutions with normative power. Unless the agents of a legal regime understand themselves to be merely issuing commands backed by force, they must aim to exercise legitimate authority, though their actions misfire. No matter how a constitution was enacted and no matter by whom, if it contains explicit text that, if affirmed and enforced, would fail a minimal threshold of legitimacy, then that text has misfired. If a constitutive aim of adjudication is to make the law legitimate, it matters not whether to do so a judge must interpret a statute, interpret a constitutional clause, strike a statute, or—clutch your pearls—strike a constitutional clause. The judge's moral and legal authority to make the law legitimate in all of these cases is the same.

CHAPTER 6

Despotism

The argument that constitutional constraints on majority rule are not despotic depends in part on a revisionary view of how to best specify the "currency" of political equality: the good, resource, capability, liberty, right, power, or status that is to be distributed so that citizens are treated as political equals. The equality principle of legitimacy, on this view, states that "citizens are not dominated by despotism only if they have adequate and equal normative power to choose who exercises the normative powers of governance on their behalf." Citizens are to have equal normative power over selecting *who* governs them, but not necessarily equal normative power over the content of the laws and policies that govern them, nor equal *causal* power over either the who or what of governance. So understood, the equality principle is both less and more demanding than commonplace accounts of political equality: less, in that the equality principle does not require law and policy to follow from the preferences of majorities; more, in that the principle is especially stringent in equally situating those who vote for officeholders. This claim about the currency of political equality now needs defending.

Two sorts of defense are needed. First, I need to explain why the free group agency conception offers strong enough conditions for political equality. Recall that Lex in Reginaland demands to be an author of the laws that bind her, and not merely their subject, claiming that freedom is impossible without collective self-governance. If Lex is correct, why is having equal normative power to choose who makes and executes law, but not to choose the substance of that law, sufficient to turn citizens into self-governing authors? One might think that any theory of legitimacy concluding that citizens aren't entitled to equal power over *what* to decide is undemocratic, and so must be a mistaken theory. In the way that reflective equilibrium works, our considered moral judgments at all levels of generality are to be fitted together coherently, so unacceptable concrete implications count against the general principles that entail them. If the free group agency conception supports such a crimped account of the political rights of citizens, goes the objection, we should reject the conception. But in the surprising and sometimes subversive way of reflective equilibrium, the reverse also can happen: the appealing implications of abstract principles can lend support to theories that might otherwise look implausible. And that is the argumentative strategy I'll pursue. My aim in this chapter is to show that limiting the scope of the equality principle to equal normative power over who decides is an appealing, rather than an unacceptable, specification of political equality, and its appeal in turn lends support to the free group agency conception from which it arises.

To be clear, my purpose is neither to analyze the concept of democracy *tout court* nor to argue for a favored democratic conception. There are many democracies, and the ideas, institutions, and practices that fit comfortably under the large democratic tent arguably are of great value on more than one ground. Perhaps democratic procedures are more likely than other kinds of decision-making to find the right answer, or are more likely to maximize the aggregate welfare of the population.[1] These would be weighty considerations indeed to favor democratic forms of government, but they are not considerations that matter to picking that currency of political equality needed to make and keep citizens free. My task is more focused: to show that certain limitations on, or deviations from, majoritarianism are not open to the charge of despotism, and so are consistent with legitimate government.

Second, I need to defend against a challenge to my view of political equality from the opposite direction. On this objection, the question is not whether equal normative power over who governs specifies sufficient conditions for political equality, but whether political equality, whatever its currency, is necessary for legitimate government at all. Lex asserts to Rex that one who has no choice over who governs cannot possibly be free. But what if Rex, not Lex, wins that argument? If, by fanciful hypothesis, the laws of Queen Frederica the Greatest indeed are perfectly just, why does she despotically dominate her subjects? True, no empirical regime,

whether an absolute monarchy, a genuine democracy, or anything in between, will produce perfectly just laws, and we know from bitter experience that basic rights never are secure for long where there are not fair elections. But this link between freedom and democracy is instrumental,
not conceptual—Judith Shklar's faithful, permanent marriage of convenience. In the utopian world of Frederica the Greatest, where, by stipulation, there is no empirical risk of substantive injustice, why is actual collective self-rule an independent precondition for legitimate government?
I will address the second challenge first.

I. Is Political Participation Necessary for Legitimacy?

By including practical necessity, along with consent and fair play, as a path
to conscript members into a free political group agent, have I not already
granted that legitimacy does not require citizens to have actual political
power? Recall that a practical necessity is that which is constitutive of, or
a precondition for, acting upon an agent's prior commitments that the
agent either cannot or will not give up. We will to be free, and to be free,
it is necessary to live under laws that protect our freedom. Therefore, if
we are to be guided by reason, we must already will membership in a free
group agent that makes and keeps us free. If this is so, when the laws succeed in making and keeping us free, are we not already those laws' authors,
even when, as is the case in Reginaland, we have no power at all, normative or causal, in deciding who governs us? No actual government could
ever enact perfectly just laws, of course, and in all actual polities, something like equal political power is an indispensable safeguard against despotism and inhumanity. But Reginaland is an idealization, not an actual
polity, and in that utopia, the argument from practical necessity seemingly forces us to concede that Frederica the Greatest's subjects are collectively self-governing. They are not dominated by her unilateral will
because her legislation perfectly tracks the general will, and so her subjects are not tyrannized by despotism.

Since no actual government could ever enact perfectly just laws, who
cares that some imaginary queen isn't a despot? We care, or should. If
Frederica isn't a despot, then having political power makes and keeps
us free only for instrumental and contingent reasons. If there are any circumstances under which normatively powerless citizens are nonetheless

collectively self-governing, then the connection between normatively powerful citizens and free citizens is causal, not constitutive. In the actual world of imperfect institutions, some forms of government will come closer to protecting the basic rights of citizens than others, and some will come closer to empowering all citizens than others. If Frederica the Greatest isn't a despot, then the empowering of citizens matters to their freedom only insofar as the exercise of such power predictably protects basic rights. So if some novel institutional design came closer to the full protection of those rights by limiting the normative power of citizens, this would come at no cost to their freedom. To resist this conclusion, we must find Frederica despotic.

And so we do. The practical necessity argument cannot rescue Frederica from the charge of despotism because, to be subject to practical necessity, one must have the capacity to will those means that are necessary to one's ends. Frederica's subjects are disabled from exercising any political means, so they are incapable of willing political ends. This is not to say that Frederica's subjects are not agents at all. The queen's benevolent laws enable them to will private ends, for the laws secure her subjects' capacities to exercise their innate, developed, and acquired powers necessary for realizing those private ends. But her subjects are not capable of political agency. This is so even if, because of Frederica's benevolence, all of their political wishes happen to come true, and all of their political needs happen to be met. One cannot face a practical necessity to will means that are impossible to will. Frederica's subjects cannot will to be members of a free political group agent or will to be collective authors of its laws, because their disempowerment renders them mere political patients to be acted upon, not political agents capable of acting. By depriving her subjects of political agency, Frederica remains a despot.

To support by analogy that this is so, recall the difficulty of justifying paternalism. A paternalizes B when A restricts B's liberty for B's own good. That A is right about B's own good is not sufficient to justify restricting B's liberty. Rather, B's capacity for competent self-governance must be seriously defective. Slightly defective won't do. Even though it is empirically the case that none of us is perfectly competent all of the time, we rejected the position that a little bit of impairment justifies a little bit of paternalistic coercion. Why? Because that would fail to recognize our normative powers to choose our own purposes, our authority over ourselves. We would be treating each other merely as moral patients owed protection, rather than as moral agents owed respect. Similarly, by disabling her subjects' normative power to set their own political ends, Queen Frederica treats them as mere political patients, creatures with less dignity than they are entitled to have, and this is a grave violation of their freedom.

The paternalist A who knows B's good better than B does might also try to invoke the argument from practical necessity, and claim that, if B wills his own good, insofar as he is guided by reason, B must also will A's intervention, and so what appears to be coercion is actually freely willed. This audacious claim justifies all paternalistic interventions: the competent B already wills the intervention, and so has no justified complaint; the seriously impaired B has no justified complaint on the usual grounds; the somewhat impaired B, out of respect, is to be treated *as if* he is competent, and so as if he already wills the intervention. Now, clearly this invocation of practical necessity has gone off the rails. Why? Because the argument of practical necessity applies only to agents, not to patients. A patient may have wishes, but to will, to set an end, one must have the capacity to act, to have the power to take means towards that end. The paternalist takes the paternalized person to be a mere patient, and by overbearing or undermining the target's ability to act over the scope and duration of the paternalistic intervention, constrains the target to be a mere patient with respect to the relevant end. If one cannot freely take an action, one cannot will to take that action. So too, Frederica's subjects. Though they are fully capable of agency in their personal lives, they are mere patients with respect to political action. Whatever they might wish for politically, and however well the Queen gratifies those wishes, her subjects are politically disempowered, and so disabled from taking means towards constituting a group agent that will make and keep them free. If they have no normative power to exercise collective self-government, then they cannot will to exercise collective self-government.

Wait, you say. Isn't the punchline of "All Foundings Are Forced" that most of the citizens of legitimate political societies are conscripted into membership through the route of practical necessity? But before the free group agent that makes and keeps its citizens free is constituted, no one has the normative power to exercise collective self-governance. If one does not have the power to take a means towards an end, one cannot will to take that means towards that end. So practical necessity fails to do its job of conscripting membership in political societies. The answer is that the question is poorly posed when asked from the *ab ovo* point of view. *In medias res,* the citizens of a legitimate society do have the capacity to exercise normative political power, so it is possible for them to will membership in the group agent that makes and keeps them free. Therefore, insofar as they are guided by reason, they will the necessary means to their freedom. It's not that individuals, wandering about in a state of nature, are conscripted by practical necessity into membership in a free group agent at the moment of its constitution. That is no less a myth than the story of individuals wandering about in a state of nature gathering together to hatch a social contract through their actual consent. Rather, the argument of practical necessity is addressed to individuals who find themselves in a political society that already protects their freedoms, and explains why they are already members of that society, with all the powers and rights, liabilities and duties that come with such membership.

II. Do Deviations from Direct Majority Rule Threaten Legitimacy?

If those who are disabled from exercising any political power are governed despotically, how is power to be denominated, and under what principle distributed, so that the governed are self-governing, and therefore free? Consider this argument about what political equality demands:

> **Political Equality as Direct Majority Rule**
> 1. Citizens are treated as political equals only when they have equal and adequate normative power.
> 2. Citizens have equal and adequate normative power only when they have equal say over public choices.
> 3. Citizens have equal say over public choices only when they are able to participate equally and directly in making decisions by majority rule.
> *Therefore:*
> 4. Citizens are treated as political equals only when they are able to participate equally and directly in making decisions by majority rule.

Clearly, if this formulation or something close to it specifies the currency of political equality aright, so that the ideal of collective self-governance calls for direct majority rule, then limiting the reach of the equality principle of legitimacy to equal normative power over choosing who governs is mistaken. What, then, is the correct specification of the ideal of political equality?

Majority Rule

Any theory of politics that professes to be democratic must recognize that every active citizen is entitled, in some sense, to an equal say in collective self-governance. One important part of the history of modern democracy has been the story of how the idea of active citizenship has expanded (in fits and spurts, and not without reversals) to relax exclusions by creed, class, color, sex, and origin. My concern here, however, is not with specifying the proper boundaries of active citizenship, but with specifying the proper sense in which such citizens are entitled to an equal say. I do not deny that these two specifications might interact. Wider conceptions of membership may go together with shallower conceptions of equality.

When I refer to citizens, I am supposing a background in which all of the permanent inhabitants of a country are citizens of that country, and all of the competent citizens are active citizens. I don't have a full account of citizenship, except to say that everyone on the planet is entitled to the rights and powers of citizenship somewhere. Though I take no stand here about who is entitled to settle within a jurisdiction, anyone who has settled is entitled to citizenship. We of course need an account of what is owed by whom to stateless persons, refugees, and voluntary migrants, but I abstract away from that problem here, except to say that it is repugnant for a state to ignore the moral anomaly of millions of people permanently living within its borders as dependent political patients deprived of the full protection of the law.

To explicate what it is to have an equal say in governance requires specifying three notions: what it is to have a say, over what choices everyone is to have a say, and what it is for everyone's say to be equal. At this point, a picture of ideal active citizenship often springs to mind: to have a say in governance is to participate directly with voice and vote in public decision-making. If one's imagination is vivid, these citizens are draped in white linen tunics under the warming Attic sun. To have an equal say is a bit less specified in this picture. Perhaps it requires that each citizen-participant have equal speaking time in the public forum, or even equal resources to expend on political speech, though it cannot require that each citizen be equally influential, for some arguments made by some people are rightly more convincing than other arguments made by other people. At least, it would appear that an equal say in governance requires that all public choices be put before all citizens for a vote, that each citizen have an equally weighted vote, and that collective decisions be made in accordance with the simple majority of these equally weighted votes. If individual self-governance is the exercise of a competent individual will, and collective self-governance is the exercise of a competent collective will, then an equal say in collective self-governance requires that the will of each competent individual on each question of governance be counted, that each counted will be given equal weight, and that in turn demands majority rule, or so it would seem.

Yet even a cursory review of decision procedures in titular democracies turns up facial deviations from majority rule, both by not satisfying the one person, one vote standard and by requiring supermajorities. California has sixty-eight times more people than Wyoming, but both states have the same two seats in the US Senate. Of the hundred members of the Senate, the fifty from the least populous states represent only one-sixth of the total population. Assuming uniform turnout across states, it is arithmetically possible for a US president in a two-way race to be elected with only 22 percent of the popular vote. This is no mere theoretical exercise, of course. In two recent American presidential elections, the Electoral College winner lost the national popular vote, and a constitutional amendment to eliminate the Electoral College procedure that makes such a result possible could be blocked by states containing under 4 percent of the population. Party-sensitive drawing of congressional districts permits disproportionate anomalies. In the 2016 elections for the US House of Representatives, Wisconsin's Democratic candidates, with 52 percent of the statewide vote, won only 37.5 percent of the congressional seats, while North Carolina Republicans, with 53 percent of the statewide vote, won 77 percent of their delegation. When North Carolina State Representative David Lewis was asked in an open legislative hearing why district boundaries were so skewed, he answered, "I propose that we draw the maps to give a partisan advantage to ten Republicans and three Democrats because I do not believe it's possible to draw a map with eleven Republicans and two Democrats."[2]

There are reasons to condemn these procedures as violations of political equality, but several constitutional democracies deviate from simple majority rule in ways one can argue are permitted or even required by political equality. India reserves parliamentary seats for scheduled castes and tribes. France, Spain, and Portugal mandate nearly equal numbers of women and men on party candidate lists. In New Zealand, those who identify as Maori and choose to place their names on a separate electoral roll fill seats in proportion to the number of Maori voters. In Belgium, where the Dutch-speaking Flemish outnumber the French-speaking Walloons, certain legislation must be supported by a majority of representatives from each linguistic community.

Why, in the social contract tradition, is majority rule presumed to be the default procedure for public choice? Locke invokes a mechanistic metaphor: if each member of society exerts force on the public decision, the sum of these forces gives the decision to the majority, like the winners of a tug-of-war: "it is necessary the Body should move that way whither the force carries it."[3] In supposing that each voter has equal force, Locke gives some due to the moral equality of persons. He fails, however, to give an adequate explanation of why this vector sum of forces counts as the will of the people. Recall Korsgaard: a bag of mice will move, but cannot act. Hobbes takes the challenge of creating a unified will out of the multitude more seriously: unity is to be found in the representative, not the represented. However, when the representative is itself an assembly, rather than a crown worn by one natural person, Hobbes must resort to his own metaphor:

> And if the Representative consist of many men, the voyce of the greater number, must be considered the voyce of them all. For if the lesser number pronounce (for example) in the Affirmative, and the greater in the Negative, there will be Negatives more than enough to destroy the Affirmatives; and thereby the excesse of Negatives, standing uncontradicted, are the onely voyce the Representative hath.[4]

Unity is achieved because each pair of yes and no votes "destroy" each other, leaving the surplus of no votes an unopposed, and so unified, will. The violent imagery here is pointed. Since consent to Hobbes's original contract is not binding unless coerced, it is not too fanciful to picture drawn swords in the assembly, the larger faction threatening to physically destroy the smaller unless unanimous consent is granted. Hobbesian unity out of multitude is delivered by either threat or death.

Never mind the violence: Hobbes poses the right challenge in demanding unity. Ideally, the people govern themselves with a unified will in perfect satisfaction of equal political freedom when the constituent members of the people are unanimous in all of their choices. The near-impossibility of such unanimity for any group larger or longer-lasting than the male passengers of the Mayflower on their last day aboard launches the quest, perhaps quixotic, for a realizable group decision-making procedure short of unanimity that nonetheless has the normative force of unanimity. Should we not then first examine decision rules in the close neighborhood of unanimity? How about 100 percent minus one? Since at least 10 percent of the population will be insane on any particular question, how about 90 percent? At three-quarters plus one, the yeses and noes destroy each other and still leave a bare majority of the whole. Two-thirds is decisive. The golden ratio, 61.803 percent, is beautiful. *Any* supermajority decision rule is closer to unanimity than a bare majority, and therefore, presumably, closer to the united will of the people.

The retort, of course, is that every supermajority decision procedure also symmetrically enacts a form of super*minority* rule. If two-thirds of the popular vote is needed to replace a government, then that government can be reelected by only one-third of the electorate, and what argument can possibly support that? But this supposed symmetry is fatal only when the failure to achieve a supermajority delivers a minority victory. It is a matter of institutional design whether this is so, not a requirement of arithmetic: the minority or the *status quo ante* needn't win. When the College of Cardinals gathers *cum clave* in the Sistine Chapel to choose a new pope by two-thirds supermajority, the prior pope is not the default, who in all but one case since 1415 is dead. More balloting under lock and key is. Indeed, a decision procedure that is widely taken to instantiate democratic egalitarianism is trial by jury, in which decision-makers are chosen more or less randomly, the decision rule for conviction or acquittal is unanimity, and the default in the case of a hung jury, at the discretion of the prosecution, is a do-over. One can always design a supermajoritarian procedure that avoids defaulting to minority rule, though often at the cost of indefinite indecision. The advantage of a bare majority rule procedure in a choice between two alternatives is that, except in the case of a tie, the procedure guarantees a unique winner, but this is no great achievement. There is no way to narrow a social choice to two alternatives that isn't extremely sensitive to, and therefore manipulable by, the method for narrowing the alternatives.

Consider a simple illustration. The well-known median voter theorem predicts that, in an election with two candidates and voters distributed evenly along some dimension, rational candidates in equilibrium will position themselves near the center of that distribution. But the more extreme preferences of party activists whose support politicians need to succeed in the nomination process lead to much greater polarization of the candidates than the median voter theorem predicts. Suppose voters are uniformly distributed and the two candidates position themselves at the two extremes—perhaps because each has an extreme billion-dollar donor who demands this. In such a case, winner-take-all majority rule is a preposterous solution to the problem of creating a unified will out of the multitude. All but two voters would prefer a less extreme candidate, and a third candidate occupying the median voter position would get twice the votes of either rival.

It gets worse, of course. With more than two candidates, no general solution to the problem of social choice satisfying reasonable criteria, such as transitivity and nondictatorship, is possible. We have known this informally for at least 235 years, since Condorcet, and with increasing formality and generality for about 70 years, since Arrow.[5] The plurality rule procedure of most American elections is especially vulnerable to violations of the independence of irrelevant alternatives criterion, hence the odd result that a candidate who would lose in a one-on-one contest against every single opponent can still win the election.[6] This is no mere theoretical possibility: it afflicts the American primary system. That the various impossibility proofs have made little dent in the folk theorems widely held by ordinary citizens in modern democratic societies is an embarrassment to civic education. To state the truth plainly: there is no purely procedural rendering of the will of the people short of unanimity over an unrestricted set of alternatives. Like the free will problem, the only solutions to the general will problem that do not succumb to magic or illusion are *normative* solutions, for neither logic nor mathematics nor metaphysics delivers a unique answer.

I do not deny that, for many public decisions, under certain background conditions, some form of first-past-the-post majority or plurality rule over options that have been narrowed through some prior majoritarian agenda-setting procedure is a procedure that has some desirable attributes. Nor is there a shortage of voting schemes that are alternatives to first-past-the-post (though none escapes Arrow's sting): instant runoff voting (used to elect the Australian House of Representatives), the single transferable vote (used to elect the Australian Senate), the Borda count (employed by the Pacific island nation of Nauru to pick its parliament), approval voting (used in UN Security Council straw polls to recommend a candidate for secretary general), and various Condorcet methods (one of which is used in the Swedish Pirate Party primaries). There are theoretical arguments and empirical evidence to suppose that different voting rules will promote or discourage two parties or multiple parties, coalition-building or dissent, centrism or polarization, stability or instability, and there are normative arguments to assess the appeal of these various attributes on the grounds of goodness or justice broadly considered. Our concern, though, is restricted to the normative question implicit in Lex's objection to Queen Frederica: which election procedures avoid domination by despotism? We should not be lulled into thinking that the formal satisfaction of one person, one vote is always sufficient to satisfy the demands of political equality, nor should we accept, without argument, that majority rule succeeds in creating unity out of multitude and authors out of subjects, thereby solving the puzzle of collective self-governance. It's not as if someone more clever than Hobbes or Locke will analytically prove that some majoritarian procedure or other delivers equality and unity. We unavoidably are in the land of the *as if*.

Direct Participation

Representative democracy, under the simple "equal say" picture, is always an imperfect realization of the democratic ideal, because the many citizens that one representative represents almost certainly have different and conflicting wills formed in light of different and conflicting reasons, interests, and judgments. Since the representative has only one voice and one vote in the legislative assembly, she cannot possibly represent all of the conflicting wills of her constituents.[7] In contrast, in a direct democracy it is up to every citizen-participant, for each legislative decision, to make her choice in light of the considerations that she holds to be most relevant, so the possibility of misrepresentation or underrepresentation cannot arise. Either there is no representation in direct democracy, or each citizen represents only one, herself. Direct democracy appears to eliminate the irreducible puzzles that threaten whenever one represents more than one by eliminating the need for the arithmetic that generates these puzzles. In ideal form, direct democracy appears to be a pure procedure constitutive of political equality: the equality principle of legitimacy is satisfied whenever the procedure is followed, however citizens vote and whatever the outcome. This is why Demi of Majoritaria's argument has initial plausibility.

On this line of reasoning, direct democracy cannot misrepresent, so direct democracy constitutes a pure procedure, so direct democracy is the ideal form of democracy. But the initial premise is false, unless the polity is without children, incompetents, or visitors—that is, a polity in which all inhabitants are active citizens. It also would need to be a polity without future generations who are owed duties of fairness, past generations who are owed duties of fidelity, or contemporary inhabitants of other countries who are owed duties of humanity, at least. Once we are reminded that even direct democrats do not represent themselves only, we remember that voting is a public office, not a private entitlement. Legislators are to legislate for the good of all, not merely for the good of themselves, and this is so even when every citizen is a legislator. If voting is a public office, your vote is not an inerrant enactment of your individual will or good, but a possibly erroneous judgment about the will or the good of all others, possibly erroneously combined. So, even in a one-generational, one-polity world, where everyone who needs to be represented is an active citizen, it is still the case that direct participants can misrepresent each other by making mistakes in judgment about what justice and goodness requires for, and therefore of, all. Because the wills or good of others might be misunderstood, mismeasured, miscounted, misjoined—that is to say, misrepresented—direct participatory democracy is not a pure procedure. This is Libby of Majoritaria's argument.

But does this view not confuse representation with respect and consideration? True, we have moral duties to those who fall outside the boundaries of active co-citizenship, and these duties might be very demanding and constraining, but is there not an important difference between representing another and respecting or considering another? A proper representative is normatively empowered and required to act *for* the represented, to enact the will of, or advance the interests of, the represented in the stead of, and in the name of, the represented. Surely not all duties to others are fiduciary duties of this sort. Your lawyer has various positive and negative duties to other parties that shape and limit what may be done on your behalf—she may not lie to the judge or withhold discoverable evidence from your adversary—but your lawyer represents only you, not these other parties. Your baker should sell you fresh and wholesome bread and make correct change at the cash register, but your baker does not bear your person. Though an elector in a direct democracy has duties to others, both citizens and foreigners, they are not all the duties of a representative. Alternatively, if such duties are the duties of a representative, is there not something better than representation? Why wouldn't the argument for the direct democratic gold standard reassert itself in a call for a global *demos*? Generations past and future cannot, and the seriously incompetent should not, have a direct say in collective self-governance, but all competent contemporaries on the planet can. Why shouldn't they all have a say, as proponents of an all-affected principle assert, and a direct say, as the supposed democratic ideal proposes?[8]

No, not every duty of an elector to others is the duty of a representative, but the all-affected principle is extravagant because not all who are affected are governed. All who are affected are owed a justification, but only those who are governed are owed a say. What is the difference? Having a say is having a normative power, such as a veto or a vote. Even when you have a right to use force to protect yourself when my actions are not justified, you do not (yet) have a normative power over me. You cannot, by contributing to some enactment, change my normative circumstances. My normative situation has always been that I am liable to the force of your self-protection. When you permissibly use causal power to defend yourself against my violation of your rights, you have no more authority over me than you have over a wild animal, against which force also is justified. In contrast, to have a normative power is to have the ability to perform a speech act that changes the normative situation of others. Care in drawing this distinction is one of the lessons of our earlier Hohfeldian investigations.

One is governed, on the power-liability view of legitimacy, only when one is subject to the normative power of the governor—that is to say, when one is morally liable to changes in one's normative circumstances, changes in one's institutional rights, duties, and status, changes in constitutive rules that shape one's normative abilities, and to the coercive enforcement of these changes—and not merely when one is burdened, harmed, or even wronged. Everyone affected by the choices of others is at risk of domination by inhumanity through the misuse of causal power, but only those who are *governed* by others are at risk of domination by despotism or wantonism through the misuse of normative power. Though there is a special terror in random inhumanity, only random authority dominates by wantonism as well. Past generations cannot be governed by us. Inhabitants of other countries are not governed by us merely in virtue of being affected by us, but would become governed once the web of global institutions is sufficiently thick to trigger transnational normative powers entailing transnational normative liabilities. One of the more interesting contemporary questions in global justice is how to correctly specify that trigger.[9] The equality principle, which assures each who is governed an equal say in who governs, protects against despotism. The agency principle, which assures that each who is governed is governed by a reason-responsive agent, protects against wantonism. Together, the equality principle and the agency principle satisfy whatever special claims the governed have against their governors in virtue of being governed, in addition to the more general claim, satisfied by the liberty principle, that all have against all others. So we can repose claims to representation as claims under the equality and agency principles, and claims of respect as claims under the liberty principle. On the free group agency account of collective self-governance, the distinctive problem of representation recedes in importance, and with it, the normative distinction between direct and mediated democracy. If governance is legitimate only if the governor is a free group agent constituted by individual agents who, though governed, are free, then the duties of a legislator under direct and mediated institutions are the same. Both are charged with making and keeping all who are governed (including themselves) free.

If, instead of asking whether citizens are properly represented, we ask if they are free, and if we accept that there is no pure procedure that, if only followed, would necessarily make citizens free, then we should conclude direct democracy is not an ideal towards which imperfect political institutions must aspire. We have not yet specified what it is for citizens to have equal normative power, and we have not yet described the institutions of public decision-making that either are most likely to realize this equality of normative power or are least likely to descend into despotism. But at this point in the argument, the plebiscite has no place of privilege. Procedure or pedigree alone cannot guarantee those who govern the normative powers they claim even when the claimants attempt to collectively govern themselves directly.

III. Which Inequalities of Power Threaten Legitimacy?

I have been making much of the distinction between normative power and causal power. It is time to explain the difference with more precision. The contrast is clearest when normative power is exercised through a speech act, a performative utterance that changes a subject's normative situation or creates a normatively potent social fact. A citizen or public official who exercises normative power in this way does things with words by enacting a normative change by vote or decision.[10] In contrast, causal power is the ability to affect what others do by making changes in the physical world, or by rearranging the conscious incentives of others by imposing costs and conferring benefits, or by exploiting unconscious inclinations and cognitive biases, whether by physical means only or with words too. To be sure, not all normative powers are exercised through speech acts. Sometimes agents have the normative power to employ causal power directly, as when a police officer makes an arrest. What confers upon an agent the normative power to exercise causal power in such cases, however, typically is the prior speech act of a higher authority.

In ordinary democratic politics, the causal power of some agents is regularly exercised over other agents who have normative power, inducing the others to use their normative powers in accordance with the will of the causally powerful. The ability of those who control disproportionate wealth and other resources to leverage their causal power into normative power in this way often is of great moral concern, because the exercise of unequal causal power can undermine the fair value of the equal normative power of citizens. But despite this empirical linkage, it is a mistake to conflate the normative power of citizens with their causal power. The two kinds of power are not morally important for the same reason, and they are not subject to the same principle of distribution.

What I will call the *power of reason* shares attributes with both normative and causal power, but is best thought of as a separate kind. The power of reason is the ability to change the beliefs upon which others act by offering evidence and arguments in good faith. From the third-person perspective, the power of reason may appear to collapse into causal power: a marketer does not much care why the target of advertising is moved to buy a product or vote for a candidate. But from the first-person perspective, when we are sufficiently self-aware of the factors that influence our choices and actions, we can distinguish between reasons, conscious incentives, and unconscious motives and biases. The first-person perspective prompts a conflation in the other direction, for the power of reason appears to collapse into normative power. Insofar as we conceive of ourselves as reasonable and rational, good evidence and sound argument have a kind of authority over us, and so we often defer, often rightly, to the judgment of those we judge to have superior knowledge and expertise. Still, the distinctions between the authority of reasons themselves over what one should believe, the power of an epistemic authority over what one should believe, and the power of a practical authority over what one should do are reasonably clear. Only the last is what I am calling normative power. This, as we saw, is the difference between the power of the Lithian commandments and the power of a blog post containing true propositions of political philosophy.

Citizens who vote for legislators exercise a normative power (shared with other voters), and legislators who vote for laws exercise a normative power (shared with other lawmakers). Insofar as voters choose whom to vote for and legislators choose what laws to enact in response to evidence and arguments, their exercise of normative power is guided by the power of reason. Insofar as citizens cast their ballots in response to conscious incentives or unconscious manipulation, and insofar as candidates for elected office make legislative choices in order to satisfy their desire to win elections and reelections, they are subject to causal power. I do not assume that voters never have sufficient reason to satisfy their desires, and so vote for the candidate who is likely to advance their private interests, or that elected officials never have sufficient reason to satisfy their desires, and so choose laws and policies that are likely to get them reelected. Should they have such sufficient reason to do so, they would be responsive to the power of reason. I am claiming, though, that voters and legislators who are moved *only* by such desires, and not by sound reasons to be moved by those desires, are under the power of causal forces, not the power of reason.

Now for what many readers will think is a hopelessly utopian step: the ideal of political equality is a standard specified by the proper distribution and exercise of normative power informed by the power of reason, but not by the distribution or exercise of causal power. Of course, no actual voter and no actual elected official is immune to causal power and responsive to the power of reason alone, and no society's politics approaches the ideal. But recall the two roles that ideals play in our moral thought: they are both constitutive standards that define an activity and normative standards that guide that activity. Above some threshold, we are to act as if actual political actors and practices meet the ideal, and treat political institutions as legitimate even when they fall short of the ideal, while at the same time aspiring to be guided in our exercise of normative power by the power of reason. This view has substantial practical bite: it asks that we take a charitable stance towards our political opponents and not disparage their motives for political gain at every opportunity. Our own actions too, witting or not, are under the sway of causal powers, and we too are vulnerable to the charge of bad faith. Rawlsian reciprocity again is called for: we have a duty of civility, within bounds, to accept one another's defects, even as we struggle to overcome our own. When, however, voters and politicians fail to be guided by the ideal at all, fail to recognize that the ideal ought to guide them, or worst of all, hold the ideal in contempt, they are open to justified moral criticism. And when those who engage in politics and rule us drive us further and further from the ideal of exercising normative power informed by the power of reason, we need not continue to act *as if.* Locke invites us to imagine we are on a ship whose captain, though disrupted by crosswinds, leaks, and shortages, keeps steering towards Algiers. Though the ship's course is neither direct nor certain, are we not entitled to conclude that we are on our way to lose our freedom in the Barbary slave markets?[11] When we are governed by political actors who not only exercise power over us in ways that fail to be informed by the reasons that are relevant to making and keeping us free, but who actively undermine our collective commitment to those reasons, there is little comfort in noting that we have not yet reached despotic shores. There are limits to the charitable practice of thinking and acting *as if.*

The free group agency conception of legitimacy is uncompromising in its requirement that citizens have equal normative power in their collective self-government. Free group agency's stance on the equal distribution of *causal* power, in contrast, is entirely contingent on whether the incentives and inclinations triggered by the exercise of causal power make and keep citizens genuinely equal in their capacities to exercise normative power. Candidates in all actual democracies will be moved by the incentive to remain in office, and so act to please their constituents, or a subset of their constituents, or their party bosses, or their large donors. Voters in all actual democracies will be moved by the incentive to have their private interests served, and so vote for candidates who will advance those interests, or will be manipulated by messages that trigger emotional or cognitive biases that track neither their interests nor their reasons. With the right combination of ordinary virtue, wise institutional design, and good fortune, these incentives and inclinations can align with and support the equal distribution of the normative power of citizens. One of the most important tasks of political science is to discover which arrangements of causal power sustain legitimate government and which do not. Experience and prudence tell us that our rights and liberties are safer when causal power is widely dispersed. But legitimacy does not require, or even favor, the equal distribution of causal political power on first principles, only the equal distribution of normative power. To take an exceptionally American example, a constitutional right to keep and bear arms might or might not be a contingently prudent way to deter tyrannical government, but the Second Amendment tracks no prior moral right of citizens to wield lethal power in the way that the Fourteenth and Fifteenth Amendments and the Lithian Tablet track prior moral rights of citizens to wield normative power. Similarly, the correct account of distributive justice has a great deal to say about how causal power and the material resources that enable it are distributed, but unless there is an instrumental connection between inequalities of causal power and inequalities of normative power, the correct account of legitimacy is indifferent to unequal resources. If wealth can buy votes, the free group agency view of legitimacy cries foul, but if wealth can buy only yachts, legitimate governance isn't threatened. If serious economic inequality creates a dependent lower class that votes out of fear or favor, then the fair value of equal normative power has been debased, but economic inequality needn't create such dependence. Within bounds, legitimate rule need not be just rule.

What legitimacy does require is that voters and elected officials exercise their normative powers by performing speech acts in ways that establish and maintain a free group agent constituted by free citizens. Speech acts, though, can misfire, and fail to enact the normative change the actor intends. Two people saying "I will" under certain conditions—in front of an officiant authorized by the state in the presence of witnesses and absent various disqualifying circumstances—constitutes the act of marrying. Said by two people who are under age, or currently married to others, or of the same sex in a jurisdiction that has not yet enacted marriage equality, "I will" misfires, and fails to enact a marriage, despite the couple's joint intention. The same words, "I will," spoken in response to an anxious relative's inquiry, is merely a prediction or statement of an intention to perform a speech act in the future, but not in itself a performative.

Under what circumstances do the speech acts of voters and legislators misfire? There are the obvious cases where the agent who attempts the speech act does not have the normative power claimed: the voter who mails in an absentee ballot after the deadline, or the tourist in the Senate gallery who calls out "yea" on a voice vote. Less obvious but more important, the normative powers of governance misfire when their exercise fails to establish or maintain the free group agent that is needed for legitimate governance. When free group agency fails, citizens are incapable of exercising normative power at all, let alone equal normative power. When citizens are incapable of exercising normative power at all, what appears to be legitimate collective self-governance is nothing other than the exercise of the causal powers of the strong or more numerous over the weak or less numerous, the mere domination of some lawless individuals over others.

When does free group agency fail? Recall that the free group agency view was first presented as an *in medias res* virtuous circle. We don't look for founding moments, but for happy equilibria, where free citizens constitute a free political group agent that in turn makes and keeps its citizens free. Nothing, however, guarantees that majority rule by citizens casting equally weighted votes will constitute such a free political agent. Not only can there be no assurance that laws enacted under such procedures will protect basic rights and liberties. Even if the supporters of basic rights and liberties win an election, some configurations and distributions of prior political views simply cannot be combined to achieve the sufficient unity needed to constitute all citizens into a free group agent. Again, Rawls is instructive. Political stability for the right reasons is possible when the comprehensive moral doctrines of citizens, though in disagreement about personal morality, form an overlapping consensus in support of a family of political conceptions that are justifiable to one other on grounds that citizens seeking fair terms of social cooperation can share. Rawls asks,

> When may citizens by their vote properly exercise their coercive political power over one another when fundamental questions are at stake? Or in the light of what principles and ideals must we exercise that power if our doing so is to be justifiable to others as free and equal? To this question political liberalism replies: our exercise of power is proper and hence justifiable only when it is exercised in accordance with a constitution the essentials of which all citizens may reasonably be expected to endorse in light of principles and ideals acceptable to them as reasonable and rational. This is the liberal principle of legitimacy.[12]

Reasonable pluralism about conceptions of the good is a fact of life under free institutions, eliminable only by suppression, compatible with social unity in support of legitimate law, and so not to be regretted. But *unreasonable* pluralism also is possible. Rawls is clear: an overlapping consensus, and so the requisite unity, might not be possible among the conceptions of the good and of the right that people happen to hold at any historical moment. Rather, it is a society's good fortune, or else the hard-won lesson of bitter and bloody sectarian strife, that the prevailing moral views are reasonable, in that their followers accept the idea of reciprocity between free and equal citizens.

Instead, a political society may suffer the ill fortune of containing antagonistic factions that cannot be reconciled under a widely shared conception of reciprocity. One or more factions, or possibly all factions, could hold intransigent political views that do not meet the test of public reason. Germany in the early 1930s was such a society, in which the fascists, the conservative nationalists, and the communists were all committed to the downfall of the fragile social democratic center. This is why it is no irony, let alone a deep normative puzzle, that Hitler rose to power by winning a plurality of seats in consecutive substantially free and fair Reichstag elections. Under the circumstances, no voting procedure could have rescued the feeble Weimar Republic for long. The fall of Weimar is the most horrific instance of a general truth about social choice procedures: from some initial configurations of political views, no procedure can constitute a group agent, much less a free group agent. This is why the conditions for political legitimacy must in part be substantive, and therefore why its procedures must sometimes be outcome-sensitive.

We ordinarily ought to act as if free and fair elections are instances of pure procedural legitimacy whose winners necessarily bear the normative power to govern, but this is because ordinarily the winners of democratic elections do not go about violating basic rights and liberties, undermining the political equality of voters in subsequent elections, or ruling wantonly, so that the government fails the test of free and competent group agency. Similarly, we ordinarily ought to act as if laws enacted in accordance with the procedures of democratic legislatures are legitimate simply in virtue of being enacted because ordinarily such laws do not violate basic rights and liberties, strip citizens of their equal normative power to vote, or fail a minimal test of rationality.

The main criticism of representative democracy is that it weakens the causal power of the electorate by introducing a gap between what a majority of the people would choose and what elected officials do choose, a gap that cannot be reliably closed by threat of electoral defeat. But it is a mistake to think that procedures that do not guarantee citizens equal causal power over law and policy for that reason fail to secure their equal normative power. The reverse can be true: citizens who attempt to exercise equal normative power may collectively misfire if, by their aggregated actions, they undermine the unity of the group political agent that is necessary for securing their individual freedom.

The upshot of this chapter so far is this: the choice among plurality, majority, or supermajority decision rules and the division of moral labor between citizens and their representatives are both governed by one overriding consideration—to design a system of group decision-making that constitutes an independent and self-governing group agent that makes and keeps citizens independent and self-governing. A system of group decision-making that fails to do this fails to endow anyone at all with normative power, and when citizens are incapable of exercising normative power, what appears to be democratic politics is the mere domination of one another through the exercise of causal power. Yes, this is unabashedly outcome-sensitive, and so rigged towards a family of results. But, just as was the case with constitutional constraints discussed through the tale of Lithia, this sort of rigging of electoral and legislative procedures is demanded by, rather than forbidden by, the correct account of political legitimacy. The free group agency account of legitimacy therefore leads to the conclusion that normative power and causal power are subject to different criteria of distribution.

These reflections on majority rule, representation, and the distinction between normative power and causal power suggest the following revision to the specification of political equality:

Political Equality as the Fair Value of Equal Normative Power
1. Citizens are treated as political equals only when they have equal and adequate normative power to choose who governs on their behalf.
2. Citizens have equal and adequate normative power to choose who governs on their behalf only when they have an equal vote, their vote has fair value, and their vote has normative power.

3. The vote is equal when citizens have equal access to cast votes of equal weight.
4. The vote has fair value only when the will of voters is not overborne by coercion, undermined by deception, or dependent on the fear or favor of others.
5. The vote has normative power only when voters are governed by legitimate law.
6. Both the fair value of the vote and the stability of legitimate law are sensitive to the distribution and regulation of causal political power.
7. Causal political power should be distributed and regulated so as to assure the fair value of the vote and the stability of legitimate law.

Therefore:

8. Citizens are treated as political equals only when they have an equal vote for those who govern them and when causal political power is distributed and regulated so as to assure the fair value of that vote and the stability of legitimate law.

The rest of the chapter illustrates some of the implications, in specifying the currency of political power, of distinguishing normative power from causal power and distinguishing the power to choose who governs from the power to choose the content of governance. In Section IV, the difference between normative and causal power explains why some outcome-sensitive electoral procedures satisfy the equality principle, while other procedures that achieve identical outcomes violate the equality principle. In Section V, the distinction helps interpret the mutual incomprehension between those who embrace current practices of campaign financing in the United States as a protected form of political speech and those who condemn the practice as a kind of legalized corruption. In Section VI, the difference between the power to choose laws and the power to choose lawmakers explains why public officials are morally permitted, and sometimes required, to defy the wishes of the citizens they serve, and supports a revisionary account of the moral force of campaign promises.

IV. Do Outcome-Sensitive Voting Rules Threaten Legitimacy?

It is not my purpose to provide a full moral theory of voting rights, let alone contribute to US constitutional doctrine, which has swung widely, and not entirely coherently, in districting cases. Rather, I will use some of the new moving parts in the revised propositional argument, such as the distribution and regulation of causal political power and the fair value of the vote, to help loosen a knot in our judgments about outcome-sensitive voting procedures.

Justice Douglas clearly is correct when he writes, in an early dissent, "There is more to the right to vote than the right to mark a piece of paper and drop it in a box, or the right to pull a lever in a voting booth. . . . It also includes the right to have the vote counted at full value without dilution or discount."[13] Before the United Kingdom's Reform Act of 1832, the rotten borough of Old Sarum, with its seven inhabitants, and the ancient county of Lancashire, containing the great industrial city of Manchester, each sent two members to Parliament. Though the handful of voters in Old Sarum and the several thousand freeholders enfranchised in Lancashire each cast one vote per seat, surely they did not have equal normative power to elect members of the House of Commons. (Of course, unequally sized districts were hardly the only deviation from political equality in nineteenth-century Britain.)

Still, "one person, one vote" is an aphorism, not yet a criterion backed by argument. Justice Goldberg surely is right to rule against Georgia's lopsided scheme for nominating US Senate candidates in an opinion where he thunders, "The conception of political equality from the Declaration of Independence, to Lincoln's Gettysburg Address, to the Fifteenth, Seventeenth, and Nineteenth Amendments can mean only one thing—one person, one vote."[14] But if the venerable texts he cites can mean only one thing, "one person, one vote," that one thing can in turn mean many things. A bemused Justice Frankfurter, in a failed attempt to head off the doctrine of vote dilution from the start, also is right (though not in the way he intends), when he says,

> Talk of "debasement" or "dilution" is circular talk. One cannot speak of "debasement" or "dilution" of the value of a vote until there is first defined a standard of reference as to what a vote should be worth. What is actually asked of the Court in this case

is to choose among competing bases of representation—ultimately, really, among competing theories of political philosophy.[15]

Just so. As I argued at the end of Chapter 5, insofar as they are able, judges ought to read the law in a way that makes it legitimate, and they cannot know what the legitimate reading of the law demands without engaging in political philosophy.

Consider a fable that explores outcome-sensitive voting. Kyklos is a roundly shaped metropolis of three million people—one million black and two million white. Although whites and blacks live throughout the city, the black residents of Kyklos tend to be concentrated in the city center. Although whites and blacks are distributed across the income scale, blacks in Kyklos tend to have lower incomes. Race in Kyklos does not perfectly predict one's vote, but most whites and most blacks choose different candidates. Though its black residents have been equal under law for some time, the history of Kyklos is marked by racial discrimination and its economic and social sequelae.[16]

Kyklos is entitled to three seats in a national legislative assembly. For many years, the city has filled these positions through an at-large election in which voters cast ballots for up to three candidates, and the candidates who receive the three highest number of votes are seated. Kyklos has never elected a black legislator and has never elected a legislator who was the first choice of its black residents. The fair-minded residents of Kyklos are uneasy with this result, though all acknowledge that a formal one person, one vote principle is respected: there are no dirty tricks of voter registration or ballot access to suppress the black vote. The good people of the city have suggested four proposals for reform:

PIZZA SLICE: Divide Kyklos into three equal districts running from the outer edge of the city to a point in the center, where a monument to political equality is to be erected. The candidate who receives the most votes in each district wins.

BAGEL RING: Divide Kyklos into three districts by drawing concentric rings. The outer ring will be nearly all white and affluent. The middle ring will be economically mixed with a white majority. The inner circle will be largely black and poor. The candidate who receives the most votes in each district wins.

RESERVED SEAT: Set aside one of the three seats for black voters. Each voter can vote for up to three candidates. The candidate who gets the most votes from voters who voluntarily self-identify as black is seated, and the other two seats are filled by the two candidates who have the most votes overall.

MODEST PROPOSAL: Give every black citizen in Kyklos two votes, and others one vote.

The Modest Proposal's transparent directness is unsettling because Bagel Ring, Reserved Seat and Modest Proposal all deliver the same expected electoral outcome in Kyklos: one legislator who is the first choice of black voters, and two legislators who are preferred by white voters. Insofar as blacks and whites in Kyklos comprise distinct and stable political blocs, each of these three plans distribute causal political power between the two groups in the same way. So shouldn't these schemes stand or fall together? Or are normative distinctions to be made among these outcome-sensitive plans?

Perhaps, but first we need to distinguish among the various outcomes to which these plans are sensitive. The subject of the equality principle is the normative power to choose who governs, the power to change normative circumstances through the speech act of voting. Voters are co-authors of enactments that grant winning candidates the normative power to exercise the normative powers of public office. The equality principle requires that this normative power to choose who governs be shared equally among active citizens, else the domination of despotism threatens. We need to specify what counts as an equal share of normative power, but it is not the same thing as an equal share of causal power. Citizens exercise causal power in politics when they are able to get other political actors to do what they want through persuasion and incentives such as rewards and penalties, offers and threats. When I tell a candidate I will vote for her only if she supports my issue, persuade other voters to vote for her only if she supports my issue, organize a demonstration to show how many other voters support my issue, or contribute money to her campaign only when she supports my issue, I am attempting to exercise causal power over her. I exercise normative power only when I cast my vote (and, as we shall soon see, that vote has normative power only over who governs, not over my issue).

Increasing the causal power of the disadvantaged is likely to bring about good outcomes, just outcomes, and outcomes that support the three principles of legitimacy. If historically disadvantaged groups gain causal political power, we are likely to see a stronger realization of the liberty principle through increased protections of basic rights, a stronger realization of the agency principle through more reason-responsive public decision-making, and, in the register of the equality principle, stricter adherence to free and fair election procedures. But just as it is illegitimate for Queen Frederica the Greatest to bring about good and just outcomes despotically, it would be illegitimate to do so through the Modest Proposal if it does not meet the test of equal *normative* power, properly understood. As Lex in Reginaland reminds us, legitimacy demands that we be co-authors as well as co-subjects of government. The challenge of the Modest Proposal, then, is to show that one black, two votes, though a deviation from one person, one vote, nonetheless satisfies the equality principle's requirement that each active citizen has an equal share of normative power in choosing who governs, under the correct interpretation of the equality principle. The Pizza Slice plan has a symmetrical challenge: if, under the correct interpretation of the equality principle, the alternative Bagel Ring scheme satisfies the equal normative power requirement, then there is nothing *per se* illegitimate about the outcome sensitivity of the hole in the bagel, and indeed, considerations of distributive justice may demand such outcome sensitivity to redress background unfairness in causal power. Severe imbalances in causal power may in themselves undermine the fair value of an equal vote, but legitimacy does not—indeed cannot, without violating the liberty principle—demand *equal* causal power under conditions of free political competition.

So, does the Modest Proposal meet the demands of the equality principle? Equal normative power in choosing who governs requires that the condition of nondictatorship be satisfied, for there is no clearer case of despotism than if one and only one identified person has the power to unilaterally decide who rules. So too if only two identified persons have that power, or three. The logic of nondictatorship unspools to support some sort of anonymity condition. In a way that needs to be specified, who governs must not depend on the personal identities of voters. Suppose that, under some voting procedure, citizen A votes for candidate X in jurisdiction P and citizen B votes for candidate Y in jurisdiction Q. Then the electoral outcome should not change if, instead, A and B swap both candidates and jurisdictions, so that A votes for Y in Q and B votes for X in P.

The Modest Proposal violates this anonymity condition by granting some citizens unequal powers of authorship in virtue of who they are. Nor would it much matter if the charge of treating race as an essential property of voters was addressed by revising the Modest Proposal to "one *self-identified* black, two votes." Why is race still an essential, rather than contingent, property of a voter if black voters needn't and white voters could identify as black? If those with no black heritage self-identified as black in numbers, the scheme would collapse in self-defeat, so it is apt to consider blackness here a necessary but not sufficient essential property to effectively self-identify as black, and that is enough, I think, to flunk the anonymity condition. Under a stable, self-sustaining implementation of the revised Modest Proposal, black voters in Kyklos will have one normative power (the power of self-identification) that other voters lack, to invoke another normative power (the power of two votes) that other voters lack. Nor do we need to wait and see whether black voters in fact invoke that first power. Domination is relational and potential, not necessarily actual. Queen Frederica the Greatest claims the normative power to rule by her unilateral will, so Reginaland is a despotism even if all of her commands were in fact welcome by all. So if one black, two votes sounds in the key of domination, so does one self-identified black, two votes.

If Modest Proposal violates the anonymity condition by granting unequal normative power in virtue of essential properties of different citizens, doesn't Reserved Seat violate anonymity for the same reason? If so, then must the well-intentioned identity-sensitive voting schemes around the world mentioned earlier, such as setting aside parliamentary seats in India for castes and tribes and spots for women on party lists in Europe, fail the test of equal normative power as well? Not necessarily. Suppose we randomly divided rigidly designated voters into virtual districts by their proper names, but each vote had equal weight and each virtual district had an equal number of voters. If this strictly violates the anonymity condition, it is an innocuous violation, without a hint of domination by despotism. Yes, voters are assigned to districts based on a rigid identifier, but this differential treatment does not result in unequal normative power. There may be other objections to such a scheme: this method reproduces sameness and suppresses a diversity of voices in the legislature just as the Pizza Slice plan does. It disperses people who share interests or face common problems. It blunts one of the advantages of the freedoms of movement and association, the ability to choose one's co-constituents. If other kinds of injustice can be remedied by nondespotic procedures, then fairness requires that they be adopted. But these objections to random districting by proper name are not that the procedure is a form of despotism. Now consider the Reserved Seat proposal to create a virtual district of black voters. Here too, if the virtual constituency is equal to the others in population, each vote has equal weight. So if Reserved Seat violates the anonymity condition, it too is an innocuous violation. There may be other objections: perhaps the plan will undermine cross-racial coalition-building, or it will stoke resentment. But the Reserved Seat proposal does not select who governs in violation of the equality principle.

My tentative conclusion is that an outcome-sensitive solution along the lines of the Bagel Ring plan both satisfies the equal vote criterion and is required by the fair value of the vote criterion. The entrenched causal disempowerment of black voters of Kyklos under the existing at-large procedure, when combined with their persistent poverty, creates a dependent class that is inconsistent with the independent and self-governing citizenship the free group agency conception is meant to underwrite. Though Pizza Slice satisfies the equal vote criterion, it does not secure the fair value of the vote, for it does nothing to remedy the dependence of black voters on the causally dominant white majority. Yes, Bagel Ring wears its race-consciousness on its face, but this is no defect in the dimension of normative legitimacy. Unlike Justice O'Connor in *Shaw v. Reno*, we should not, like some Captain Renault in *Casablanca,* be shocked, *shocked,* to find that race-conscious districting is going on here.[17] Still, when possible, territorial remedies such as the Bagel Ring proposal or—better yet—schemes of proportional representation such as the single transferable vote are preferable to the remedy of reserved racial constituencies. Why? You have just read a justification of the Reserved Seat proposal, but you might not have been convinced, and you might not be the only one. Though in the first chapter I insisted on distinguishing genuine legitimacy from perceptions of legitimacy, perceptions of course affect causal power, often in profound ways. Imposing a remedy to political inequality that is mistakenly but widely seen as illegitimate or mistakenly but widely seen as unfair risks triggering resentment that impedes the cause of social justice. This, I am aware, is a political judgment, not a philosophical argument.

Modest Proposal does not fare as well as Bagel Ring. The landmark Supreme Court case *Reynolds v. Sims* is correct in holding that one person, one vote can be violated by dilution or concentration, even when voting weights are equal.[18] One black, two votes, however, despite its consequence of a more equal distribution causal power, does not satisfy the equal normative power criterion. It doesn't follow from the logic of *Reynolds v. Sims* that political equality *isn't* violated when voting weights are made unequal to *counteract* dilution or concentration.

Recall the work the equality principle is meant to do: secure the independence of citizens from the unilateral will of others by defeating domination by despotism. Having an equal say in who governs is necessary (but not sufficient) to solve the puzzle of how we can be both free and ruled, how we can be both subject to and author of our common constraints. But we should not expect too much out of a principle that governs the selection of who governs, because we should not expect too much out of *any* procedure. No procedure by itself will secure the independence of citizens from domination by inhumanity (a tyranny by practice) or from domination by wantonism (a tyranny of unreason). Nor will any procedure by itself deliver all the kinds of equal or fair treatment that justice demands. If legitimacy is the normative power to govern, then it is conceptually possible that a legitimate government fails, in some ways, to be a just government. Though I have called the principle that governs who governs the equality principle, it is not that principle's burden to remedy all unjust inequalities.

The Modest Proposal of one black, two votes is make-believe. Meanwhile, actual proposals have been adopted across the United States that violate political equality through the selective imposition of one person, no vote. Since 2010, over twenty states have adopted measures that increase obstacles to voting by requiring stricter identification at the polls, by making voter registration more difficult, or by aggressively purging the registration rolls. Why? The reason given is to reduce voter fraud.

No one who is entitled to vote should be denied the vote, and no one who is not entitled to vote should be permitted to vote. A perfect election system would distinguish perfectly between the two, but no election system is perfect. Since we cannot eliminate all errors in both directions, we must choose among a continuum of policies that trade off enfranchising eligible voters (at the cost of allowing some fraudulent or otherwise improper votes) and reducing voter fraud (at the cost of suppressing the vote of some eligible voters). As Justice Stevens said about fraud reduction measures in Arizona, "At least two important factual issues remain largely unresolved: the scope of the disenfranchisement that the novel identification requirements will produce, and the prevalence and character of the fraudulent practices that allegedly justify those requirements."[19] There are two dangers, disenfranchisement and fraud, neither can be eliminated, and so some balance must be struck. Sounds reasonable, no?

No. Wildly implausible facts about the electorate would have to be true before it became remotely reasonable to risk voter suppression in order to minimize voter fraud. A simple hypothetical example shows why. Consider a state that has ten million citizens who are eligible to register and vote. Because the perfect election system is impossible, suppose that the best impartial experts in electoral design can do is offer us a choice between two pretty accurate schemes, Low Fraud and High Vote. Low Fraud reduces voter fraud to zero, but with the foreseeable and unavoidable consequence that ten thousand eligible citizens are mistakenly denied the ballot. High Vote allows every eligible adult citizen into the polling booth, but with the foreseeable and unavoidable consequence that ten thousand persons who are not eligible to vote are mistakenly given a ballot as well. By construction, both policies distort the election returns by up to about 1 percent, and therefore, every so often, in very close elections, this 1 percent distortion will be decisive and swing the election. Are there grounds to choose between Low Fraud and High Vote?

Of course there are. In both, the weight of each valid vote has been mistakenly diluted or concentrated by about 1 percent, but in Low Fraud, ten thousand citizens also have been completely deprived of the basic right of exercising normative power at all, let alone equal normative power. Not a single citizen in High Vote has been completely denied such a right. True, *equal* normative power can be violated by dilution or concentration, even when voting weights are formally equal. But if vote dilution on the order of 1 percent is considered a violation of equal normative power, the magnitude and seriousness of that denial are identical under both policies, and equally shared by all who cast valid votes under both policies. With regard to the dilution of votes and the possible distortion of electoral outcomes, the two schemes are symmetrical.

Low Fraud, however, inflicts an additional indignity: ten thousand eligible citizens are directly denied their normative power to vote. Old people without driver's licenses are turned away at the polls. Black and brown people who share names with felons are challenged. Poor people who move frequently are purged from the voter rolls. Low Fraud inflicts massively greater violations of the fundamental political powers of citizens than High Vote. In High Vote, insofar as there is any violation of the equality principle at all, it is merely a 1 percent deviation from strictly equal normative power, and the deviation is the same for everyone in the eligible voting population. In Low Fraud, all normative power is wrongly denied to a concentrated few.

Of course, in the real world of American elections, the risks of fraud and of suppression are not symmetrical at all. Credible allegations of in-person voter fraud are an infinitesimal fraction of the vote. In Federal elections from 2000 to 2014, researchers found only thirty-one instances out of a *billion* ballots cast, or about one in thirty million.[20] At this prevalence, only *five* of the 139 million ballots cast in the 2016 election would be expected to be fraudulent. Meanwhile, over ninety-two million eligible voters didn't vote.[21] Do we know how many of them were prevented from voting by burdensome registration and identification barriers? We do not, but the number surely is greater than five. What we do know is that about one in ten registered voters do not have a driver's license or other form of government-issued identification, and that states purged about sixteen million registered voters from the voting lists before the 2016 election.[22] Even if the prevalence of fraud is greatly underestimated, no reasonable person could conclude that this is a close question about what political legitimacy demands. "It were better that Ten Suspected Witches should escape, than that one Innocent Person should be Condemned," wrote Increase Mather.[23] Reverend Mather does not tell us if ten is his exact threshold, but surely he has a finer sense of justice than we do. In our day's witch hunt for fraudulent voters, we are condemning an unknown but surely not small number of innocents, lest a handful escape.

Is this a case where we are to act *as if* our imperfect empirical political practices and institutions are ideal, or are we to conclude that these practices and institutions pervert that ideal? The natural duty of civility instructs us to bear the inevitable defects in democratic politics with grace, but we need not, and sometimes must not, forbear in the face of a campaign to undermine the principle of political equality itself. When officeholders, to remain in office, fraudulently invent a nonexistent problem of widespread voter fraud, and, under color of law, systematically disable the normative powers of large numbers of citizens, they pervert legitimate law. As citizens responsible and autonomous, we are to judge for ourselves whether unlawful dissent is the fitting retort to voter suppression.

V. Does Money in Politics Threaten Legitimacy?

All serious discussions of free speech make the commonplace observation that "speech" is a partially moralized concept that needs further specification if we are not to assume our conclusions or talk past each other. The utterance "I promise to pay you one million dollars if you kill the opposing candidate" is speech in the plain dictionary sense, and is aimed at a political outcome, but no reasonable person holds that a verbal contract to assassinate a political rival is a type of speech born with a presumptive protection that then needs to be rebutted. It is a category mistake to think that, to criminalize conspiracy to commit murder, some exception from, or limitation of, free speech doctrine is required. Conversely, no reasonable person holds that writing, painting, composing, or singing about political topics are *not* presumptively protected types of political speech, though these forms of expression and communication are not spoken. We are not going to settle the proper place of money in politics by arguing whether a campaign contribution is or is not "speech." Conceptual analysis marks off aptly sized arenas for normative disagreement, but does not decisively settle them.

To some, the entrenched practice of raising campaign funds from large and interested donors is plain bribery—lawful bribery, as US law currently reads, and not necessarily bribery that enriches the private pockets of public officials, but bribery nonetheless. In a randomized field experiment, members of a liberal activist group were more than three times as likely to get a meeting with a member of congress or senior staffer if they identified themselves as "active political donors" rather than "local constituents."[24] Nor do legislators still pretend that big donors get no more than access in return. After unsuccessful attempts to repeal the Affordable Care Act, Colorado Senator Cory Gardner reportedly told his colleagues, "Donors are furious. . . . We haven't kept our promise."[25] When asked by a reporter if his donors were pleased with the 2017 tax cut proposal, New

York Representative Chris Collins replied, "My donors are basically saying, get it done or don't ever call me again."[26]

To others, just as plainly, campaign contributions are protected under any plausible conception of the right to free speech. To ban or limit contributions to fund political campaigns is as much a violation of the freedom of expression as to ban or limit the publication of newspapers. Not everyone can own a newspaper. On some tellings, this inequality in newspaper ownership is merely the bad luck of the paperless, and on other tellings, unequal newspaper ownership is unfair, and may require remedy of some sort. But on no plausibly liberal view is the remedy shutting down printing presses. And because not everyone owns a newspaper or popular website or advertising agency, and because not everyone is a brilliant debater or articulate spokesperson, and because associating with and assembling with and petitioning the government with like-minded citizens is a basic political liberty, Donor's material support of Candidate's protected speech at least sometimes must count as Donor's protected speech. This follows, of course, from our account of free group agency, which explains not only how governments, under the right conditions, speak for their people, but how the associations of civil society—organizations, universities, congregations, labor unions, and political parties—under the right conditions, speak for their members.

So which is it? In the 2018 midterm election cycle, $5.7 billion was spent on congressional campaigns, less than 17 percent of which came from small donors.[27] Are the billions that rich and powerful corporate and ideological contributors spend to influence the outcomes of elections bribes or presumptively protected speech? The answer is that they are, or could be, both, which is part of the reason that each side finds the views of the other incomprehensible. It is here that the distinction between normative and causal power has purchase. If we suppose that there is a causal, though of course probabilistic, positive connection between the quantity of paid political communication in support of a candidate or issue and the behavior of voters, then unfettered campaign contributions give wealthy interests more causal power. There are reasons to think this unfair. But there are also reasons to think that no inequality of *normative* power, and so no despotic domination, has been perpetrated. To think so is to treat the voter as a manipulable tool subject to causal forces, rather than a self-governing moral agent. From the third-personal point of view of the social and behavioral sciences, *of course* the voter is subject to causal forces.

To hold otherwise is to engage in the magical thinking that we are somehow unhooked from the laws of physics. Nevertheless, from the first-person perspective, we have no choice but to conceive of ourselves as reason-responsive, self-governing agents whose vote is not determined by the vector sum of the paid political advertising that bombards our eyes and ears, but by an act of our self-governing will. Therefore, one explanation for the campaign financing controversy is a disagreement about the proper range of *as if* idealization of the choices of our fellow citizens.

From the point of view of an intendedly self-governing voter, she is exercising normative power in response to reasons when she votes, and it is insulting to tell her that she needs to be protected from political advertising. From the point of view of a political scientist, insofar as campaign expenditures are identified as a causal factor in election outcomes, voters are subject to the causal power of these expenditures. From the point of view of those who support poorly funded candidates, parties, and causes, the fair value of their normative power has been undermined by their opponents' efficacious causal power over the electorate. Notice that there is a disrespectful asymmetry built into the loser's complaint: we, who are attempting to exercise our equal normative powers that are responsive to the power of reason, are unfairly thwarted by those of our co-citizens whose moral agency is impaired by advertising agencies, and so who lack the self-governance to exercise their own normative power freely. Doesn't the duty of civility require that we extend to our co-citizens the respect that we take ourselves to be entitled to as well? My tentative conclusion, therefore, is that we ought to treat our fellow voters *as if* they are capable of competent self-governance, consider speech aimed at honestly persuading them protected speech, and so consider money that supports speech aimed at persuading voters protected speech.

Might there be a non-insulting reason to reduce the barrage of campaign advertising?[28] If we are sufficiently reflective, we can recognize that we fall short of the ideal of reason-responsive self-governance ourselves. To make up our own minds about how to exercise our normative power of voting, we therefore have reason to free ourselves, insofar as we are able, from manipulative causal power by creating a media environment that is rich in information and argument of high quality, and perhaps that can be achieved through limitations on campaign spending. So those who seek to reduce the causal power of political advertising needn't be motivated by doubts about the rationality of their co-citizens, but by doubts

about their own rationality. Returning to our earlier analysis of paternalism, we can now describe three different reasons one might have to
regulate campaign financing: to protect the self-governance of other
voters from the causal power of large contributors, to protect one's own
self-governance from the causal power of large contributors, and to protect the fair value of one's own vote from dilution by the causal power of
large contributors on other voters. The first reason is straightforwardly
paternalistic, and so arguably disrespectful to others; the second reason
is a kind of self-binding that imposes collateral restrictions on those who
see no need for self-binding and so must be justified to them; the third
reason is not paternalistic, in that it does not restrict the freedom of others
for their own good, but it does depend on the disrespectful premise that
other voters are not internally free. I needn't decide whether any of these
reasons provide adequate justification to regulate money in politics. My
purpose is to explain the standoff.

There is no parallel disrespect, however, in protecting the outer freedom
of our co-citizens from being violated by coercive political practices
that overbear their independence. Imagine that the Godfather, turning
from organized crime to electoral politics, makes voters at the polling
station an offer they can't refuse: "Either my name or your brains will be
on your ballot," he says. To enforce his threatening speech, Luca Brasi
stands by his side, gun drawn. Clearly, the Godfather is committing
wrongful coercion, and though the threat is spoken, it is not presumptively protected speech. Nor is Luca Brasi engaging in the support of
presumptively protected speech, nor are the financial contributions to
the Godfather's campaign used to purchase Luca Brasi's bullets presumptively protected speech. We do not say that the Godfather's threat,
and the resources raised and purposed to make the threat credible, are a
kind of political speech that is presumptively protected, though that
presumption is rebutted under the circumstances because the speech is
used to coerce. Rather, nothing about this political tactic is protected
speech at all.

In addition to being an ordinary moral wrong, is the Godfather's coercion of voters a violation of any of the principles of legitimacy? Wrongful
coercion is the archetype of domination, by which an individual's will is
overborne by the unilateral will of another. If the coercion of voters is not
an isolated event but an institutional practice, then the liberty principle
has been violated, and voters are dominated by inhumanity, a tyranny in

practice. That the site of this systemic coercion is the voting booth is incidental to the liberty principle as understood under the free group agency view: had the Godfather instead extorted praying in church under pain of death, the violation of liberty would be of the same kind. That the site of coercion indeed is the voting booth, not the pew, engages another condition of legitimacy, the principle of equality. Clearly, voters whose votes are extracted against their will are deprived of all normative power over who governs, let alone equal normative power, so the Godfather commits domination by despotism, a tyranny in title. Nor is there any *as if* treatment that we are disrespectfully failing to invoke. The Godfather's victims have no grounds to be insulted if we do not act as if they are bulletproof. Under different circumstances, the facts may be uncertain. Instead of issuing a direct threat, the Godfather might have a dominating relationship with voters, and command their obedience through more subtle paths of fear and favor. So the case may be difficult to prove. But note that acting *as if* is not a response to factual uncertainty, but to the practical inevitability of falling short of an ideal.

Now imagine a candidate who seeks to win public office by deceiving voters, rather than by coercing them. Our initial judgments about political deception are shaped by three contingent facts: partisans hotly disagree about whether a political statement is deceptive, deception in politics is endemic, and the efficacy of any political lie is impossible to prove. Indulge me, then, in another fictional example, this one suggested by the 1988 political farce, *Moon over Parador.* Richard Dreyfuss plays an actor, on location in a made-up Latin American country, who bears a striking resemblance to the local tin-pot dictator, whom he is able to mimic perfectly. The strongman dies suddenly, and his secret police chief, eager to remain in power, forces the Dreyfuss character to impersonate the dead dictator and rule in his stead. So consider a fanciful case of identity theft, in which a fraudulent candidate covers up the sudden death of a popular political figure and impersonates him. There is no factual ambiguity here: the fraudulence is total, and if Impersonator wins the election, it must be because, and only because, the deception succeeded. Should we not conclude that such undermining of the will of voters through Impersonator's deception is as much of a violation of their right to equal normative power as is the overbearing of the will of voters through the Godfather's coercion? There is no conceptual or normative reason to think that a vote gained through a material lie is any more valid than a vote gained by coercive threat: both subject the voter to the unilateral will of the candidate.

Consider now another example, still fictional but creeping uncomfortably closer to reality: a month before a presidential election, candidate Slanderer, trailing in the polls, proclaims that his rival, Slandered, was born in a foreign country and so is constitutionally ineligible to hold the office. The accusation is manifestly false and Slanderer knows it to be false. Nonetheless, Slanderer wins the election, and the false accusation is the but-for cause of the upset victory over Slandered. It's my hypothetical, so I get to say what its facts are, but if you are having trouble entering into a political world where such facts are knowable, suppose that Slandered produces not only her long-form birth certificate but DNA evidence and sworn eyewitness testimony from the physicians and nurses who attended her birth, while Slanderer produces no evidence at all; coverage of the false accusation crowds out nearly all other campaign issues in nearly all broadcast, cable, and online media outlets in the weeks before the election, and in meticulous and accurate census counts of each and every registered voter, taken both before and after the election, millions of citizens reported to the census-takers that they switched their support from Slandered to Slanderer because, and only because, they believed the accusation that she was born in a foreign land. Must we not reach the same conclusion about deceptive Slanderer as we did in the coercive Godfather and fraudulent Impersonator examples? Slanderer has intentionally undermined the normative powers of millions of voters, and so rules despotically. It is equally true, however, that Slanderer has done so through political speech.

In the nonfictional world, of course, the evidentiary hurdle of showing that deception was a necessary cause of an election victory is very high. Individuals who would have voted differently if not for the deception, however, do have a justified complaint, and all voters, whether taken in by the lie or not, whether influenced by the lie or not, have a justified complaint. Indeed, even if the lying candidate was so spectacularly inept at lying that not a single voter believed the lie, all voters would still have a justified complaint. In all cases, the lying candidate has wrongfully attempted to win an election through fraudulent speech that attempts to undermine the free choices of voters, and so has wrongfully attempted to dominate them. Sometimes, the attempted domination succeeds in undermining the will of individual voters, and when it succeeds in enough cases, it undermines collective self-governance itself.

Perhaps legal recourse for deception on the campaign trail is a cure worse than the disease, so we might end up concluding that deceptive political practices should not or even cannot be subjected to legal scrutiny, but rather, are matters for political ethics. To give an analogous example, Rawls distinguishes the idea of public reason as a criterion of liberal legitimacy and the *ideal* of public reason as a political virtue. Legislation that fails the test of public reason, in that it cannot be supported by a reasonable balance of political values that others can reasonably be expected to endorse as free and equal citizens, is incompatible with political liberalism and should be struck down by a court with powers of judicial review. Therefore, the natural duty of civility demands that citizens and public officials offer each other public reasons in support of their legislative proposals on fundamental questions of justice. But compliance with this duty of civility must not be legally required, for that would violate the right to free speech. Rather, violations of public reason may be judged only in the court of public opinion. Conversely, legislation for which sufficient support in public reason exists is to be constitutionally upheld, even if the law's proponents did not in fact offer public reasons to support it.[29] Similarly, there may be deceptive campaign practices that violate the natural duty of civility, but either should not or cannot be regulated. It would be excessively timid, however, to conclude that *anything* uttered by a politician is properly protected free speech that must be beyond the reach of the laws of defamation and fraud. Knowingly false political speech can violate the equality principle. Chapter 7, "Wantonism," shows how lying public officials can violate the agency principle as well.

We have been focused on the interaction between candidates for elected office and voters and the interaction between campaign donors and voters, have distinguished between influence that is persuasive, coercive, and deceptive, and have concluded that honest persuasive influence does not interfere with the equal normative power of voters, despite possibly unfair inequalities in causal power. When Donor pays the expenses of Candidate to speak honestly to Voter, Donor is speaking honestly to Voter, and such speech is presumptively protected. Consider now the interaction between donors and candidates for elected office. When Donor merely speaks honestly to Candidate, attempting by power of reason to influence the exercise of Candidate's normative power when in office, Donor straightforwardly is engaged in protected speech. But when Donor gives money to Candidate to pay for Candidate's speech to Voter, Donor isn't speaking to *Candidate*. The money Donor gives to Candidate plays no communicative function in their interaction.[30] Donor's normative power over Candidate begins and ends with Donor's one vote, if Donor has a vote. Donor's power of reason begins and ends with Donor's argument to Candidate (which may have been delivered through an expensive and indirect medium, but if Donor is exercising the power of reason only, what is delivered is honest, persuasive speech, not cash). If the cash itself plays any role in the interaction between Donor and Candidate, it must be causal, and therefore cannot be, in itself, protected speech. Recall our earlier description of causal power: causal power is the ability to affect what others do by making changes in the physical world, or by rearranging the conscious incentives of others by imposing costs and conferring benefits, or by exploiting unconscious inclinations and cognitive biases, whether by physical means only or with words too. Unless Donor's money to Candidate is a mere pass-through to speak identically to Voter, but having no causal influence on the exercise of Candidate's normative powers, the money is an improper interference with Candidate's exercise of normative powers subject to the power of reason, and so a cause for complaint by citizens. Their votes have been deprived of their fair value by Donor's improper causal influence, and the laws and policies enacted by a winning Candidate will be improperly responsive to the will of the Donor.

This reeks of the ideal, so why do we not extend to the interaction between Donor and Candidate the same charitable *as if* construction that we extended to the interactions between Donor and Voter and Candidate and Voter, and act as if Candidate is not causally influenced by Donor's money? Why doesn't the duty of civility require that we charitably suppose that the only power Donor has over Candidate is the power of reason? We do not because there is no ground for such charity. There can be no presumption that the money Donor gives to Candidate is protected speech to Candidate, for to Candidate, it cannot be speech at all, and so it cannot be understood as the exercise of the power of reason. There is no ideal deliberative interaction we are to suppose the money is playing a part in, so there is no occasion to act as if the interaction is ideal. There could be a factual uncertainty: perhaps the money is causally inert, because Donor and Candidate would engage in identical speech to Voter even if there were no possibility of causal influence (as could begin to be the case if all political contributions were strictly anonymous). But, as we saw in the Godfather example, the *as if* perspective is a response to the practical inevitability of falling short of an ideal, not to factual uncertainty. Even the factual uncertainty dissolves when Donor gives to opposing candidates and opposing parties, as often is the case when corporations and industry associations make campaign contributions. No power of reason is being exercised when contradictory reasons are paid for, and there is no expressive content in supporting opposing candidates. The only possible explanation is that corporate lobbying groups are exercising causal power over candidates and officials.

I have come to an unsurprising conclusion through a somewhat surprising path. The duty of civility ordinarily directs us to charitably consider the political speech of candidates to be the exercise of the power of reason between candidates and voters, and the money donors contribute to candidates as the exercise of the power of reason between donors and voters. This is so, even though as an empirical matter, donors and candidates also exercise causal power over voters. We therefore are to act as if money in politics does not undermine the equal normative power of citizens, though we must not overlook the fact that the causal power of money in politics can undermine the fair value of equal normative power. When it comes to the relationship between donors and candidates, however, the duty of civility underwrites no charitable interpretation. The money of donors is never speech to candidates, and so either exercises improper causal power over candidates or is inert, but cannot exercise the power of reason. We conclude where we began: money in politics is both expressive and corrupt.

VI. Does Legislative Independence Threaten Legitimacy?

The difference between the power to choose laws and the power to choose lawmakers explains why public officials are morally permitted, and sometimes required, to defy the wishes of the citizens they serve, and supports a revisionary account of the moral force of campaign promises. Consider two actual little cases with invented variations that help specify this distinction in the currency of political power.

Stephen McGrail, a twenty-five-year-old state senator, voted to defeat a bill seeking to restore the death penalty in Massachusetts. After being deluged by phone calls, letters, and—this was a long time ago—telegrams in support of capital punishment, he announced that he would take a "fresh sounding." After finding that nearly seven out of ten people canvassed on the streets of his district supported the death penalty, he changed his vote.

Larry Johnson of Wisconsin, a pseudonymously named and located state senator, voted against establishing the death penalty. "I know the people in my district support the death penalty," he said. "If you poll them, you will probably find that 70 percent favor the death penalty. But I don't believe in it. I've told them that. I said so during the campaign. If they want their representative to vote for it in the Wisconsin State Senate, they'll have to elect someone else. I've said that to them. And they elected me."[31]

Suppose McGrail and Johnson bump into each other in the airport on their way back from a conference on legislative ethics. While waiting for their planes, they sit down over a couple of beers to talk:

McGrail: I am a delegate enacting the will of my constituents.

Johnson: And I am a trustee serving the genuine and enduring interests of my constituents.

McGrail: So legislators can choose to occupy either the role of delegate or the role of trustee. Cheers to that!

Clearly this won't do. McGrail is treating the duties of a legislator as hypothetical imperatives: *if* you adopt the role of a delegate, *then* you should represent the will of the people; *if* you adopt the role of a trustee, *then* you should represent the genuine, enduring interests of the people. But is there no right answer to whether (or when) an elected official should be one or the other? It is faux sophistication to take a detached view and merely observe the varieties of legislative conduct. McGrail and Johnson have a real normative disagreement, whether they recognize it or not.

McGrail: I was deluged by constituents who support the death penalty.

Johnson: I told the voters in my campaign that I'm against the death penalty and they voted for me anyway.

McGrail: Ah, so even if there is one right way to be a legislator, we
faced different circumstances, so we both could have acted rightly.

This won't do either, for consider McJohnson. Like Johnson, 70 percent
of McJohnson's voters supported the death penalty. McJohnson told them
during the campaign that she was against capital punishment and they
voted for her anyway. Like McGrail, 70 percent of McJohnson's voters deluged her after the election, demanding that she support the death penalty. What does she say to her constituents at her next town meeting?

McJohnson: Sorry, but I believe the death penalty is unjust.

The 70 percent: But we voted for you, you represent us, and we now
want you to support the death penalty.

McJohnson: And violate my moral principles?

The 70 percent: We too have moral principles, and we believe that the
death penalty is not unjust. Why do your moral principles take
precedence over our moral principles? You work for us.

McJohnson: And break my campaign promise? I was clear during the
campaign that I oppose it.

The 70 percent: That's okay. We release you from your promise.

The 30 percent: Not so fast. We still oppose the death penalty, and you
70 percent can't release Senator McJohnson from her promise to *us*.

The 70 percent: Senator, what entitles you to make a promise to a
minority of your constituents to ignore the will of the majority?
Your duty is to represent us all. Since we don't all agree, your duty
is to represent the views of the larger part of your constituency,
and supporters of the death penalty are the larger part by far.

McJohnson: In voting for me, you empowered me to oppose the death
penalty. If you wanted to withhold such authorization, you should
have voted against me.

The 70 percent: In voting for you, we empowered you to represent us.
We did not accept a take-it-or-leave-it offer because we are not
customers bargaining with you. We are self-governing citizens.

The 30 percent: And what are we, mere subjects?

McJohnson's choices can be illuminated by a more articulated hypothetical example. Suppose the electorate is divided about two issues, whether

Table 6   McJohnson's Voters
Those "against" are single issue voters

		Nuclear Power		
		For	Against	
Death	For	45%	25%	**70%**
Penalty	Against	10%	20%	**30%**
		55%	**45%**	

to institute the death penalty and whether to build a new nuclear power plant. Although a majority of voters support the death penalty and a majority of voters support nuclear power, those who oppose hold their views so strongly that they are single-issue voters who will not vote for a candidate who supports the policy they are against. Suppose, as well, that only two candidates are running, voters who don't have an acceptable candidate don't vote, and indifferent voters divide evenly between the two candidates. The views of voters are distributed as shown in Table 6.

How should a McJohnson position herself to best represent the wishes of her constituents, and how should she position herself to win the election? The two answers can come apart. One might think that a faithful representative should side with the majority view on each issue: with the 70 percent who support the death penalty and with the 55 percent who support nuclear power. Support for both is the plurality position, the first choice of 45 percent of the electorate (top left). But if she does so, the 55 percent of the electorate who oppose one or the other policies will not vote for her. All 55 percent, however, will vote for an opponent who opposes both policies, a pair of positions held by only 20 percent of the electorate (bottom right).

Well then, perhaps opposing both policies is the pair of positions that best represents the will of her constituents, considering the uncompromising views of the one-issue voters, even though that pair of positions is the first choice of only 20 percent of the electorate. But a candidate who opposes both policies can be defeated by a candidate whose positions are the first choice of only 10 percent of the electorate! A candidate who opposes the death penalty but supports nuclear power (bottom left) will also get the votes of the 45 percent who support both policies and win with 55 percent of the vote. Then *that* candidate can be defeated by an opponent who commits to supporting death and opposing nukes (top right) who, though the first choice of only 25 percent of voters, will win 47.5 percent to 32.5 percent, with 20 percent abstaining. He in turn can be defeated by our original plurality candidate supporting both policies (top left), by 45 percent to 25 percent, with 30 percent abstaining, completing the intransitive cycle. If both candidates choose their platforms simultaneously, there is no stable equilibrium, and the candidate who chooses first can always be defeated by the candidate who chooses second, however the first mover moves.

What is the lesson? Not only that the pairwise preferences of voters over policies can be intransitive—the upshot of Arrow's impossibility theorem is clear. Not only that a candidate who wants nothing other than to conscientiously represent the will of her constituents often has no clue how to do so—that too clearly follows, for it is impossible to do the impossible. In addition, the example illustrates how difficult it is to disentangle four different and possibly contradictory reasons that can be offered to justify the actions of candidates and elected officials. This is so, not merely for the obvious reason that candidates and officials are not transparent about their true motivations, but for the subtler reason that purposes often cannot be inferred from their actions even after the fact. McJohnson might be acting on moral principle, or keeping a campaign promise, or doing her best to faithfully represent her constituents, or making a strategic take-it-or-leave-it offer to the electorate to win an election. Because often there is no unambiguous or even coherent answer to what course of action would follow from these purposes, candidates and officials are quite unconstrained in what they can say to justify their choices to us (and to themselves).

You might think that the model of candidates bargaining with voters is all we can expect and all that we need from representative democracy: calculating candidates offer *prix fixe* menus of positions, voters select candidates with the offerings that are most appealing, the winner of the election attempts to serve up what was promised, those who voted for losing candidates have no complaint about what is put on their plates, and if enough voters aren't satisfied with the meal, the politician is defeated in the next election by an opponent offering a more palatable menu. Alas, though it may be that this is the most we can expect from typical democracies, it falls far short of what we need. No procedure for nominating candidates and selecting platforms can make it the case that voters are presented with those options that, on any plausible criterion, are the most worthy of their consideration, and if offered more than two options (for surely the worthy ones number more than two) there is no procedure meeting a short list of reasonable criteria that can reliably choose a definitive winner.

Audiences for books like this being who they are, I suspect most readers believe that McJohnson should stick to her principles and continue to oppose the death penalty. Why? Does her campaign promise morally bind her to the 30 percent? Does her campaign promise give her a permission, but not an obligation, to disappoint the 70 percent? Or is she bound by her moral principles, whether or not she promised, and whether or not her promises obligate? If you think the last, then consider McJail, who promises in his campaign to institute the death penalty, wins the election, but is subsequently inundated by calls from his constituents, 70 percent of whom oppose the death penalty, pleading with him not to impose cruel and discriminatory punishment. Don't you want from McJail less *Profiles in Courage* and more responsiveness? What accounts for this flip, other than the simple view that legislators should act on the *right* moral principles, period, and none of these finer points about representation, promising, or conscience matter?

This simple view is correct, or nearly so. I say nearly so, because, though it is true that legislators should oppose unjust laws, even if those laws are supported by their constituents, this truth provides little guidance in the face of disagreement about which laws are the unjust ones. For moral prescriptions to be action-guiding, they need to be framed from the first-personal perspective of a reasonable agent who faces a moral choice. Perspectivalism is neither relativistic nor skeptical, and an agent's actions are always appraisable from the perspective of omniscience. But that perspective is not available to a conscientious agent making choices under the factual uncertainties and normative disagreements that are a permanent feature of democratic politics. Yes, we wish we could convince McJail that the death penalty is unjust. But having failed to do so, are there honest second-order reasons we can give him to defer to his constituents opposed to the death penalty that wouldn't as well be reasons for McJohnson to defer to *her* constituents who *support* the death penalty?

The free group agency conception of legitimacy cuts through this tangle of views on representation with a revisionist account of electoral mandates and campaign promises. Legitimacy is normative power, and those who are elected to public office through properly enacted procedures that satisfy the equality principle acquire the normative power to govern. Call this normative power a mandate, if you will, but then the only mandate of an elected official is the authority to exercise those legal powers that in turn have been authorized by legitimate law under a legitimate constitution. Like turtles, it's normative power all the way down. Normative political authority varies in scope and jurisdiction, but it comes in only one strength. Just as legislation passed by a one vote margin is as much law as legislation passed unanimously, a president or prime minister elected by a margin of one ballot (or one Electoral College delegate or one parliamentary seat) has as much authority to exercise the full normative powers of office as someone elected in a landslide. To be a bit more accurate, whether mandates have strength is contingent on the procedural details of a legitimate constitution. A constitution *could* titrate the powers of an elected official to vary with her margin of victory, and one can understand the US Constitution's provisions for the presidential veto and the congressional override to be something similar. But I am unaware of an electoral procedure that scales an official's normative powers to the margin of her popular victory. To be clear, one's *causal* power may vary with one's margin of victory, as it may vary with changes in public opinion polls after one is elected. Politicians are able to leverage their popularity into legislative victories because they can disappoint many voters on many issues without being turned out of office and they can reward and punish potential legislative allies. But unless provided for by legitimate law, the magnitude of an electoral victory confers no more *normative* power than the results of a public opinion poll. Senator McGrail's "fresh sounding" of his district may have been a useful stunt, but it had no moral force.[32]

So on this view, when Scott Brown, a Republican, was elected US Senator from Massachusetts in a 2010 special election, ending the Democratic party's filibuster-proof supermajority, the reaction of Massachusetts Representative Barney Frank, a Democrat, was unnecessarily accommodating. The Senate had already passed its version of the Affordable Care Act, known as Obamacare, and the bill was before the House of Representatives. Frank said that the Democratic Party's approach to health care reform was "no longer appropriate," and that "our respect for democratic procedures must rule out any effort to pass a healthcare bill as if the Massachusetts election had not happened." Although Frank was one of the most principled and effective legislators in Congress, he was mistaken here about what democratic theory and political ethics require. There is no will of Congress independent of its proper votes. Legislation passed by a lame-duck Congress (or a Supreme Court nomination by a lame-duck president) is not lacking in legitimacy. A sitting president who vetoes a bill the day after losing an election has no less legitimate authority than if she had vetoed it the day before the election. A properly enacted measure that has low approval ratings in the polls is no less law than a measure that has widespread popular support. So there would be nothing at all inappropriate or disrespectful of democratic procedure for the House to pass the Senate bill as is. On what plausible account of respect for democratic procedures is a newly seated Senator owed a redo? So, while there may have been considerations of strategy that would counsel against the House enacting the legislation passed by the Senate before Brown's arrival, these were not ethical considerations.

Nor do electoral mandates, understood normatively, have direction. All elected officials are morally bound to support good, just, and legitimate laws, policies, and actions, but elected officials are not morally bound to support what their constituents, either most of them or most of those who voted for them, *think* are good, just, and legitimate laws, policies, and actions. There are at least three reasons why elected officials have no such duty of responsiveness. The first, which I have repeatedly pointed out, is that often there is no coherent answer to social choice questions, so there is no coherent answer to what representing the will of the voters would require. The second reason involves a different impossibility result. Recall our example in Chapter 3, "All Foundings Are Forced," of the Libyan ministers making a group decision. I used that as a proof of the possibility of group agency, since it showed how a group could combine its judgments about logically related premises in a reasonable way that would give a different result than if their individual conclusions were combined in a reasonable way. But suppose, instead, that the members of the group insisted that both their aggregated judgments about premises and their aggregated judgments about the conclusion guide the decisions of their representative. To always satisfy all aggregated judgments in such a case is impossible. To take an unfortunately common example, suppose a constituency of three persons has the views about cutting or raising taxes, cutting or raising spending, and balancing the budget or running a deficit shown in Table 7, and suppose as well—the claims of supply-siders notwithstanding—that it is impossible to balance the budget if taxes are cut and spending is raised.

Table 7   Inconsistent Aggregation of Judgments

A:	Cut taxes	cut spending	balance budget
B:	Cut taxes	raise spending	run deficit
C:	Raise taxes	raise spending	balance budget
Majority:	**Cut taxes**	**raise spending**	**balance budget**

Though each of the three constituents is individually consistent, their aggregated views are not: a majority wishes to cut taxes, a majority wishes to raise spending, and a majority, *per impossibile,* wishes as well to balance the budget. Christian List and Philip Pettit have shown that, for at least three agents deciding about at least three logically related propositions, even when all agents are internally consistent, an inconsistent set of conclusions can always be constructed.[33] Nothing, of course, guarantees that the choices of voters are internally consistent: there is no shortage of voters who individually demand tax cuts, spending increases, and balanced budgets.

The most important reason that mandates do not have direction, however, is moral, not logical: even when legislators can identify the preferences of their constituents, they need not defer to them. Legitimate governance requires the satisfaction of three different principles—equality, liberty, and agency—in order to escape three different kinds of domination—despotism, inhumanity, and wantonism. Citizens are treated equally under the equality principle when they have an equal say in choosing who governs them. This is the lesson of Reginaland. Citizens are not, however, owed an equal say in choosing the content of law and policy or the methods by which law and policy are selected. This is so because nothing guarantees that the preferences of a majority of constituents will not violate the basic liberties or violate the conditions for competent group agency. These are the lessons of Majoritaria and Randomark. When citizens vote for a candidate in an election that satisfies the demands of the equality principle, they exercise one and only one normative power: the power to have an equal say in choosing who governs. Though they may believe otherwise, and though candidates may believe otherwise, citizens are not exercising normative power over the content of law and policy. They exercise that power only when they participate in binding referendums provided for under legitimate procedures. The electoral mandate of an American president is to exercise the legal powers granted by the Constitution, as interpreted by the courts, insofar as those powers are legitimate, and insofar as the powers claimed by the courts to interpret the president's powers are legitimate. True, an election to fill an office is a speech act, a way of bringing about a normative change in the world by enacting something through words in accordance with some procedure, but this speech act is rather inarticulate, capable of uttering no more than a name. If, in accordance with proper procedures, the people say "Roosevelt," they thereby make it the case that Franklin Delano Roosevelt has the normative powers of the presidency. But what moved these voters to say "Roosevelt," what these voters thought they were expressing when they said "Roosevelt," what their hopes and fears were when they said "Roosevelt," is of no genuine normative significance, either for the voters or for President Roosevelt. If this is so for the 1932 election, one of the most consequential landslides in American history, it is *a fortiori* so for lesser contests of more ambiguous significance. A survey can tell us what lots of separate persons want and perhaps why they want it. Only an election is an act of the group will of the people, and when only a name is on the ballot, the people exercise normative power only to choose who governs.

It follows from this view that elected officials ought not to make campaign promises, and have no moral obligation to keep promises that are made. Campaign promises are void *ab initio*. Why? To make a campaign promise and to take it as morally binding is to fail in one's duty to legitimately govern all citizens, and therefore to fail in one's duty not to preempt consideration of reasons and arguments about good, just, and legitimate laws and policies. A candidate may of course announce a policy platform, expound principles, or exhibit virtues, and voters will make reasonable predictions about the candidate's intentions and capacities to govern in accordance with these policies, principles, and virtues. But a candidate must not—indeed, efficaciously cannot—promise away the duty to govern legitimately, justly, and wisely in accord with the best reasons, arguments, and facts available at the time of decision. Electoral mandates have no direction and cannot be given direction.[34]

Voters will, predictably, seek evidence and assurance that the candidates they elect will support the voters' views about politics and policy. Candidates will, predictably, provide such evidence and assurance, and if those who win elections also wish to win reelections for themselves and their parties, they have strong incentives not to disappoint their supporters. This is an accurate description of the incentives candidates and voters face and of the likely outcomes in equilibrium. But whether this predictable mechanism is something to cheer or bemoan depends on whether the laws and policies elected officials enact are consistent with the liberty, equality, and agency principles, and not whether they are consistent with the preferences of voters or with promises made to voters.

The normative impotence of a campaign promise is most easily seen when the policy promised is a violation of basic liberties. Suppose Senator McJail, having promised to reinstitute the death penalty in his campaign, later is persuaded by the 70 percent of his constituents who oppose the death penalty that capital punishment is a grave injustice:

> *McJail:* I've made a terrible moral mistake, but fortunately it's not too late to undo it. Justice requires that I vote to commute the capital sentences of prisoners recently condemned to death under the new law.
>
> *The 30 percent:* Sorry, Senator. It *is* too late to undo it. We don't believe that the death penalty is unjust, you promised us that you would enact it, and we don't release you from your promise.
>
> *Prisoner:* Yeah, and I was going to change my mind about doing the hit because I had an epiphany that murder is wrong, but since I promised my client and had already taken his deposit, I was duty-bound to go through with it.

Clearly, nothing turns on whether it is 30 percent, 70 percent, or 100 percent of Senator McJail's constituents who are holding him to his promise. From his current moral point of view, he had made an immoral promise, a promise that he now sees was void *ab initio* no less than the promise of the assassin sitting on death row. Perhaps McJail faces some sort of moral remainder, such as a requirement to apologize to his constituents. Perhaps the penitent contract killer should have given back the down payment. But neither senator nor hit man should fulfill his promise. A promise to violate basic liberties is not morally binding, because an official cannot efficaciously commit to undermine a precondition of legitimate governance.

Just as a promise to violate the liberty principle is void, so too is a promise to violate the equality principle. The preferences of voters can undermine the equality principle by enacting illegitimate election procedures, and this is so even when the procedures used to enact the illegitimate procedures are themselves facially legitimate. Suppose that, in Kyklos, bagel ring apportionment satisfies the equality principle but the preexisting at-large scheme does not. The electoral reform movement succeeds in enacting bagel ring districts, from which one black and two white representatives are elected. Made uneasy by the discomfiting issues raised by the city's first black representative, however, a majority of voters wishes to return to the old at-large system, under which all three representatives are likely to be white. Is this not a moment for legislative courage? No representative should support returning to procedures that violate equal political liberty, no representative should promise to do so, and no representative, having promised to do so, should keep such a promise. This is so, even when an overwhelming majority of her constituents who elected her under procedures that satisfy the equality principle wishes her to do so. Because the conditions for legitimacy are in part substantive, and not entirely matters of pedigree and procedure, a legitimate authority is capable of acting illegitimately. This is the lesson of the bastard Edmund.

What about a campaign promise about less morally fraught issues? Much of law and policy involves contested matters of the public good on which citizens reasonably disagree. Should we encourage trade or protect jobs? Pave roads or lay track? Raise taxes or cut spending? Conserve energy or build nuclear reactors? How can a people be self-governing if its representatives owe no deference at all to what the people want, even when what they want is not unjust or illegitimate? And if representatives do owe such deference, why shouldn't voters be able to demand promissory commitments to particular policies and expect adherence to these commitments?

The answer requires an explication of the third condition of the free group agency conception of legitimacy: the agency principle. To be free, a people must avoid wantonism, or domination by unreason. To avoid wantonism, a people must be governed by a self-governing group agent constituted by self-governing citizens. To be a self-governing group agent, the government must have the functional capacities of considering, willing, and doing in ways that are responsive to the reasons that apply to its citizens. Deferring to majority preferences and keeping campaign promises are neither necessary nor sufficient ways for officials to perform as a self-governing group agent, and so avoid wanton domination. To an explication of wantonism we now turn.

CHAPTER 7

Wantonism

To solve the puzzle of how each of us can be self-governing while being governed by coercive institutions, it is not sufficient to wave the talisman of collective self-governance. We must explain, without recourse to spookiness, how two tricks are performed: first, how a group is capable of independent and self-governing action, and second, how that group action is connected to the individual members of the group in ways that make and keep those individuals independent and self-governing. Chapter 3, "All Foundings Are Forced," sketched an explanation that begins by noting that the three essential components of agency—considering, willing, and doing—are functions but not necessarily mental states in wet brains, and so action might be a capability of artificial as well as natural persons. We then explored three mechanisms by which group agents are constituted—shared aims and plans, representation, and procedure—and three routes by which individuals are conscripted into group membership—consent, fair play, and practical necessity. Chapter 4, "Forcing a People to Be Free," explored defective group agency, and showed why there is no contradiction in judging a political society to be a failed or impaired group agent, and so possibly a proper target for paternalism, even if no natural individual within that political society is a failed or impaired agent. The task now is to explain why being governed by a failed or seriously defective group agent is a form of tyranny, and so a great wrong, not merely a burden or inconvenience or inefficiency.

I. Does Incontinence Threaten Legitimacy?

A wanton, on Harry Frankfurt's telling, is an individual who lacks the capacity to form second-order volitions, and so merely follows the strength and direction of his first-order desires.[1] Someone who is blown about by the vector sum of his desires, who has no critical, reflective view about which desires he wills to have, and either isn't able to or doesn't see the point of evaluating and choosing which of those desires he will act upon, either fails to be a competent agent or fails to be an agent at all. In Frankfurt's arresting terms, such an individual is not a person. A toddler is a clear case of a wanton. So is a tiger, who, more so than a toddler, is capable of taking effective means towards its ends, and so is capable of instrumental rationality. But a tiger (as far as we know) is incapable of reflecting about, and so endorsing or rejecting, its ends. Tigers neither identify with their predatory nature nor contemplate vegetarianism. A group wanton, then, is an entity that lacks the capacity to combine either the first-order desires or the second-order volitions of its constituent members into a second-order group volition. An anthropological group can fail to constitute a normative group, and so be a group wanton, even if every natural member of the group is a competent person.

An individual wanton may, contingently, be a danger to itself or to others, depending on the content of its effective desires and how they are shaped and directed by its environment. A well-minded toddler can be kept safe and a well-fed tiger made safe. Still, a human wanton is a misfortune, because even wantons that are benign are missing a quality of great moral importance. Their ends may not be due respect merely in virtue of being their ends, and so, though wantons retain all the claims of moral patients, they are not always entitled to be treated as moral agents.[2]

We all are wantons some of the time about some things: willing to have the will we want to have or ought to have is a constant human struggle of attention and control that we do not always win. So Frankurtian personhood or unified agency is best thought of as a regulative ideal that we should strive for, though we may never reach. Looking at ourselves from the third-person point of view of the behavioral and social sciences, we all are somewhat impaired some of the time. A moral empiricist might then conclude that some impairment justifies some paternalistic interference. In contrast, as noted earlier, a Kantian approach to paternalism would direct us to respect each other *as if* we are fully capable of self-governance over some range of actual imperfect rationality until it is perverse to continue to do so. A great deal then turns on whether, and to what extent, we should respect our actually flawed institutions *as if* they were fully capable of autonomous and independent collective self-governance, until it is perverse to continue to do so.[3]

There is one important reason why the considerations of nonideal theory are triggered sooner in the case of failing artificial persons than failing natural persons. Unlike individuals, wanton governments are *necessarily* dangerous, even if they contingently turn out to be benign. A wanton government dominates all who are subject to its misrule, for arbitrary law is no law at all. Lawlessness is a state of mutual domination, where each, as self-legislator, self-judge, and self-enforcer, cannot help but coerce each. What makes wrongful coercion wrong is that the will of the coerced is at the mercy of the will of the coercer, stripping the coerced of independence. The wrongfulness of wanton domination is, in some sense, more terrifying, because those subject to it are at the mercy, not of the will of another rational person, but of the will of an impulsive toddler or an appetitive tiger.

Why does Randomark, a direct democracy with a Bill of Rights that instantiates the equality of its citizens by choosing it laws by random lottery, violate the agency principle? A competent group agent must have the three functional capacities: considering in light of relevant reasons, choosing (that is, willing) in light of relevant considerations, and doing in light of relevant choices. The random legislative procedure of Randomark is incapable of considering relevant reasons at all. Individuals who submit legislation to the legislative lottery might be adequately responsive to reasons (though not, in our case, the author of the Circle Simplification Act), so if Randomark gets lucky, any particular winning proposal could end up being a reasonable statute. But the group that is Randomark is incapable of responding to reasons and assessing whether the winning proposal is reasonable. Furthermore, even if each proposal, taken on its own, is reasonable, Randomark has no mechanism for ordering and reconciling these proposals so that they cohere into a purposeful, endorsable plan. Though a particular randomly enacted statute might be in accord with the second-order volitions of that law's proposer, and so be the competent action of one competent agent, a second-order volition of an individual has no more standing in the formation of the will of a self-governing group agent than a first-order desire has in the formation of the will of a self-governing natural agent. Until the proposal is reflectively endorsed in some way by the group, it is simply one of many competing and inconsistent preferences in need of governance—one more mouse in Korsgaard's bag.

Consider a Hotspur, who acts impetuously on the strongest desire of the moment, for to him, "thought's the slave of life."[4] Hotspur is ungoverned, a wanton, and this is so, even if each desire, considered alone, has rational support. What he lacks is the capacity to order his desires into a consistent intention, giving himself reasons why some desires should be endorsed and others rejected. A group decision-making procedure that merely aggregates the preferences of the individuals that make up the group, acting on the most numerous individual preference or on the vector sum of individual preferences, is simply a group Hotspur. A collection of individuals that lacks the capacity to order the preferences of the many into a consistent intention, giving reasons why some preferences should be endorsed and others rejected, is ungoverned, a group wanton. This is so, even if each individual's preference is, considered by itself, a reflectively endorsed intention, so that none are individual Hotspurs.

Now consider Randoman, an individual who decides to act on desires at random: exercise or dessert, fidelity or promiscuity, Philosophy or Wall Street, all are treated equally by a fair coin toss. Randoman is in one respect even more the wanton than Hotspur. Hotspur simply is ungoverned. But as Richard III is "determined to prove a villain," Randoman is determined to prove a wanton, and thereby shows utter contempt for his powers of self-government.[5] Now suppose Randoman decides to give odds to his desires in proportion to their strength: if his desire to eat a slice of butter cream chocolate cake is much stronger than his desire to work out on the elliptical trainer this evening, he tosses a die and if he rolls a six he works out, otherwise he pigs out. This still mocks self-governance. In weighting his desires, Randoman is even more explicit about rejecting the authority of reasons over his actions and embracing his wantonism. For if he believed, in a Humean spirit, that the strength of a desire were sufficient reason for action, he would choose chocolate cake, not weight chocolate cake in a lottery. (Yes, we can construct for Randoman a utility function under which weighted randomization is responsive to reasons—for instance, if he wants to exercise once a week but is indifferent about when, or if he has a third desire, to be surprised—but suppose that is not his motivation for randomizing.)

Back to Randomark. Suppose Cirque, the author of the Circle Simplification Act, wants to improve his odds. So he goes to the next-door neighbor and offers to bake her a chocolate cake if she submits an identical proposal to the lottery, and she agrees, so the probability of enacting $\pi = 3.2$ doubles. He next calls up his old high school classmates to remind them of how they suffered at the hands of their mean geometry teacher, and adds a few vengeful copycat proposals. Cirque then goes across the street and offers to submit that neighbor's legislative proposal next week (a plan for universal health care) if the neighbor puts $\pi = 3.2$ into the lottery this week. Cirque succeeds in rounding up enough support to make passage of his legislation very likely, though his supporters do not support the Circle Simplification Act because it is a good idea for Randomark, nor can they explain why it is a good idea for Randomark. Cirque has become a gifted politician, but Randomark is not any closer to having a unified will than Randoman is when he weights his lottery in favor of chocolate cake. If support for the Circle Simplification Act is unanimous, then the citizens of Randomark are, in a way, estopped from complaining, since their injury is self-inflicted, but the nature of the injury still merits description. Though the statute has the superficial shape of law, Randomark has failed to constitute itself as a competent agent that has the capacity to give itself law—it is incapable of self-governance. Insofar as the Circle Simplification Act attempts to exercise normative power over teachers and schoolchildren by coercively enforcing what is taught—leave aside how it would or could be imposed on Randomark's engineers and architects—it succeeds only in exercising brute force. Since all legislation in the country has been enacted by lottery, it is not extravagant to say that all of Randomark is a tyranny of unreason, its subjects dominated by arbitrary whim. This is so, even if the Randomarkian Supreme Court steps in to strike down statutes that violate its Bill of Rights, and even with respect to accidentally sensible legislation. Had the universal health care proposal of Cirque's neighbor been enacted by lottery, rather than the Circle Simplification Act, the subjects of Randomark would of course be better off. But they would be no less tyrannized than the subjects of that despot on the other side of the mountain, Frederica the Greatest, and a lot worse off overall, for Queen Frederica's laws are reliably, rather than accidentally, reasonable. Randomark's Bill of Rights protects its subjects from domination by inhumanity, and its even-handed lottery protects them from domination by despotism, but Randomark is still dominated by wantonism. Though it is true that, for group agents of sufficient scale, unity is not possible without procedure, *not any procedure unifies*. Randomark has a procedure that delivers a decisive choice, but decisiveness is not sufficient to achieve unity out of multitude. Hamlet berates himself for overthinking.

> And thus the native hue of resolution
> Is sicklied o'er with the pale cast of thought,
> And enterprises of great pitch and moment
> With this regard their currents turn awry,
> And lose the name of action . . . [6]

But perhaps the young prince of Denmark gets it backwards, for the greater threat to the name of action is not insufficient resolution, but insufficient thought.

Randomark illustrates a failure to consider reasons for action, a form of impulsiveness or incontinence. We have already noted two other procedural misfirings that undermine the other two capacities of competent agency: choosing in response to considering and doing in response to choosing. A group may have thoughtfully considered the reasons for and against several proposals, but, as we saw in the example of McJohnson choosing her positions on nuclear power and the death penalty, its decision procedures produce intransitive rankings, so the group is not competent to make a decisive choice that follows from its considerations. If confronted with sequential pairwise comparisons, the group will be inconstant. Or a group may have the capability to choose decisively, but be unable to take coherent action that follows from its choices. We saw this in the example of inconsistent judgment aggregation in Chapter 6. On three logically interrelated propositions, the group decides to cut taxes, raise spending, and balance the budget. The group may have thoughtfully considered the reasons for and against each proposition, and they may have decisively chosen what to do about each. But they enacted a practically inconsistent set of directives that cannot possibly be turned into coherent action. Their procedures allow a form of collective *akrasia*, a weakness of (the general) will, and so the group fails to achieve the coherence in action required of a competent agent.

What if, impossibly, the citizens of Randomark unanimously consented *ex ante* to the procedure of random legislation? As in the case where they all submit Cirque's Circle Simplification Act to the legislation lottery, they are estopped from complaining in one sense. Insofar as there is truth to the doctrine *volenti non fit injuria,* they are not wronged as moral patients. But they fail to become a self-governing group agent and so fail to respect each other's purposes. In a consensual Randomark, a gap opens between not treating each other as means and sharing in each other's ends.

II. Does Unreflectiveness Threaten Legitimacy?

I have located three misfirings of agency—incontinence, inconstancy, and incoherence—in the nascent will of the toddler (though they are readily identifiable, and much less amusing, in grown-ups), and argued that group agency can misfire in the same three toddlerish ways. It is less clear why an instrumentally rational tiger is a wanton and why a group agent that acts in tigerish ways has misfired. A competent agent chooses reason-responsive purposes and is capable of adapting the choice of purposes to changes in, or revised understandings of, the relevant reasons, even if, upon proper reflection, the agent's purposes remain constant, or if acting upon different purposes is not possible. There is a puzzle here: to be a competent agent, one needs to be purposeful, which requires the capacity for constancy, but one also needs the capacity to reflectively endorse one's purposes, and that requires that one consider the counterfactual of having different purposes, or inconstancy.

"I meant what I said and I said what I meant. . . . An elephant's faithful one hundred percent!" proclaims Horton, and the youngest of readers admire the commitment of the egg-hatching pachyderm, though they are not yet ready for such constancy themselves.[7] The commitments of the North-Going Zax and South-Going Zax, in contrast, are instantly seen as preposterous. Standing foot to foot and face to face, blocking each other's meridional path, both refuse to step aside:

"And I'll prove it to YOU," yelled the South-Going Zax,
"That I can stand here in the prairie of Prax
For fifty-nine *years!* For I live by a rule

That I learned as a boy back in South-Going School.
Never budge! That's my rule. *Never budge in the least!*
Not an inch to the west! Not an inch to the east!
I'll stay here, not budging! I can and I will
If it makes you and me and the whole world stand still!"[8]

Though the standoff occurs on the prairie of Prax, praxis is what neither Zax achieves: not because they do not move—Horton also refuses to budge—but because their fixed ends are not reflectively endorsed.

It is not in the nature of a Zax to step aside, you say. But neither is it in the nature of an elephant to hatch an egg:

"Why, of all silly things!
I haven't feathers and I haven't wings.
Me on your egg? Why, that doesn't make sense . . .
Your egg is so small, ma'am, and I'm so immense!"[9]

But Horton overcomes his elephant nature, and so becomes a person, when he thinks critically about his ends, and concludes that the care of another creature is a worthy commitment. It was hard to keep his commitment, and he might have failed, the way that every empirical agent sometimes is defeated by external circumstances or internal weakness of will. Or, assessing the reasons for and against sitting on the egg, Horton might have declined. He might have concluded that he did not want to overcome his elephant nature. Horton's personhood does not depend on choosing to sit on the egg, or on persevering to hatch the egg, but on his capacity to consider whether or not he has reason to sit on the egg. The Zax, in contrast, do not consider at all, at least not in the text that has come down to us. They might have offered reasons why it is so important to follow the *Never budge in the least!* rule, or reasons why it is important not to offer such reasons, as some persons of faith might say about their belief in God, without threat to their personhood. (I don't hold that individuals, let alone governments, are wantons if they don't meet the demanding requirements of Kantian or Millian autonomy. I mean for the free group agency account to be compatible with Rawls on public reason.) But that is not what the South-Going Zax says. Instead, he offers a causal explanation: I learned the rule in South-Going School. The Zax have fixed ends: going north only or going south only. The end is not to arrive in the north or in the south, but to go north or go south without deviation. They are instrumentally rational, in that they do take the best available means to their ends. Presumably, had a bicycle with a fixed handlebar been on offer, a Zax would have used it, and instrumental rationality does not guarantee success. But the Zax are not competent moral agents because they lack the capacity to ask themselves "Why go north?" and "Why go south?" Young children delight in this story because they see something the Zax do not: there is no good reason, no reason in the whole world, to follow the rules of the North-Going Zax and South-Going Zax.

A group that lacks the capacity to reflectively endorse its purposes also fails to be a competent group agent, even if it is effective at taking the means towards its ends. This at first sounds impossibly demanding, for it appears to rule out whole classes of instrumentally rational group agents that we belong to and rely on daily. The chamber orchestra has a fixed purpose and doesn't contemplate becoming a football club. The football club isn't open-minded about aiming to lose their matches, and the homeless shelter that contemplates converting to a luxury hotel is having one thought too many, to borrow a thought from Bernard Williams. We create these groups and depend on them to be tigerish. Must we say that none of them succeed at agency?

The answer, I think, is that natural persons can successfully constitute limited fixed-purpose artificial persons, including the associations and clubs, organizations and churches that make up civil society, but only for certain kinds of limited fixed purposes that do not threaten the free agency of its members or of others. Take the simplest case of constitution by representation. A multitude of hungry students constitute a unified agent for the limited purpose of buying pizza by each handing Hal five dollars and saying, "Hal, I authorize you to provide me pizza for dinner." Each contributing student is an author of Hal's action, as long as Hal buys pizza. If no one further limited Hal's discretion by specifying the toppings, then whether Hal returns with tomato and cheese pizza, arugula and truffle pizza, or gluten-free tofu pizza, the students, through Hal, have successfully performed a group action. If Hal returns with burritos, however, with the explanation that, upon reflection, he thought Mexican was a better choice, group agency has misfired, and Hal's friends have a justified complaint. This is a clear case where instrumental rationality in pursuit of fixed purposes succeeds and more open reflection fails. But there are other circumstances under which a solely instrumentally rational Hal would fail to act for the students. If he robbed the pizzeria because he was short on cash, the group action also would have misfired. If Maryam decided that she wasn't really hungry, so Hal forced a slice down her throat in order satisfy the instruction "provide me pizza for dinner," Maryam would not be the author of her forced feeding. If no pizzeria in town is open, a great taqueria is, and communication with the students is not possible, then Hal has an interpretive problem about the terms of his authorization. Did it come with the unstated conversational implication "or something else if the pizzeria is closed"? Should Hal act upon hypothetical authorization, and ask himself "what would the students have asked me to get for dinner had they known the pizzeria is closed?" (Notice that these two formulations are not the same, just as interpreting an advance directive and employing substituted judgment in deciding medical care for others are not the same.) Now, I don't want to overstate the case: under no construal is Hal tasked with reflecting on the final ends of individual members of the group. It's just about pizza. But even a group action as simple as buying pizza might require more than only means-ends reasoning. This is why the pizza group probably fails to constitute a competent group agent if Hal is a robot, even if the hungry students are the sharpest artificial intelligence programmers at MIT (though perhaps this is just a failure of imagination at the other end of Mass Ave). Not all coordination mechanisms or solutions to collective action problems constitute normative group agents in our sense because algorithms merely select the best means to achieve an end. An agent must be capable of deliberating about and choosing ends themselves—functional capacities that machine learning cannot yet instantiate. I say yet: recall that what makes group agency possible is that these functional capacities needn't be mental states.

The puzzle posed by Hamlet, Horton, and the Zax, of resolution warring with thought, can now be at least partially resolved. To be an agent, one must have ends, and something isn't an end unless one is committed to take means towards it—otherwise what poses as an end is merely a wish. But not all ends are reasonable, not all means to ends are reasonable, and whether ends and means are and are thought to be reasonable might shift over time in light of changing circumstances and deeper reflection. Limited-purpose groups, such as intermediate associations in civil society, lack agency if they lack purpose, which is why the more established of such groups usually have written constitutions or bylaws. But they usually have officers or decision-making bodies as well, who are tasked with interpreting the group's purposes, adapting them to changing and unforeseen circumstances, and—most important—insuring that instrumentally rational action in pursuit of the group's ends does not violate the freedoms of its members or of others.

Governments, in contrast, are not limited-purpose group agents. This is not to say that the powers of government, properly understood, are not limited. Our rights and liberties sharply limit what governments are permitted to do to us and for us. But on the free group agency view of legitimacy, the purpose of government is nothing short of protecting our autonomous and independent moral agency itself. If the puzzle of freedom under constraint is to be solved, our free agency is protected only when our government is a self-governing group agent constituted by all of us. So a government, to be legitimate, cannot be merely instrumentally rational the way that limited-purpose intermediate groups can mainly be. Government undermines its purpose if it conceives of our freedom only as its limited purpose, to be pursued instrumentally. Our freedom is not the government's instrumental purpose because we are not free if we are treated as moral patients upon which the government operates. This is the lesson of Reginaland. Part of what makes us free is that we are authors as well as subjects. To be such authors, our collective creation must have the functional capacity to reflectively endorse its ends in a way that parallels the capacity of an autonomous natural agent to reflectively endorse her ends. To see how this can be so, we must uncover the secrets of the second trick: how group action can connect to the individual members of the group in ways that make and keep those individuals independent and autonomous. This much can be said now: the trick is not landed by the conventional view of campaign mandates and promises. The conventional view turns our elected officials into either toddlers or tigers—they either become incontinent, inconstant, and incoherent, or they become instrumentally rational fixed-purpose agents. Either way, they tyrannize us by unreason, and we are dominated by wantonism. To answer the question posed at the end of Chapter 6, this is why campaign promises are void *ab initio* even in cases where basic liberties are not at stake.

III. Does Dishonesty Threaten Legitimacy?

At a March 2013 public hearing of the US Senate Committee on Intelligence, Senator Ron Wyden, Democrat of Oregon, questioned General James Clapper, President Obama's Director of National Intelligence, about the mass surveillance of American citizens:

> *Wyden:* I hope we can do this in just a yes or no answer, because I know Senator Feinstein wants to move on. Last summer, the NSA director was at a conference and he was asked a question about the NSA surveillance of Americans. He replied, and I quote here, "The story that we have millions, or hundreds of millions, of dossiers on people is completely false." The reason I'm asking the question is, having served on the Committee now for a dozen years, I don't really know what a dossier is in this context. So, what I wanted to see is if you could give me a yes or no answer to the question—does the NSA collect *any* type of data at all on millions, or hundreds of millions, of Americans?
>
> *Clapper:* No, sir.
>
> *Wyden:* It does not?
>
> *Clapper:* Not wittingly. There are cases where they could inadvertently, perhaps, collect, but not wittingly.
>
> *Wyden:* All right. Thank you. I'll have additional questions to give you in writing on that point, but I thank you for your answer.[10]

Three months later, we learned from the striking revelations of Edward Snowden that the National Security Agency indeed was collecting massive amounts of telephonic and electronic data on hundreds of millions of Americans. The FBI and NSA secretly enlisted the major telecommunications companies to hand over records of all telephone calls in the country, and intelligence agencies gathered the addresses emailed and websites visited of all internet users, which were then stored for subsequent searching.

Senator Wyden was not trying to find out the truth, which he already knew from the classified briefings given to the Congressional intelligence oversight committees. Two years earlier, when the Patriot Act was up for renewal, Wyden and his colleague Mark Udall wrote an opinion piece asking, "How Can Congress Debate a Secret Law?"

As members of the Senate Intelligence Committee we have been provided with the executive branch's classified interpretation of those provisions and can tell you that we believe there is a significant discrepancy between what most people—including many Members of Congress—think the Patriot Act allows the government to do and what government officials secretly believe the Patriot Act allows them to do.[11]

Nor was Wyden's purpose to catch the witness off guard, for the senator had sent his questions to the director in advance, thereby giving Clapper time to think about how to answer. Wyden's subtextual question to Clapper was, "When are you going to reveal to the rest of Congress and to the American people the secret legal arguments you have relied on to justify conducting mass surveillance programs, so that those programs and the arguments you have made to support them can be subject to public scrutiny, political debate, and legal challenge?" Clapper's subtextual answer to Wyden was, "Never, if I can help it."

What was the secret legal interpretation that Senator Wyden was trying to bring to light? The Fourth Amendment of the US Constitution limits the government's power to search persons and their things without good reason and specific authorization:

The right of the people to be secure in their persons, houses, papers, and effects, against unreasonable searches and seizures, shall not be violated, and no Warrants shall issue, but upon probable cause, supported by Oath or affirmation, and particularly describing the place to be searched, and the persons or things to be seized.

For decades, the courts have understood that, like papers, conversations counted as the sort of thing that could be searched or seized, so the Fourth Amendment included protections against at least some kinds of surveillance of communications, such as electronic eavesdropping and telephone wiretaps. The intelligence agencies held that, though listening to telephone calls and reading emails between Americans requires particular search warrants, collecting massive amounts of what is known as metadata—telephone numbers and the time and duration of calls, email addresses, IP addresses, and website visits—does not.

The spy agencies did not proceed without *any* legal authorization. These collection programs repeatedly were approved by the Foreign Intelligence

Surveillance Act Court, set up by legislation to review applications by intelligence agencies to engage in electronic surveillance within the country, and so provide judicial oversight of the searches of constitutionally protected citizens and residents. Members of the FISA Court are Federal judges appointed by the Chief Justice of the Supreme Court. They conduct their reviews in secrecy, and their decisions to allow surveillance are in practice difficult to review. The government may appeal a denial of authorization to a FISA Court of Review, and a telecommunications company may contest an order to collect, but there is no knowing target of surveillance to protest a grant of authorization. The Court of Review did not convene for the first twenty-three years of its existence.[12] In an ordinary criminal investigation that leads to a public prosecution, the accused can challenge the legality of searches at trial and on appeal, so that, over time, the constitutionality of various surveillance practices is openly argued and settled. In contrast, the primary aim of intelligence gathering is national security, not law enforcement, so the vast majority of those subject to surveillance by intelligence agencies are never prosecuted, do not find out that their communications have been monitored, and therefore have no opportunity to challenge the legality of the search. The FISA Court repeatedly granted the NSA blanket permission to surveil hundreds of millions of people, presumably on the theory that the bulk collection of metadata does not constitute a "search" in need of a particularized warrant. Until the Snowden leaks, the targets of these collections could not have known that they were being surveilled, so they could not have appealed the constitutionality of bulk collections in a higher and open forum. Although not foreseen by the drafters of the original Foreign Intelligence Security Act, who were trying to institute more oversight over domestic intelligence activities, not less, the FISA Court was empowered to interpret the scope of the Fourth Amendment in secrecy and, in effect, with finality.

The surveillance programs exposed by Edward Snowden raise a number of fascinating and important normative questions: Do we have a moral right to privacy that a just constitution would recognize and protect? If so, when is that right to privacy properly limited by considerations of national security? When, if at all, is the illegal disclosure of classified information morally justified, and how should the law treat leakers and whistleblowers? I will attend to a complementary but separate question: How, if at all, can secret governmental policies be reconciled with democracy? In particular, is secrecy compatible with the liberty, equality, and agency principles of the free group agency account of legitimate governance?

Director Clapper lied under oath. Lying is a highly, though not completely, moralized act description, a presumptive moral wrong in need of justification. Perjury by a public official is a serious crime. Secrecy, in contrast, is more normatively flat, with no presumption of wrongdoing built in. Others are not owed answers to all questions: we are entitled to keep many matters private, and often keeping the confidences of others not only is admirable but obligatory. So we might at first see an important moral difference between lying to the Senate about the massive collection of the electronic communications of the American people and merely concealing such a program. Perhaps, as well, an institutional division of moral labor between the branches of government permits even more concealment than would be the case if not for the opposing institutional roles occupied by senators and spymasters. Just as, in adversary legal proceedings, lawyers are allowed to conceal some material facts from each other but not allowed to make false statements, perhaps officers of the executive branch are allowed to withhold some information from legislators or judges but not allowed to lie to them.[13]

From the perspective of self-governing democratic citizens, however, to be subject to secret government policies does not appear to be any less damaging to political freedom than to be deceived about those policies. Though official liars commit an added moral offense, why aren't official concealers already violating the conditions for democratic governance? Self-governing people must in some way author the laws to which they are subject, and—deconstructive literary theory notwithstanding—one cannot author actions in ignorance. Yes, a people can give general *ex ante* authorization for a policy of specific *ex post* secret actions. Democracy does not demand that the movements of troops or of interest rates be announced in advance, and more to our point, there is no contradiction in a people approving a general policy of secret surveillance in particular circumstances. But if citizens cannot possibly approve an unknown general policy, can they still be self-governing? Senator Wyden appears to have a damning complaint.

Does this book's conception of legitimacy recognize the senator's complaint? There are two reasons to think that it cannot. First, the view I argue for replaces any requirement for the actual consent of the governed with the requirement of free group agency, so the complaint that citizens have not consented to secret policies is misplaced: their consent is not needed. Second, the equality principle demands that citizens have equal normative power to choose *who* makes their laws, but not necessarily power over the content of those laws. When the group agent is constituted by representation and procedure—as it must be in all but the smallest of polities—the complaint that citizens have not had a voice in fashioning the content of secret policies also is misplaced, for their voice is not directly needed. Earlier, I drew from the equality principle the counterintuitive conclusion that campaign promises are void *ab initio*. Am I now committed to the repugnant conclusion that transparency in government is superfluous? That would be a damning complaint against the free group agency conception.

For citizens to exercise their equal normative power over who governs, they do need to be informed in a timely way about the words and actions of those who govern them. But it follows from the distinction between normative power and causal power that citizens are not, on first principles, entitled to some specified amount of causal power over their legitimate representatives. In rejecting the view that representative democracy necessarily is inferior to direct democracy, we rejected the claim that the citizenry collectively is entitled to maximal causal power over its officials, reducing legislative and executive discretion to zero. Nor could we endorse, or even plausibly interpret, a right to equal causal power for individual citizens. Recall that we had good reasons to reject Senator McGrail's account of legislative mandates. Voters do not need equal casual power over the content of law and policy to be political equals, so if the main argument for full transparency is that openness assures voters such control, the equality principle doesn't demand full transparency.

Nor does the liberty principle support a general demand for transparency. As we saw in Majoritaria, whether substantive rights are more or less secure under popular control is a contingent factual matter that will vary with how popular the right in question is. The Snowden revelations led to a popular outcry against warrantless bulk collections against all Americans, but I doubt that the public disclosure of a warrantless collection program targeting only Muslim-Americans would have met with equal outrage. Earlier, we concluded that whether or not a high court with powers of judicial review is necessary to protect basic rights and liberties is a matter of contingent fact and institutional design; so too, whether or not the practice of maximal transparency is necessary to protect basic rights and liberties is a matter of contingent fact and institutional design.

Perhaps the example of secret surveillance law exposed by Edward Snowden shows how the liberty principle *necessarily* demands transparency. Secret laws about our rights and duties are intolerable because, to be genuinely free, one must know what the law requires, prohibits, or permits one to do. Secret law is perverse for the same reason that *ex post* law and strict criminal liability are perverse. If one either cannot know what the law demands or cannot avoid breaking the law whatever one does, the law becomes to us an inscrutable god impossible to appease. One either is crippled by fear of arbitrary punishment or unmoored by reckless fatalism. Either way, one's genuine freedom and self-governance are compromised.

The secret FISA Court rulings, however, did not establish secret rights and duties, but secret powers and liabilities. The liberty principle and the Fourth Amendment require reasonable limits on surveillance, and a government that oversteps those limits violates the rights of its citizens. But that is so whether or not the policy of excessive surveillance is revealed or concealed. In contrast, suppose that the substance of some surveillance policy falls within the morally permissible bounds, in that it gives due consideration to both privacy and public safety. Is there any affront to freedom if such a policy is kept secret? What is kept secret is the extent of the government's power to search and seize, and so the extent of a subject's liability to search and seizure. What is not kept secret is which activities by subjects are lawful or not. It is a mistake to think that one has a right to commit those crimes that can only be detected through impermissible search. One ordinarily has no right to commit a crime. One has a right to be protected from unreasonable search. So the government's secret power to search does not, by itself, impose unknown duties on subjects.

I am not making the morally clueless claim that those who break no laws have nothing to fear from invasions of privacy. The government surely can violate my right to privacy whether I have something unlawful to hide or not. But the way in which my freedom of action is inhibited by unknown liabilities to government power is a subtler thing than the way my freedom is violated by unknown duties. US law considers those who are subject to surveillance, including those who are lawfully surveilled unawares and never subsequently questioned or charged, "aggrieved persons," which gets it right: to be a target of surveillance, even if not otherwise affected, is to be burdened with something grave, and so a cause of grief.[14] But not all burdens are wrongs. Nature can burden us with accident and illness, and other people can burden us by thwarting our plans or setting back our interests without wronging us. We take prudent precautions against the risk of being burdened by nature and by society, and the avoidance of this risk sometimes shapes and limits our actions. I may have dreams of opening a bookstore on the beach but be rationally deterred by hurricanes and Amazon. Similarly, a person who greatly values her privacy but cannot know the extent of the government's powers of surveillance might rationally curtail innocent actions and self-censor harmless speech to avoid exposure to prying eyes and ears. But if freedom is independence from the domination of the will of another, we are not necessarily less free when we limit our actions to avoid burdens. To conclude that being liable to secret power violates our freedom, we must show that we are dominated (and not merely burdened) by the secrecy of the power (and not merely by its content).

Surprisingly, the demand for transparent government finds its strongest support in the agency principle, rather than in the equality or liberty principles, which is why the discussion of the Wyden-Clapper exchange appears here, and not in earlier chapters. To avoid dominating its citizens by wantonism, and so becoming a tyranny of unreason, a government must have the functional capacities of a free agent responsive to the reasons that apply to those who constitute it. Only then are citizens co-authors of the laws that bind them, and not merely the subjects of those laws. Insofar as the promulgation of secret law, or government deception and secrecy more generally, undermine the group agent's three capacities of considering, willing, and doing, or undermine the responsiveness of the group agent to the reasons of its constituent members, group agency misfires and wantonness threatens. An individual agent ignorant of, or deluded about, her choices, or an author blind to, or tricked about, what he has authorized, clearly has not succeeded in acting freely. When competent willing is undermined from within by ignorance, weakness of will, or self-deception, the agent fails to be internally free. When the will is undermined or overcome by the deceit or fraud of others, the agent fails to be externally free. So too with group agents: the conditions of constitution or of conscription can misfire because of false beliefs that are fatal to unified group agency.

To be clear, an individual who has second-order volitions does not become a wanton when she is deceived by another individual external to her. The deception I am considering here is internal to the deliberative mechanisms of the group agent. If group agents are agents because they reproduce the functions (though of course not the psychology) of individual agents, then there will need to be interactions among the group's constitutive members that reproduce the three functions of considering, willing, and doing that go on inside of an individual agent. The wanton individual is wanton because he cannot or will not make consideration-responsive choices in ways that give him a coherent, unified will. The wanton is either puzzled by, or indifferent to, the question of which competing consideration or choice should win out. He lacks the unity that makes one an agent because he lacks, or does not use, internal deliberative capacities to unify the competing parts of his self. Now, what is the parallel failure in a would-be group agent? It is the inability or unwillingness to combine (I don't say aggregate) the possibly conflicting individual second-order wills of its members into a unified, coherent whole, and creating such unity is possible only by following some sort of admittedly imperfect procedure. Now suppose a group member undermines this unifying procedure by cheating or deceiving in ways contrary to the internal procedure. Then the deliberative mechanism that seeks coherence and unity itself is faulty. Considered as two natural persons, when one public official lies to another, the deceiver has undermined the other's external freedom, or independence. Considered as two constituent members of an artificial person, when one public official lies to another, the group agent suffers self-deception, a defect in its internal freedom, or self-governance.

This is why the dance of words between the courteous Senator Wyden and the mild-mannered Director Clapper is such a serious matter. Clapper's lie was not an offense against Wyden, who, as Clapper knew, already knew the truth. Nor was it a direct offense against the American people, who, if my account of the equality principle is correct, are not owed transparency in real time. Rather, Clapper's lie undermined the capacity of the Senate to play its part in the constitution by procedure of a free group agent. Senator Wyden had some reason to believe that Congress did not intend in the Patriot Act to authorize warrantless bulk surveillance, and, in any case, had reason to believe that such surveillance violated constitutional protections against warrantless search and seizure. Clapper's perjury kept these secret powers claimed by the executive branch hidden from review by Congress and the Supreme Court. The normative magic conjured by the constitution of group agency by procedure is the creation of a unified will out of a multitude of conflicting wills. A necessary (but hardly sufficient) condition to work this magic is that the procedures of constitution be followed. The procedures that constitute legislation and adjudication as group actions of the United States do not require full transparency in real time between branches of government, but do require, at a minimum, that public officials not lie under oath to each other.

What if Clapper had merely refused to answer in public session, an option that was lawfully open to him? Then whether or not keeping the surveillance programs secret was a failure of group agency would have turned on a difficult substantive judgment: does the mechanism of the separation of powers (or, as Richard Neustadt illuminatingly rephrased it, separate institutions sharing powers) in practice provide enough opportunities for the officers of government to uncover those truths that are essential for them to play their roles in enacting the three functions of considering, choosing, and doing in a timely way?[15] The legislature is not entitled to full disclosure by the nation's spymasters in real time. Though we must reject the Panglossian foolishness that stipulates some Invisible Hand always guides institutional mechanisms towards good, just, or even minimally legitimate equilibria, no matter what the mechanism, we must also recognize that well-designed procedures justify some sorts of division of moral labor and the division of epistemic labor that follows. As the hypothetical example of the three Libyan ministers shows, genuine group decisions do not require uniformity of belief and judgment of the group's members. This is a relief, because such uniformity rarely is possible. Once Clapper lies under oath, however, this judgment about the substantive adequacy of the procedures for forging unity out of multitude is superfluous, for perjury triggers a formal failure of group agency. Like a candidate stuffing ballot boxes in an election or a prosecutor tampering with witnesses at a trial, a public official lying to Congress triggers a misfiring of normative power, clouding the government's clear authority to act on its secret legal interpretation.

Adherence to the rule of law is seen, quite properly, as a precondition for the free and equal treatment of citizens, protecting them against domination by inhumanity and domination by despotism. If the free group agency conception of legitimacy is correct, then the rule of law serves another crucial role. Because it is a necessary condition for the constitution of group agency by procedure, and so a necessary condition for creating a unified will out of multitude, the rule of law protects citizens from domination by wantonism as well.

IV. Does Incoherence Threaten Legitimacy?

The core insight needed to solve the trick of how the reasons of the constituted group agent are to be responsive to the reasons of the group's conscripted members is that the subject of the equality principle is *who* decides, not how to decide or what to decide. Counting procedures must be central to choosing who governs because that is the only way to instantiate the political equality of all citizens. In contrast, counting procedures need not be central to the how or what of governing. Start from the idea that every citizen must share, somehow, in the normative power to govern, else she is not an author also but a subject only. So imagine that, in the Village of Lithia, across the green from the Lithian Stone, stands a very large, hollow cube hewn from obsidian in which citizens enter and public decisions are made (in compliance, of course, with the Lithian Commandments). We, the observers, don't know what happens inside, but we know who is let in, and we know what decisions come out. If only one person is let in, only one person can possibly contribute to public decisions, so that one person despotically dominates the rest. If all but one person is let into the black box, the one excluded person can't possibly contribute to public decisions, so that one person is despotically dominated by the rest. We saw this reasoning earlier in another guise: the logic of the nondictatorship criterion supports a nonoligarchy criterion, which supports an anonymity condition, which supports universal suffrage and an equally weighted counting procedure.

The Black Box of Lithia, though very large, is likely to be too crowded, too hot, too noisy. So, instead, imagine this is how the box is filled (and imagine, as with the Lithian stone, it has always been so—no smuggling in some legitimate procedure for legitimating procedures). Citizens arrange themselves into pairs. How they do so is up to them, but the members of a pair both have to agree to be in that pair. Then, by mutual agreement, the members of the pair designate one of the two to enter the black box. Under favorable assumptions about how the pairs are formed and the designee selected—we might suppose that family members or like-minded friends comprise the pairs, and the pairings and designations occur without threats, bribes, or collusion—this procedure of reducing the entrants to the black box by half preserves the political equality of every citizen. If, instead, some pairs are entitled to send both of their number to the black box, and others none at all, then—still, without knowing anything about what happens inside the black box—we would have to conclude that the political equality of the citizens of Lithia had been violated. This example supports the judgment that the normative power of all citizens to select those who are empowered to exercise normative power over all citizens must satisfy the demand of equality, properly understood, if collective governance is not to be despotic. Everyone does not have to directly participate in the substance of governing to remain autonomous and independent, which is why everyone does not have to enter the black box. But if all subjects are not to directly participate in governing, then the mechanism for reducing the number of subjects who will directly participate must treat every subject as a moral equal, for only then are subjects treated as citizens.

But this judgment does not extend—or I should say, my judgment does not extend—to the equal treatment of the beliefs, desires, values, and proposals of these same citizens, and it certainly does not extend to the notion that the equality of citizens demands an equally weighted counting procedure to aggregate their beliefs, desires, values, and proposals. If we thought that, our objection to the randomized legislative procedure of Randomark would be limited to the damage it does to good public policy, not the damage it does to freedom. The entrants to the black box are charged with forging a reason-responsive unity, and as we have noted again and again, no particular kind of aggregation is sufficient or necessary for creating such unity.

What should go on inside Lithia's black box? Let us begin by listing standards to be met, starting from the most innocuous. For the black box to meet these standards, it will have to have a way to go about it, a method, and so procedures will be needed. But as we will see, these standards call for *imperfect* procedures—procedures that aim at, but might not meet, a standard that is independent of, and not constituted by, the procedure itself. Two conclusions follow from the crème brûlée test: following the best recipe does not guarantee pudding, and we can know when we do or do not have pudding without knowing the best recipe for pudding. Now, a sampling of conditions.

The Grammar Condition. The text of any legislation emerging from the black box must meet current standards of grammar, otherwise the plain meaning of the text can misfire and fail to instruct citizens and implementing officials about their legal rights and duties. So if the Grammar Condition were cast in stone, and the Lithian Commandments included

THOU SHALT NOT ENACT UNGRAMMATICAL LEGISLATION,

no Lithian legislator or citizen would have reason to complain on democratic grounds.

How to implement the Grammar Condition? Several imperfect procedures might have adequate accuracy: using a grammar and spellchecker software program, employing a nonpartisan proofreader, appointing a legislative subcommittee on grammar, giving power to a minority of some size (ranging from 1 to $N/2 -1$) to block passage of legislation by invoking the Grammar Condition, or locating the powers of grammatical review in an independent Court of Grammar whose grammarians have lifetime appointments. True, such procedures might be used tendentiously to thwart group agency, because all imperfect procedures are, well, imperfect. Perhaps the best procedure is simply to leave judgments of syntax and semantics to the majority of legislators. But if the best way to ensure that legislation can be parsed is to remove that function from the authority of legislators, there is no loss—*no loss at all* (to echo Ronald Dworkin)—to Lithian democracy.[16] This is so, even if a nonmajoritarian procedure has been chiseled on the Lithian Stone:

THE GRAMMATICAL POWER SHALL BE VESTED IN ONE COURT
OF LITERACY.

Indeed, the opposite is true. The legislative and executive institutions of Lithia lose the normative power to perform speech acts if they are unable to speak with sufficient clarity to be understood, and a polity is ungoverned if its government is unable to perform speech acts.

The Arithmetic Condition. As with grammar, so too with arithmetic. The text of any legislation emerging from the black box, insofar as it contains sums, fractions, or percentages, must comply with the axioms of arithmetic, otherwise the plain meaning of the text can misfire and fail to instruct citizens and implementing officials. The line items of an appropriation bill must sum to the total appropriation. If a budget is declared to be in balance, then expenditures cannot exceed revenues. So what objection could be leveled against the following commandment?

THOU SHALT NOT ENACT LEGISLATION THAT VIOLATES THE
AXIOMS OF ARITHMETIC.

The power to enforce this condition can be vested anywhere from a young intern with a calculator to a High Court of Numeracy. As with all of these conditions, the wisest course might be to vest the legal power with the decision-makers in the black box themselves, but we must not confuse exercising a legal power and exercising a moral power. A legislature that adopts legislation violating the axioms of arithmetic, and that therefore doesn't add up, has misfired and abused its moral power. Whatever else we think reason-responsiveness demands of the black box, it demands being responsive to arithmetic. This is so because whatever else we think reason-responsiveness demands of a citizen of Lithia, it demands that the citizen be responsive to arithmetic.

Other basic requirements of rationality similarly follow, such as a non-contradiction condition, which requires that a law not command "do A" and "not do A," or assert "B" and "not B," and a consistency condition, which requires that if one law commands "do A" or asserts "B," a second law must not command "not do A" or assert "not B" without rescinding the first law.

The minimal conditions for reason-responsiveness do not stop here. If, to be a unified group agent, the black box must be responsive to reason, then participants in the black box ought to be able to articulate the reasons they are being responsive to, both to each other and to their co-citizens outside the box. So another condition of successful group agency is that participants offer arguments to each other in support of their proposals. Insofar as these arguments depend on assertions of empirical fact, participants should support their assertions with evidence; insofar as these arguments depend on normative premises and logical deductions, participants should support their proposals with normative and logical arguments. In short, participants have a duty to deliberate in good faith, answer good faith objections, and explain to each other why they find arguments for one proposal stronger than other arguments for another proposal. It is not excessive that these arguments be made explicit, in either writing or speech, and it is not excessive that these arguments be subject to scrutiny by citizens outside the black box, so that the output of the black box not only is legislation, but a coherent case for the legislation supported by factual evidence and normative argument. We expect from courts not only decisions but opinions supporting decisions, and when a court splinters in its reasoning, with members supporting a decision for incompatible reasons, there is a sense that, though decisive, the court has misfired. Why can't we expect from public officials coherent and honest explanations of their actions?

Lest you think that I am veering off again into an unrealistic utopia, I should be clear that, as Rawls convincingly argues, the burdens of judgment under free institutions make it completely unreasonable to expect unanimity in choices, let alone unanimity in reasons for choices, and certainly not unanimity in reasons for choices that go all the way down—that would be inconsistent with public reason and the fact of reasonable pluralism. There will inevitably be disagreement about public purposes and some sort of voting—though not necessarily winner-take-all simple majority rule—will be needed to provide the decisiveness that also is a condition for action. But that is compatible with practices of reason-giving and truth-telling, and it is compatible with the adoption of at least some imperfect procedures that aim at standards of reason-giving and truth-telling that are independent of the procedure itself. No, we probably should not have a High Court of *Modus Ponens* or a High Court of Empirical Inference, lest we end up with, not merely the Lithian Stone, but the Lithian Stonehenge. But it is not utopian for public officials to hold themselves and their colleagues to the standards of a college freshman term paper and to view the failure to meet such standards as a serious misfiring of free group agency and a slide towards wantonism, the tyranny of unreason.

Clearly, the agency principle calls for exacting and extensive deliberation among legislators and public officials. To what extent, then, does the free group agency conception of legitimacy track the larger idea of deliberative democracy, and in what ways does it differ? There is much overlap in extension between the prescriptions of the free group agency view and many versions of deliberative democracy, so in that sense, my account is a wholehearted endorsement of democratic deliberation. In the free group agency account, however, deliberation is a solution to a particular problem that most deliberative democrats do not explicitly pose, the problem of constituting a self-governing group agent out of a multitude of individuals. A self-governing group agent must have sufficient capacities to consider, choose, and act, to have such capacities, the group agent must be sufficiently unified, and to achieve sufficient unity, the individual members of the group must in some way reason together, and not merely aggregate their prior preferences.

In turn, on the free group agency account, deliberation is *not* meant to be a solution to a number of other problems posed by the various conceptions of deliberative democracy. Some theories of democracy hold up the direct participation of citizens as an ideal, and so call for deliberation among citizens and between citizens and their elected officials.[17] I do not deny that such deliberation ordinarily is a great good, but I don't think that legitimacy demands it. On the free group agency conception, deliberation is necessary for legitimacy only when a unified group agent is necessary, and citizens ordinarily are constituted as a unified group agent when their elected representatives achieve the requisite unity with each other. Therefore, it is not necessary on my view for the requisite unity to be achieved among citizens as long as it is achieved by their government, which is why the equality principle guarantees citizens equal normative power over the choice of who governs, but not over the content of laws and policies. On this, Hobbes is right: "For it is the Unity of the Representer, not the Unity of the Represented, that maketh the Person One."[18]

On other accounts of deliberative democracy, deliberation is the procedural solution to the supposed impossibility of grounding legitimacy on substantive standards, either because there are no substantive standards or because we will never agree about what they are.[19] One of the main arguments of this book, of course, is that we always have a place to stand from which we can ask if those who follow a procedure, deliberative or otherwise, for achieving legitimate government have succeeded in achieving legitimate government. True, reciprocity and mutual respect require that our imposition of coercive law on each other be supported by reasons we can share, and virtuous citizens and officials will offer each other such reasons. But it is not a condition for law's legitimacy that all citizens actually accept each other's reasons, even when deliberating in good faith, because not all citizens are reasonable, and not all offered reasons are reasons we can share. The measure of the reasonableness of a proposed law or policy is its conformity with substantive principles that are exogenous to any actual democratic deliberation.

It follows that a substantive constitution, such as a Bill of Rights, and counter-majoritarian institutions, such as a Supreme Court with the normative power to strike down unconstitutional legislation, are compatible with reciprocity and mutual respect among citizens. Some deliberative democrats contrast deliberative democracy with constitutional democracy, and hold that removing issues from the legislative agenda by entrenching certain rights and liberties in a constitution may fail to show sufficient respect for the moral disagreements of citizens. For these theorists, democratic deliberation is the solution to the problem of mutual justification in the face of disagreement, and such justification is achieved only when reason-giving citizens (or their representatives) are in principle open to reconsidering previously rejected reasons.[20] In contrast, the Lithian Stone argument claims that constitutional constraints on majoritarian decision-making are justified if they are the correct constraints, because majorities do not have the legitimate authority to enact laws that do not have legitimate authority. Yes, a constitution that removes too much from the legislative agenda would be disrespectful, but so would a constitution that removes too little. As the crème brûlée argument against proceduralism claims, we always have a place to stand from which to make these judgments about legitimacy.

V. How Can We Pull Ourselves Together?

When an individual natural agent commits basic offenses against reason by mouthing (or tweeting) unparsable utterances, arithmetic impossibilities, contradictory intentions, and incoherent commands, his attempted speech acts misfire. Such an individual at that moment does not have an ordered mind or a unified will, and so is incapable of competent action. So too with a group, artificial agent. Though each member be a rational and competent author of individual action, together they might fail to author a rational and competent group action. Procedural constraints on such failures of collective rationality (if they reliably hit their target) do not constrain collective self-government: because the precluded irrationalities make collective willing impossible, there is no tradeoff between democracy and rationality in these instances. Of course, people will disagree about whether a misfiring of rationality has occurred, disagree about whether the procedural constraints have hit their target, and so will raise the question, yet again, "Who is to say?" The answer is the same: unless we are to succumb to thought-numbing and action-paralyzing skepticism, it is up to the judgment of those who are normatively empowered to judge, and it is up to the judgment of each of us to judge the judges. Crème brûlée is exacting.

Procedures that prevent certain failures of rationality, however, are not sufficient to assure success. I still need to explain with greater specificity how the choices of a group agent are responsive to the reasons of its members even when those members disagree about what choices to make. It is not enough to say that, since unanimity is exceedingly rare, some sort of counting rule is necessary. I must show how some counting rules are able to fend off the charge of wantonism. The problem is this: if an individual wanton is someone who simply acts on his strongest desire without willing that his strongest desire be his will, why isn't a collective body that simply enacts its strongest desire through some counting rule a group wanton? When Locke says "it is necessary the Body should move that way whither the force carries it," he not only fails to justify majority rule, he fails to show how *any* counting procedure, majoritarian or not, constitutes unified group action.[21] Where resides the person in the legislative machine that considers whether the group agent wills the will that it has, reflectively endorses the results of its counting rules, and so escapes both toddlerhood and tigerhood? And what can that reflective, endorsing person be, other than another mechanism in search of personhood? Do we not face personless mechanisms all the way down?

The futility of this search is familiar, of course, because the same regress threatens the freedom and autonomy of all natural agents. From the outside looking in, no individual is empirically self-determining, simultaneously and miraculously both detached from prior causal chains and yet capable of choosing and pursuing nonarbitrary purposes. Nonetheless, since you have no choice but to conceive of yourself as an individual reason-responsive agent, you do manage to pull yourself together, however imperfectly, to commit yourself to your ends by attempting to take effective means to realize them. The alternative to purposeful agency is to find oneself lounging in bed like Ivan Goncharov's character Oblomov, curious (or not) about whether that human animal with your particular causal makeup will be moved by something or another to display wake-up behaviors.[22] You don't first pull yourself together into a unified, self-governing agent, and then go about setting and pursuing that agent's reason-responsive, consistent, and coherent ends. You can't do it that way because there is no unified you yet to do the pulling. Rather, as Christine Korsgaard convincingly tells the story, you become a unified agent by struggling to set and pursue reason-responsive, consistent, and coherent ends.[23] To put it another way, you become self-governing by acting *as if* you are self-governing.

Suppose—yes, I realize this is a big supposition—this is a correct sketch of how, without the help of some prior tiny person within, some Cartesian ghost in the machine, an individual with conflicting and incoherent purposes becomes a unified, self-governing agent. What then is the analogous picture of how a collection of individuals with conflicting and incoherent purposes becomes a unified, self-governing agent? How do groups pull themselves together? Earlier we explored three routes to group constitution and three ways to conscript members to the group. But since we did not yet have the threat of wantonism in clear focus, we did not consider how these mechanisms are able to defeat the threat.

Constitution by shared aims and plans by members conscripted through consent appears to be the most assured way for a group to pull itself together into a unified agent, but also the most demanding and, for political societies, most fanciful. No polity is formed and maintained by the unanimous consent of its citizens to shared ends and means. Indeed, any collection of individuals capable of such stable unity would have little need for political institutions at all. Our challenge is to show how a group agent that is neither consensual nor unanimous, such as the city-state of Lithia, nonetheless can pull itself together. Lithia's stony commandments either fell or might as well have fallen from the sky, so Lithians cannot rely on some illusion of a bygone consensual founding or a moment of ratification. The commandments cannot be repealed, and this is so even if an overwhelming majority of Lithians wants to harvest organs, enact legislation by lottery, or suspend the axioms of arithmetic, so the authority of its constitution does not depend on the ongoing endorsement of its content. Earlier, I said that if the practices and procedures of Lithia's officials comply with the agency principle in that, in the requisite sense, the actions of the Lithian government follow from competent group intentions that follow from competent considerations, then the Lithian commandments are not wanton. But what is that requisite sense? To state the worry more sharply, for Lithia to be a free group agent, its constitution must accomplish three tasks: it must be responsive to the reasons for action of every Lithian; it must knit these reasons for action together to form a unified agent; and it must do so in a way that makes and keeps each citizen free. I have argued that the Lithian Commandments can satisfy the liberty condition and that admission to the Black Box of Lithia can satisfy the equality condition. Until Lithia's governance can be shown both to respond to the reasons of individuals and to the reasons of a unified group agent, however, I have not explained how Lithia can satisfy the agency condition.

Competent agency requires, among other things, that the agent's choices be responsive to the relevant considerations. But relevant considerations need not be first-order substantive considerations only. One can have a wide array of content-independent reasons to act in some way that do not turn directly on the merits of the action. One could have sufficient reason to follow some directives, fulfill some promises, grant some requests, or enact some procedures even when one would not otherwise have sufficient reason to act in that way on the substantive merits alone. I am not making any controversial claims here about the scope or preemptive force of second-order reasons, merely the commonplace observation that there are such reasons. When it comes to groups, if not for second-order reasons, group agency would not merely be limited to constitution by shared aims and plans. Group agency would be even more severely limited to that subset of group agents constituted by shared aims and plans whose individual intentions were aligned from the start or who engaged in the mutual adjustment of their intentions on first-order substantive grounds only.

Note as well that to form a shared intention, members of a group agent do not have to share all underlying motivations, beliefs, and interests that support that intention. Voluntary and informed contracts are shared intentions, which is why entering into a binding contract ordinarily is an expansion, not a restriction, of one's freedom. But the end that contractors share need not be any thicker than the end of performing the terms of the contract in good faith. They need not share interests or beliefs all the way down. When we bet on a ballgame, we have different beliefs about and stakes in who will win, but as long as we share the intention to carry out the terms of the bet, we have succeeded in constituting a group agent—though for a limited purpose and duration, to be sure.

Collective self-governance of course is not a limited transaction—I have argued that it cannot be a transaction at all—so satisfying the agency principle is likely to be correspondingly more demanding. For a group agent like Lithia to be a competent group agent, its choices must be responsive to those considerations that are relevant, rational, and reasonable for an agent of its kind, which in turn must be responsive to the considerations that are relevant, rational, and reasonable, under the circumstances, to the natural agents that constitute it. But the agency principle does not require that those natural agents respond to identical first-order, substantive considerations.

One reasoned consideration is a precondition for all others: the consideration that a free group agent governing Lithia must exist and continue to exist. For group agents less capacious than polities, there is no such precondition. No particular voluntary association or movement is necessary. Whether such groups should exist, and whether any one should be a member, turn on the contingent ends that groups and their potential members happen to have. Not so for polities. I have followed Kant here in holding that being in a lawful condition is a practical necessity, a precondition for living with others without wrongly dominating them and being wrongly dominated by them in turn. Therefore, under the *in medias res* circumstances in which they find themselves, the officers and inhabitants of Lithia face a compelling second-order reason to recognize the claimed authority of the Lithian stone, whether or not they agree with its particulars on the merits, as long as the liberty and equality conditions are otherwise satisfied. So there is a sufficient reason for the group agent that is Lithia and its officers to enforce the Lithian commandments, and that reason follows from the sufficient reason that each natural agent who makes up this group agent has to recognize the normative power of the Lithian commandments. To will governance by a free group agent that creates and protects one's free agency is a practical necessity; under the *in medias res* circumstances that Lithians find themselves, coordination around the existing Lithian commandments constitutes just such a free group agent, and there is no path to constitute some alternative group agent that doesn't traverse the physically and morally dangerous territory of lawless mutual domination. It goes something like this: you already conceive of yourself as a self-governing individual agent with purposes and principles that constitute your identity, so you already have a dispositive reason to conceive of yourself as free to pursue your purposes in accord with your principles, so you already have a dispositive reason to live with others under collectively self-governing institutions that realize and protect such freedom, so you already have a dispositive second-order reason to see the results of at least some non-unanimous procedures as the choice of the unified group agent of which you are a part, even when you disagree with the substance of the choice.

Not any non-unanimous procedure will do. Rather, to fend off the threat of wantonism, the decision-making procedures inside of the Black Box of Lithia must struggle to achieve reflective endorsement through the back and forth of giving reasons for actions and sincerely defending proposals against sincere objections. When first-order disagreements about the good cannot be resolved through honest argument, deliberators should be prepared to engage in second-order reasoning about the just. When disagreements about the just cannot be resolved through honest argument, deliberators should be prepared to engage in higher-order reasoning about legitimacy.[24] Disagreement will of course always remain, often contentious and bitter, and then the only route to decisive choice is a voting procedure, with each member of the decision-making body deciding for herself which first-order, second-order, or higher order considerations are dispositive.

Transparent reason-giving by all parties to a controversy is crucial to overcoming the threat of wantonism. Those who vote for a proposal are to publicly justify their choice, and to do so, they must give reasons that others, insofar as they are reasonable, would accept as fitting reasons, though those others might have in the end have judged differently. Under the discipline of transparent reason-giving, as an elected official you are pressed not merely to further the private interests of your constituents, much less your own electoral chances, but to explain why, for the issue under consideration, you have sufficient reason to further such interests, rather than pursue the common good. You are pressed to articulate an account of justice and fairness to justify why you are supporting the claims of the few against the claims of the many. You are pressed to articulate an account of legitimacy to justify why you have a duty of civility to accept defeat when your proposals are outvoted and to continue to search for common ground with your adversaries on other matters of great public importance. You are pressed to articulate the factual claims that underpin your positions, backed up by evidence and judgments about evidence. You are pressed, under the pains of the charge of incontinence, incoherence, and inconsistency, to explain how your various votes over time hang together, or else explain why you were mistaken in the past or have good reason to change your mind now. I am not so naïve as to believe that this discipline of reason-giving will produce honest arguments and not rationalizations. Then again, the discipline of judicial reason-giving does not guarantee that courts will produce honest arguments and not rationalizations. Nonetheless, when arguments, objections, and responses to objections are part of the record of public decision-making, open to scrutiny and—depending on how the Black Box standards are procedurally implemented—formal review, we will have come as close to the ideal of a self-governing group agent, and as far from a group wanton moved by the vector sum of causal forces, as any empirical government can achieve.

I said that, in collective choice, disagreement will always remain, but individual choice often is no different. We try to pull ourselves together by considering reasons for our actions, and when reasons are in conflict, we try to reconcile them by further reflection about which reasons apply under the circumstances or about whether we have higher order reasons to recognize the force of some considerations over others. We do not always succeed in decisively defeating competing considerations, and sometimes we weigh or judge in ways we know, or ought to know, are insufficiently supported, but choose we must. We make mistakes, have regrets, are open to criticism. We might delude ourselves, like Ishiguro's Mr. Stevens. We might be inconstant, like Dickens's Richard Carstone. We might choose grotesquely, like Tolkien's Gollum. We might fall apart, like Shakespeare's Ophelia. There is no pure procedural route to individual unity out of our multitude of desires, interests, values, and beliefs, and there is no pure procedural route to political unity out a multitude of legislators and citizens with their own multitude of desires, interests, values, and beliefs. Again, we might collectively delude ourselves or be inconstant or choose grotesquely or fall apart. But when it comes to pulling ourselves together, we have no choice but to act as if success is possible.

Conclusion

This account of legitimacy has taken us quite some distance from many commonly held views. Consider several ways in which this is so:

Normative legitimacy is conceptually prior to descriptive legitimacy, and it is a confusion to think that legitimacy simply means beliefs about legitimacy. Perhaps the source of this fairly recent but endemic error can be traced to sloppy readings of Max Weber.

The idea of legitimacy is conceptually distinct from the idea of legality. Any connection between law and legitimacy is a matter for substantive moral argument, not conceptual analysis. This is so despite the etymology and early senses of the *word* legitimacy and its cognates.

The idea of legitimacy is not essentially tied to notions of procedure or pedigree. This too is a matter for substantive moral argument, not conceptual analysis. This is so despite the linguistic and historical association of the word illegitimacy with bastardy. We learn this lesson from Edmund.

It is true that citizens and officials who seek to live under legitimate government will adopt procedures that best predict success. But following the best method for producing legitimate government doesn't constitute legitimate government any more than following the best recipe for crème brûlée constitutes crème brûlée. The proof of the pudding is in the eating, and the standards for legitimate government are in part substantive, not purely procedural.

Legitimacy is a moral power that entails moral liability, but it does not entail moral obligation, and it does not entail immunity. This is so despite the conceptual baggage that may have been left behind by divine command theory and its secular successors. The connections between legitimacy, obligation, and immunity must be established by normative argument, not conceptual analysis.

To be legitimate, government must make and keep us free in two senses: we must be internally free, understood as the capacity for self-governing moral agency, and externally free, understood as independence from domination.

The answer to the puzzle of how we can remain free while governed is that we are both authors and subjects of the normative power to govern. When a people is governed by a free group agent constituted by its free citizens, those citizens are as free as they can hope to be.

A moral agent has the capacity to consider in response to reasons, choose in response to considerations, and do in response to choice. Since these three capacities do not refer to psychological states, a group of individual agents might together possess these three capacities to an adequate degree and so be a unified group agent.

A group agent is constituted by three mechanisms: shared aims and plans, representation, and procedure. Individuals are conscripted as members of a group agent by three routes: consent, fair play, and practical necessity.

A government legitimately governs its citizens only if the government is a free group agent constituted by free citizens. A government is a free group agent only if it has the functional capacities of considering, willing, and doing. Citizens are free only if they are not dominated in any of three ways: Citizens are not dominated by inhumanity only if each has an adequate set of basic rights and liberties consistent with an equal set for all *(the liberty condition)*; Citizens are not dominated by despotism only if each has equal normative power to choose who governs *(the equality condition)*; Citizens are not dominated by wantonism only if their government has the functional capacities of a free agent responsive to the reasons that apply to those who constitute it *(the agency condition)*.

Legitimacy and justice are neither identical in concept nor in extension, though they clearly overlap. The subject of justice is the distribution of rights, duties, and advantages by social institutions. The subject of legitimacy is the specification of the normative power to impose normative liabilities, or, more colloquially, the right to rule. One could of course view questions of legitimacy as a proper subset of questions of justice and count the normative powers and liabilities that are the concern of legitimacy as one category among the many rights, duties, and advantages that are the subject of justice. This is no mistake, and it naturally follows from an inquiry that begins with the question of what justice demands. But if one's inquiry begins with the question of who has legitimate authority over whom, one finds coherent answers that are detached and insulated from the other rights, duties, and advantages that are the main concern of theories of justice. Recall James I's insistence that his authority is not dissolvable by tyranny or infidelity (or by heresy, apostasy, or acts of the pope).

Though I have made conceptual room for a substantive conception of legitimacy that imports many of the requirements of justice, I have resisted an easy conclusion, which is that institutions are legitimate only if they are substantively just, or nearly so. I have made no suppositions about the connection between justice and legitimacy, and instead I posed the modern puzzle of legitimacy as the reconciliation of collective rule with individual freedom. The solution, somewhat surprisingly, is both less and more demanding than the most plausible accounts of substantive justice. Less, in that the fair distribution of income and wealth beyond an adequate minimum, though a requirement of justice, does not appear to be a precondition for legitimate governance because citizens can be self-governing and independent agents under at least some unfair conditions of distribution. More, because the preservation of the autonomy and independence of citizens as agents puts requirements of unity and coherence on governing institutions that are more demanding than what substantive justice requires. Wanton governments destroy our free agency even when our basic rights and liberties are unthreatened. This is the lesson of Randomark. So legitimacy is not to be understood as simply justice-lite.

There is no Law of the Conservation of the General Will, such that legitimacy can neither be created nor destroyed, only changed from form to form. Though the idea of a state of nature is most illuminating as a hypothetical abstraction, not an historical condition, it remains true that an anthropological people can suffer the moral disaster of failing to be organized under legitimate laws and institutions and so fail to be a normative people.

Our folk theorems about legitimacy mislead. We have loaded myths about founding moments and the consent of the governed with moral freight they cannot bear. All foundings are forced, and we should not look to the egg for the source of legitimate governance or for the primal procedural scene. Free group agency is the test of legitimate collective self-governance, and it is a recursive construction that we either succeed or fail at constituting here and now. We create a unity out of a multitude of persons in the polity through law and institutions in parallel with how you create unity out of a multitude of desires, interests, values, and beliefs in your mind through reflection and endorsement.

The liberty, equality, and agency principles control three distinct aspects of governance: The liberty principle controls what decisions should be made. The equality principle controls who has the normative power to make these decisions. The agency principle controls how decisions are to be made. These are the lessons of Majoritaria, Reginaland, and Randomark. One might have thought that collective self-governance entails an equal say for all subjects in the substance of the laws and policies that govern. Not so. Collective self-governance requires only that all have an equal say in *who* governs.

The three principles of liberty, equality, and agency set out a demanding regulative ideal of legitimacy, which citizens and officials should strive for, but may never reach. When, inevitably, our actual political institutions fall short of this ideal, what are we to do? Kant's prescription, to act as if all empirical governments are legitimate and not rebel, the way that we should treat our empirically impaired neighbors as if they are competent and not paternalize, has its lower limits for failing governments as well as for failing neighbors.[1] It is of great moral importance, but in the end, a matter of moral judgment, to decide when the lower threshold has been crossed, collective self-governance no longer exists, and we have been returned to a state of nature (or collective self-governance has not yet been established and we have not yet escaped a state of nature). A virtue of the power-liability view is that we are not without resources in the face of governments that are judged to be above the minimal threshold of legitimacy but are far from the ideal and slipping farther. There are forms of dissent and disobedience, resistance and even outside intervention, that are consistent with treating nonideal governments as if they exercise legitimate normative power over us. Power entails liability, but not necessarily duty, and not necessarily immunity. This is the lesson of Clamdigger and Motorist.

Responsibility for judging whether claimed legitimate authority is genuine or not cannot be avoided. Any appeal to higher authority simply pushes the inquiry back a step. Similarly, responsibility for judging whether a legitimate authority may nonetheless be disobeyed cannot be avoided. The answer to Locke's question, "Who shall be Judge?" ultimately is *You shall be Judge.*[2] Moral reasoning about legitimacy requires judgment all the way down.

In the beginning, the greatest threat of domination was violence and force. The established democracies continue to threaten the citizens of other countries with unjustified violence and force, and continue to threaten their own citizens who commit, or who are suspected of committing, or who look like those who are suspected of committing, crimes, so there is much work to be done. Still, the greatest risk to the legitimacy of democratic government no longer is the inhumanity of tyranny by practice.

The exclusion of most of humanity from the authorship of the constraints that coerce them has historically rendered most governments tyrannies without title, but the spread of universal suffrage has gone far in reducing that source of domination. Formal violations of political equality persist in disproportionate voting procedures, the bad faith suppression of voting rights through the manipulation of ballot access continues, and the private financing of political campaigns is barely better than legalized bribery. Again, there is much work to be done, but the greatest risk to the legitimacy of democratic government in established democracies no longer is despotism.

Lies are the weapons of the weak and evasions of the precarious: ask any child or any woman under a man's thumb. In part because of codes of honor, in part because of fear of heavenly judgment, the great and powerful relied on violence and force more than dishonesty to get their way. Although there is not much to mourn about the passing of violent honor cultures, it is no small irony that, at least in constitutional democracies, the lie has replaced the sword as the weapon of choice of the great and powerful. The greatest danger to the legitimacy of contemporary democracies, I believe, is the threat of wantonism. Deception undermines the will as assuredly as coercion, force, and violence overbear the will. The opacity of the aims and actions of those who claim normative power can deprive citizens of their self-governance and independence as assuredly as barring them from the voting booth. The contempt of elected officials for not only the findings of science but truths about what J. L. Austin called "moderate-sized specimens of dry goods," the trashing of reasoned argument, the dismissal or distortion of ordinary data and analysis, the near universal acceptance in our political discourse of what Harry Frankfurt famously analyzed as "bullshit," is more than ugly, more than burdensome, and more than unfair.[3] If these affronts to truth and truthfulness so damage the deliberative capacities of democratic institutions that they are rendered incontinent, inconstant, and incoherent, and if these affronts to transparency and reason-responsiveness are so corrupting that the connection between the governors and the governed is cut, then we will have sunk into domination by wantonism, a tyranny of unreason. A king of false shreds and deluded patches cannot govern himself, and a government that cannot govern itself cannot legitimately govern others.

Notes

Introduction

1. John Rawls, *A Theory of Justice* (Cambridge, Mass.: Harvard University Press, 1971), p. 5.
2. John Locke, *Two Treatises of Government* (1689), ed. Peter Laslett (Cambridge: Cambridge University Press, 1960), *Second Treatise,* § 235, p. 422.

1. Legitimacy in a Bastard Kingdom

1. William Shakespeare, *King Lear* (1606), eds. David Bevington and David Scott Kastan (New York: Bantam Books, 2004), 1.2.
2. *Lear,* 1.1.
3. For a chilling hour-by-hour reconstruction of these shameful events, see David Rohde, *Endgame* (New York: Farrar, Straus & Giroux, 1997).
4. First by the UN General Assembly in the 2005 World Summit Outcome Document, ¶¶ 138–139, later reaffirmed by UN Security Council Resolution 1674 (2006), ¶ 4.
5. Independent International Commission on Kosovo, *The Kosovo Report* (Oxford: Oxford University Press, 2000), p. 10.
6. *Kosovo Report,* p. 290.
7. Or rather, the Commission held that the illegality of the campaign was straightforward, which is all that is needed here. Some have argued that the Kosovo intervention made new international law. I do not have a considered view about how new international law is made, except on a point that I hope is not controversial: if international law is simply

whatever international bodies do, then such "law" is not recognizably law-like because it does not guide or constrain prospective action.

8. *Kosovo Report,* pp. 288–89.

9. "Meet the Press," NBC News Productions, December 17, 2000, https:// search.alexanderstreet.com/view/work/bibliographic_entity%7Cvideo _work%7C232712, at 31:05.

10. Bush v. Gore, 531 U.S. 1046, 1047 (2000) (Stevens, J., dissenting); citation omitted.

11. Bush v. Gore, 531 U.S. 1046 (2000) (Scalia, J., concurring).

12. Bush v. Gore, 531 U.S. 98, 157 (2000) (Breyer, J., dissenting).

13. Ronald Brownstein, "The Presidential Transition: Bush Has Legitimacy, But It's Fragile," *Los Angeles Times,* December 17, 2000, p. A1.

14. Max Weber, *Economy and Society* (c. 1920), ed. Guenther Roth (Berkeley: University of California Press, 1968), vol. I, chap. III.1, p. 213.

15. *Economy and Society,* vol. I, chap. III.1, p. 213.

16. *Economy and Society,* vol. I, chap. III.2, p. 215.

17. *God and the King: or, A Dialogue shewing that our Soveraigne Lord King James, being immediate under God within his Dominions, Doth rightfully claime whatsoever is required by the Oath of Allegeance* (1615).

18. Jean-Jacques Rousseau, *The Social Contract* (1762), I:1.

19. See J. P. Sommerville, *Politics and Ideology in England, 1603–1640* (London: Longman, 1986).

20. More ink has been spilled on attributing all or parts of the *Vindiciae* than in assessing it as a work of political philosophy. Skinner definitively gives it to Mornay. See Quentin Skinner, *The Foundations of Modern Political Thought* (Cambridge: Cambridge University Press, 1978), vol. II, p. 305. Garnett, who prepared the excellent and painstaking contemporary translation, concludes that the work most likely is the result of close collaboration with Languet. See Stephanus Junius Brutus, the Celt (pseud.), *Vindiciae, contra tyrannos: or, concerning the legitimate power of a prince over the people, and of the people over a prince* (1579), ed. George Garnett (Cambridge: Cambridge University Press, 1994), p. lxxvi.

21. William F. Buckley, "Be Skeptical about Bush 'Illegitimacy,'" *The Houston Chronicle,* December 2, 2000, p. A42.

22. Thomas Hobbes, *De Cive* (1642) 7:3, in *On the Citizen,* eds. Richard Tuck and Michael Silverthorne (Cambridge: Cambridge University Press, 1998), p. 93.

23. Bartolus of Sassoferrato, *Tractatus de Tyrannia,* in Ephraim Emerton, *Humanism and Tyranny: Studies in the Italian Trecento* (Cambridge, Mass.: Harvard University Press, 1925), pp. 119–154. The work was written sometime between 1337 and 1357.

24. Bartolus coins the terms *tyrannus ex defectu tituli* and *tyrannus ex parte exercitii*. Mornay has *tyrannus absque titulo* and *tyrannus exercitio*.

25. I thank Lucas Stanczyk for pressing me here.

26. See Arthur Isak Applbaum, "Cultural Convention and Legitimate Law," *Chicago Kent Law Review* 74 (1999), pp. 615–624.

27. This is one of Jeremy Waldron's objections to Ronald Dworkin's defense of the legitimacy of counter-majoritarian institutions and practices such as judicial review. See Jeremy Waldron, *Law and Disagreement* (Oxford: Clarendon Press, 1999).

28. See Nomy Arpaly, "On Acting Rationally against One's Best Judgment," *Ethics* 110 (2000), p. 488, where she distinguishes between a manual for rational actors and a theory of rationality.

29. See John Rawls, *A Theory of Justice* (Cambridge, Mass.: Harvard University Press, 1971), and *Political Liberalism: Expanded Edition* (New York: Columbia University Press, 2005 [1st ed. 1993]); and T. M. Scanlon, *What We Owe to Each Other* (Cambridge, Mass.: Harvard University Press, 2000).

30. For one account of the difference, see David Estlund, "The Democracy/Contractualism Analogy," *Philosophy & Public Affairs* 31 (2003), pp. 387–412.

31. *A Theory of Justice*, p. 86.

32. *A Theory of Justice*, p. 86.

33. *A Theory of Justice*, pp. 195–201.

34. *A Theory of Justice*, p. 355f.

35. *A Theory of Justice*, p. 356.

36. *A Theory of Justice*, p. 86.

37. *A Theory of Justice*, p. 201.

38. *A Theory of Justice*, p. 362.

39. *Declaration of Independence*, Dunlap Broadside, from the Papers of the Continental Congress, US National Archives Identifier 301682.

40. Thus posed, institution by consent is sufficient but not necessary. The argument can be strengthened in one direction, insisting that governments are legitimate *only if* instituted by consent and that *only* democracies satisfy that condition, and weakened in another, allowing that other conditions of legitimacy are needed. The points I shall be making do not depend on which of these variations we choose.

41. John Locke, *Two Treatises of Government* (1689), ed. Peter Laslett (Cambridge: Cambridge University Press, 1960), *Second Treatise*, § 101, p. 334.

42. *The Godfather*, directed by Francis Ford Coppola (Paramount Pictures, 1972), in Jenny M. Jones, *The Annotated Godfather: The Complete Screenplay* (New York: Black Dog and Leventhal Publishers, 2007), p. 46.

43. Thomas Hobbes, *Leviathan* (1651), ed. Richard Tuck (Cambridge: Cambridge University Press, 1991), chap. 21, p. 146.

44. *Second Treatise*, § 119, p. 347f.

45. Robert Nozick, *Anarchy, State, and Utopia* (New York: Basic Books, 1974), p. 287.

46. Rawls, *A Theory of Justice*, p. 111f, crediting H. L. A. Hart. See also Arthur Isak Applbaum, *Ethics for Adversaries: The Morality of Roles in Public and Professional Life* (Princeton: Princeton University Press, 1999), chap. 6, "Rules of the Game and Fair Play."

47. John Rawls, *Justice as Fairness: A Restatement* (Cambridge, Mass.: Harvard University Press, 2001), p. 4.

48. *The Doctrine of Right* (1797), in Immanuel Kant, *Practical Philosophy*, ed. Mary J. Gregor (Cambridge: Cambridge University Press, 1996), Prussian Academy edition, Ak. 6:318.

49. *What We Owe to Each Other*, p. 260.

2. Legitimacy without the Duty to Obey

1. See A. John Simmons, "Justification and Legitimacy," *Ethics* 109 (1999), p. 746; but see Simmons, "Voluntarism and Political Associations," *Virginia Law Review* 67 (1981), p. 23, for an earlier, contrary view.

2. Joseph Raz, *The Morality of Freedom* (New York: Oxford University Press, 1986), p. 24.

3. Raz's writings on authority are extensive and nuanced. Here, I use as my foil only one of his claims, that the exercise of legitimate authority entails a moral duty to obey. This view follows from his account, in *The Authority of Law: Essays on Law and Morality* (New York: Oxford University Press, 1979), pp. 3–27, of legitimate authority as providing exclusionary reasons, and is elaborated in *The Morality of Freedom*, pp. 23–69. I take no stand here on other major components of his view: that what normally justifies authority over a subject in some domain is that the subject is more likely to comply with the applicable reasons for action by following the directives of the authority, rather than by trying to follow the reasons that apply directly (*The Morality of Freedom*, p. 53); and that there is no general obligation to obey the law, even the laws of a good and just legal system, because obeying the law is not always the best way to comply with applicable reasons for all persons across all the decisions over which the law claims authority (*The Authority of Law*, pp. 233–249; *Ethics in the Public Domain: Essays in the Morality of Law and Politics* [New York: Oxford University Press, 1994], pp. 341–354). Raz is clear that the criteria for being a legitimate authority are extremely demanding,

legitimate authority is quite rare, and perhaps no legal system has the authority it claims.

4. Wesley Newcomb Hohfeld, "Fundamental Legal Conceptions as Applied to Judicial Reasoning," *Yale Law Journal* 26 (1917), pp. 710–770.

5. Throughout, I use "privilege," "liberty," "permission," and "justification-right" as synonyms, employing the term favored by the author whose views I am engaging.

6. David Copp argues that political legitimacy confers a bundle of various Hohfeldian advantages. See David Copp, "The Idea of Political Legitimacy," *Philosophy & Public Affairs* 28 (1999), pp. 3–45. Surely he is correct if the claim is that reasonable normative conceptions of legitimacy would include most if not all elements of such a bundle. But Copp does not make the sharp distinction between concept and conception that I am invoking. My view is that moral power, and only moral power, is at the core of the concept—what legitimacy is. Other Hohfeldian advantages, such as a claim-right to obedience or immunity from territorial interference, are what legitimacy arguably gets you.

7. *The Morality of Freedom,* p. 46.

8. See Arthur Isak Applbaum, "Are Violations of Rights Ever Right?" *Ethics* 108 (1998), pp. 340–366; also in Applbaum, *Ethics for Adversaries: The Morality of Roles in Public and Professional Life* (Princeton: Princeton University Press, 1999), pp. 136–174.

9. Joel Feinberg, "Voluntary Euthanasia and the Inalienable Right to Life," *Philosophy & Public Affairs* 7 (1978), p. 102.

10. Robert Ladenson, "In Defense of a Hobbesian Conception of Law," *Philosophy & Public Affairs* 9 (1980), pp. 134–159.

11. Ladenson, pp. 137–39. Since Hobbes clearly claims that the commands of the sovereign obligate, this third step is "Hobbesian" only on the interpretation that "obligated" in Hobbes means nothing more than "justifiably threatened."

12. *The Morality of Freedom,* p. 44.

13. Bad Person Motorist has been influenced by Holmes's bad man theory of the law. "If you want to know the law and nothing else, you must look at it as a bad man, who cares only for the material consequences which such knowledge enables him to predict." Oliver Wendell Holmes Jr., "The Path of the Law," *Harvard Law Review* 10 (1897), p. 459.

14. I am grateful to an Editor of *Philosophy & Public Affairs* for raising this point.

15. "If it be proper to state the common-law meaning of promise and contract in this way, it has the advantage of freeing the subject from the superfluous theory that contract is a qualified subjection of one will to

another, a kind of limited slavery. . . . The only universal consequence of a legally binding promise is, that the law makes the promisor pay damages if the promised event does not come to pass. In every case it leaves him free from interference until the time for fulfilment has gone by, and therefore free to break his contract if he chooses." Oliver Wendell Holmes Jr., *The Common Law* (Boston: Little, Brown, and Co., 1881), pp. 300–301.

16. See Arthur Isak Applbaum, "Are Lawyers Liars? The Argument of Redescription," *Legal Theory* 4 (1998), pp. 63–91; also in *Ethics for Adversaries,* pp. 76–110.

17. John Rawls, *The Law of Peoples* (Cambridge, Mass.: Harvard University Press, 1999).

18. See *Ethics for Adversaries,* chaps. 9 and 10.

19. Kofi Annan, "Secretary-General Reflects on 'Intervention' in Thirty-Fifth Annual Ditchley Foundation Lecture," United Nations Press Release SG/SM/6613, June 26, 1998.

20. See Frederick Schauer, *Playing By the Rules* (Oxford: Clarendon Press, 1991).

21. John Rawls, *A Theory of Justice* (Cambridge, Mass.: Harvard University Press, 1971), pp. 46–53.

22. William Shakespeare, *King Lear* (1606), 1.2.

3. All Foundings Are Forced

1. National Transitional Council of Libya, https://www.webcitation.org/5x0wuZ8r2.

2. France Diplomatie, https://web.archive.org/web/20110401172312/http://www.diplomatie.gouv.fr/en/country-files_156/libya_283/libya-national-transitional-council-10.03.11_15202.html.

3. The story of the Libyan uprising relies upon Duncan Pickard, "Claiming Legitimacy: The Founding Weeks of the National Transitional Council of Libya," eds. Arthur Applbaum and Tarek Masoud, Harvard Kennedy School of Government Case Program.

4. Considering requires more than simply responding to stimuli or desires. It demands a degree of reflection that Harry Frankfurt captures with his account of second-order volitions, or what Agnieszka Jaworska captures with her account of valuing. See Harry G. Frankfurt, "Freedom of the Will and the Concept of a Person," *Journal of Philosophy* 68 (1971), pp. 5–20, and Agnieszka Jaworska, "Respecting the Margins of Agency: Alzheimer's Patients and the Capacity to Value," *Philosophy & Public Affairs* 28 (1999), pp. 105–138.

5. *The Doctrine of Right* (1797), in Immanuel Kant, *Practical Philosophy,* ed. Mary J. Gregor (Cambridge: Cambridge University Press, 1996), Prussian Academy edition, Ak. 6:237. Here I follow the interpretation of Arthur Ripstein, *Force and Freedom* (Cambridge, Mass.: Harvard University Press, 2009).

6. So, although a normative group is not merely valued instrumentally, the source of its value is extrinsic. Think, for example, of a family heirloom or historical artifact that is neither beautiful nor expensive. On this distinction between the source of value and ways of valuing, see Christine M. Korsgaard, "Two Distinctions in Goodness," in *Creating the Kingdom of Ends* (Cambridge: Cambridge University Press, 1996), pp. 249–274.

7. Michael E. Bratman has what I think is the most plausible account in *Faces of Intention* (Cambridge: Cambridge University Press, 1999), chaps. 5–8. I loosely follow his view. Margaret Gilbert has written the seminal works on this topic, but I am not persuaded by her holism or by her views about how involuntary commitments are formed. See *Living Together* (Lanham, Md.: Rowman & Littlefield, 1996) and *Sociality and Responsibility* (Lanham, Md.: Rowman & Littlefield, 2000).

8. Thomas Hobbes, *Leviathan* (1651), ed. Richard Tuck (Cambridge: Cambridge University Press, 1991), chap. 16, "Of Persons, Authors, and Things Personated," pp. 114.

9. Unity in the representative is readily understood when the representative is a natural moral agent with one wet brain. Had Hobbes insisted that any other unity is impossible, his argument for monarchy would have been conceptual. Instead, Hobbes allows that the representative can be an assembly of men whose unity is achieved by majority rule: there are more than enough majority votes to "destroy" all the minority votes, so the excess speaks with one voice. Hobbes will need this account of majority rule later to make his initial covenant work, but it comes at the price of weakening the contrast between unity and multitude.

10. Philip Pettit has fruitfully pursued this line of argument. See especially "Responsibility Incorporated," *Ethics* 117 (2007), pp. 171–201; "Groups with Minds of Their Own," *Socializing Metaphysics,* ed. Frederick Schmitt (New York: Rowman & Littlefield, 2004), pp. 167–193; and Christian List and Philip Pettit, "Aggregating Sets of Judgments: An Impossibility Result," *Economics and Philosophy* 18 (2002), pp. 89–110. See also Lewis A. Kornhauser and Lawrence G. Sager, "Unpacking the Court," *Yale Law Journal* 96 (1986), 82–117. For a precursor, see Howard Raiffa, *Decision Analysis* (Reading, Mass: Addison-Wesley, 1968), who relies on a result later published in Aanund Hylland and Richard Zeckhauser, "The

Impossibility of Bayesian Group Decisionmaking with Separate Aggregation of Beliefs and Values," *Econometrica* 47 (1979), pp. 1321–1336.

11. John Rawls presents the principle of fairness, called in an earlier article the principle of fair play, in *A Theory of Justice* (Cambridge, Mass.: Harvard University Press, 1971), pp. 108–114, 342–350, where he credits H. L. A. Hart. Rawls originally proposed the fair play principle as a way to ground political obligation in voluntary action other than consent, and succeeds in this task better than Locke's tacit consent. Still, Rawls later conceded that ordinary citizens do not accept benefits voluntarily. I use a modification of the fair play principle to establish moral permissions, rather than obligations, in *Ethics for Adversaries: The Morality of Roles in Public and Professional Life* (Princeton: Princeton University Press, 1999), pp. 113–135. Here, the fair play idea is used to ground normative powers rather than obligations or permissions.

12. *Groundwork of the Metaphysics of Morals* (1785), in Kant, *Practical Philosophy*, Ak. 4:417. See also Christine M. Korsgaard, "The Normativity of Instrumental Reason," in *The Constitution of Agency: Essays on Practical Reason and Moral Psychology* (Oxford: Oxford University Press, 2008), pp. 27–68.

13. I am grateful to Frances Kamm for raising this question.

14. See Alan Wertheimer, *Coercion* (Princeton: Princeton University Press, 1987), for the normative conception of coercion that I follow here.

15. See Ripstein, *Force and Freedom,* chap. 6.

16. The notion of a smaller moral world comes from Christine M. Korsgaard, "The Reasons We Can Share," in *Creating the Kingdom of Ends,* p. 296.

17. I am grateful to an anonymous reader for Harvard University Press for raising this question.

18. As Alan Wertheimer was fond of saying, quoting the old Fram oil filter commercial: "You can pay me now or pay me later."

19. John Stuart Mill, *On Liberty* (1859), ed. David Spitz (New York: W. W. Norton, 1975), chap. 5, p. 88.

20. See Arthur Ripstein, "Beyond the Harm Principle," *Philosophy & Public Affairs* 34 (2006), pp. 215–245.

21. *Doctrine of Right,* Ak. 6:231.

22. John Rawls, *Justice as Fairness: A Restatement* (Cambridge, Mass.: Harvard University Press, 2001), pp. 4, 94.

4. Forcing a People to Be Free

1. "President Discusses Beginning of Operation Iraqi Freedom: President's Radio Address," Office of the Press Secretary, 22 March 2003, https://

georgewbush-whitehouse.archives.gov/news/releases/2003/03/20030322
.html.

2. Frederick Schauer, *Playing By the Rules* (Oxford: Clarendon Press, 1991), pp. 31–34.

3. Michel de Montaigne, "Of Husbanding your Will" (1585–88), in *The Complete Essays of Montaigne,* ed. Donald M. Frame (Stanford, Calif.: Stanford University Press, 1958), III:10, pp. 775.

4. DefenseLink News Transcript: Deputy Secretary Paul Wolfowitz Interview with BBCTV and Radio, US Department of Defense, 19 February 2003, https://web.archive.org/web/20061002105425/www
.defenselink.mil/transcripts/transcript.aspx?transcriptid=1936.

5. DefenseLink News Transcript: Deputy Secretary Paul Wolfowitz Interview with ITV London, US Department of Defense, 17 February 2003, http://web.archive.org/web/20061002105504/www.defenselink.mil
/transcripts/transcript.aspx?transcriptid=1934.

6. Oxford Research International, "National Survey of Iraq, February 2004," for ABC News and BBC.

7. More recently, in a March 2007 ABC News poll, 52 per cent answered somewhat or absolutely wrong, with wide disparities by faction: 98 per cent of Sunnis, 29 per cent of Shia, and only 17 per cent of Kurds. See http://abcnews.go.com/images/US/1033a1raqpoll.pdf, p. 18.

8. By faction, among Sunnis, 21 per cent said liberated and 66 per cent humiliated; among the Shia, 43 per cent said liberated and 37 per cent humiliated; and among the Kurds, 82 per cent said liberated and 11 per cent humiliated. Oxford Research International, "National Survey of Iraq, February 2004."

9. John Stuart Mill, "A Few Words on Non-Intervention" (1859), in *The Collected Works of John Stuart Mill,* ed. John M. Robson (Toronto: University of Toronto Press, 1984), vol. XXI, p. 118f.

10. John Stuart Mill, *On Liberty* (1859), ed. David Spitz (New York: W. W. Norton, 1975), chap. 4, p. 85f.

11. *On Liberty,* p. 11.

12. In his early writing, Mill clearly holds that tyranny plays a causal role in the shaping of the minds of its subjects. In "Cataline's Conspiracy" (1826), he says that an aristocracy "seldom or never reduces the human mind so completely to the level of the brutes, as a military despotism." In a despotism, the danger faced by those who cultivate their merits and talents "contributes most of all to sink the minds of the unhappy subjects of a despotism into the lowest state of brutality and degradation of which human nature is susceptible" (*Collected Works,* XXVI, p. 345f). In the posthumous "Three Essays on Religion," he returns to the idea that

self-control, unnatural to the undisciplined human being and to children, must be learned. "Savages are always liars" (*Collected Works*, X, p. 395).

13. Jean-Jacques Rousseau, *On the Social Contract* (1762), book 1, chap. 7, in *On the Social Contract with Geneva Manuscript and Political Economy*, eds. Roger D. Masters and Judith R. Masters (New York: St Martin's Press, 1978), p. 55.

14. See Masters edition, *Social Contract* 1:7, n. 37 (p. 138), and *Geneva Manuscript* 1:3 (p. 164).

15. Here I follow Arthur Ripstein's Kantian account in "Authority and Coercion," *Philosophy & Public Affairs* 32 (2004), pp. 2–35, "Beyond the Harm Principle," and Arthur Ripstein, *Force and Freedom* (Cambridge, Mass.: Harvard University Press, 2009).

16. "A Few Words on Non-Intervention," p. 122f. Elsewhere, Mill goes so far as to turn this into a constitutive rather than an empirical claim. "The attempt to establish freedom by foreign bayonets is a solecism in terms. A government that requires the support of foreign armies cannot be a free government" ("The Spanish Question" [1837], *Collected Works*, XXI, p. 374).

17. The passage in "The Spanish Question" continues: "If a government has not a majority of the people, or at least a majority of those among the people who care for politics, on its side; if those who will fight for it, are not a stronger party than those who will fight against it, then it can only have the name of a popular government; not being able to support itself by the majority, it must support itself by keeping down the majority, it must be a despotism in the name of freedom." Note that Mill simply assumes that the side that has the majority of willing fighters is the stronger.

18. Here I follow Dennis F. Thompson, *Political Ethics and Public Office* (Cambridge, Mass.: Harvard University Press, 1987), p. 153.

19. A point I owe to Mathias Risse.

20. See Tamar Schapiro, "What Is a Child?" *Ethics* 109 (1999), pp. 715–738.

21. Here, I follow the now standard accounts by Stanley Hoffmann, "Collaborationism in France during World War II," *Journal of Modern History* 40 (1968), pp. 375–395, and Robert O. Paxton, *Vichy France: Old Guard and New Order, 1940–1944* (New York: Knopf, 1972).

22. See Agnieszka Jaworska, "Respecting the Margins of Agency: Alzheimer's Patients and the Capacity to Value," *Philosophy & Public Affairs* 28 (1999), pp. 105–138.

23. See *The Doctrine of Right* (1797), in Immanuel Kant, *Practical Philosophy*, ed. Mary J. Gregor (Cambridge: Cambridge University Press, 1996), Prussian Academy edition, Ak. 6:320.

24. *Toward Perpetual Peace* (1795), in *Practical Philosophy,* Ak. 8:374, p. 341n.

25. *Doctrine of Right,* Ak. 6:307.

26. *Doctrine of Right,* Ak. 6:312.

27. *Doctrine of Right,* Ak. 6:232.

28. *Doctrine of Right,* Ak. 6:266.

29. I am grateful to an Editor of *Philosophy & Public Affairs* for directing me to this passage.

30. *Doctrine of Right,* Ak. 6:237.

31. *Doctrine of Right,* Ak. 6:312.

32. *Doctrine of Right,* Ak. 6:307.

33. *Doctrine of Right,* Ak. 6:315.

34. *Doctrine of Right,* Ak. 6:314.

35. I am grateful to an Editor of *Philosophy & Public Affairs* for pressing me on this point.

36. I thank Melissa Seymour Fahmy for pressing me on this point.

37. John Rawls, *The Law of Peoples* (Cambridge, Mass.: Harvard University Press, 1999).

38. In Iraq, we do not need to suppose. In the March 2007 ABC News poll, only a 42 per cent plurality of Iraqis thought a democracy was best for Iraq, with 34 per cent opting for a strong leader for life and 22 per cent for religious rule.

39. I thank an Editor of *Philosophy & Public Affairs* for pressing me on this point.

40. *The Law of Peoples,* p. 94.

5. The Three Tyrannies

1. Here I am influenced by Christine Korsgaard's account of two-level moral theories that distinguish ideal from nonideal conditions. See Christine M. Korsgaard, "Taking the Law into Our Own Hands: Kant on the Right to Revolution," in *The Constitution of Agency: Essays on Practical Reason and Moral Psychology* (Oxford: Oxford University Press, 2008), pp. 233–262, and "The Right to Lie: Kant on Dealing with Evil," *Philosophy & Public Affairs* 15 (1986), pp. 325–349. For the introduction of the distinction between ideal and nonideal theory, see John Rawls, *A Theory of Justice* (Cambridge, Mass.: Harvard University Press, 1971), pp. 8f, 245ff, 351ff. See also Richard Fallon, *Law and Legitimacy in the Supreme Court* (Cambridge, Mass.: Harvard University Press, 2018), pp. 25–35, who insightfully distinguishes between legitimacy as an ideal and as a threshold. For an engaging general treatment of *as if* reasoning, see Kwame Anthony Appiah, *As If: Idealization and Ideals* (Cambridge, Mass.: Harvard University Press, 2017).

2. See Christine M. Korsgaard, "Creating the Kingdom of Ends: Reciprocity and Responsibility in Personal Relations," in *Creating the Kingdom of Ends* (Cambridge: Cambridge University Press, 1996), pp. 188–221, and "Taking the Law into Our Own Hands: Kant on the Right to Revolution," pp. 258–260.

3. Christine M. Korsgaard, *Self-Constitution: Agency, Identity, and Integrity* (Oxford: Oxford University Press, 2009), pp. 27–34.

4. See Korsgaard, "Taking the Law into Our Own Hands: Kant on the Right to Revolution," pp. 256–258.

5. *A Theory of Justice,* p. 312.

6. John Rawls, *The Law of Peoples* (Cambridge, Mass.: Harvard University Press, 1999), pp. 64–67. On the power-liability account, the last condition would need to be softened to say, "imposes *bona fide* moral liabilities, some of which might be moral duties and obligations, on its inhabitants."

7. In *Political Liberalism: Expanded Edition* (New York: Columbia University Press, 2005 [1st ed. 1993]), Rawls offers a more demanding liberal principle of legitimacy, which follows from conceiving of citizens as free and equal, and not merely as responsible and cooperating. Compare *Political Liberalism,* p. xx, and *The Law of Peoples,* p. 66.

8. *The Law of Peoples,* p. 10.

9. *A Theory of Justice,* p. 390.

10. Judith N. Shklar, "The Liberalism of Fear," in *Liberalism and the Moral Life,* ed. Nancy Rosenblum (Cambridge, Mass.: Harvard University Press, 1989), p. 37; reprinted in Judith N. Shklar, *Political Thought and Political Thinkers* (Chicago: University of Chicago Press, 1998), p. 19.

11. Ronald Dworkin, *Freedom's Law: The Moral Reading of the American Constitution* (Cambridge, Mass.: Harvard University Press, 1997), pp. 7–35.

12. See Edmund Burke, "Speech to the Electors of Bristol" (1774), in *The Founders' Constitution,* eds. Philip B. Kurland and Ralph Lerner (Chicago: University of Chicago Press, 1987), vol. 1, p. 391f; James Madison, *The Federalist,* no. 10, in *The Founders' Constitution,* vol. 1, p. 128; John Stuart Mill, *Considerations on Representative Government* (1861), in *The Collected Works of John Stuart Mill,* ed. John M. Robson (Toronto: University of Toronto Press, 1984), vol. XIX, p. 433.

13. Will E. Edington, "House Bill No. 246, Indiana State Legislature, 1897," *Proceedings of the Indiana Academy of Science, 1935,* ed. Paul Weatherwax (Fort Wayne, Indiana: Fort Wayne Printing Company, 1936), pp. 206–210.

14. Henry David Thoreau, "Civil Disobedience" (1849), in *Collected Essays and Poems,* ed. Elizabeth Hall Witherell (New York: Library of America, 2001), p. 202.

15. Joseph Raz, *The Morality of Freedom* (New York: Oxford University Press, 1986), p. 30.

16. See *The Doctrine of Right* (1797), in Immanuel Kant, *Practical Philosophy*, ed. Mary J. Gregor (Cambridge: Cambridge University Press, 1996), Prussian Academy edition, Ak. 6:312, and Arthur Ripstein, *Force and Freedom* (Cambridge, Mass.: Harvard University Press, 2009), p. 168ff.

17. Ronald Dworkin, *Law's Empire* (Cambridge, Mass.: Harvard University Press, 1988), and *Freedom's Law*.

18. *Freedom's Law,* p. 11.

19. For "let us resign this commission to more obedient and suppler people," see Michel de Montaigne, "Of the Useful and the Honorable" (1585–88), in *The Complete Essays of Montaigne,* ed. Donald M. Frame (Stanford, Calif.: Stanford University Press, 1958), III:1, p. 600.

20. On matching the tactics of dissent to its justifications, see Arthur Isak Applbaum, *Ethics for Adversaries: The Morality of Roles in Public and Professional Life* (Princeton: Princeton University Press, 1999), chaps. 4, 9, and 10.

21. For a searing account of choices made by antislavery judges, see Robert M. Cover, *Justice Accused: Antislavery and the Judicial Process* (New Haven: Yale University Press, 1975).

22. *Justice Accused*, p. 170. See also Michael Les Benedict, "Wendell Phillips, the Constitution, and Constitutional Politics before the Civil War," in *Wendell Phillips, Social Justice, and the Power of the Past,* eds. A. J. Aiséirithe and Donald Yacovone (Baton Rouge: Louisiana State University Press, 2016), pp. 133–154.

6. Despotism

1. For the most nuanced and sophisticated account of epistemic arguments for democracy, see David Estlund, *Democratic Authority: A Philosophical Framework* (Princeton: Princeton University Press, 2008). The claim that democratic forms of government produce the greatest happiness of the greatest number goes back to Bentham, of course. For his account of democracy, see Philip Schofield, *Utility and Democracy: The Political Thought of Jeremy Bentham* (Oxford: Oxford University Press, 2006).

2. North Carolina Joint Select Committee on Congressional Redistricting Hearing Transcript, February 16, 2016, p. 50. Also cited in *Rucho v. Common Cause*, 588 U.S. ___, slip op. 2 (2019), where Chief Justice Roberts, though granting "excessive partisanship in districting leads to results that reasonably seem unjust," found that "partisan gerrymandering claims present political questions beyond the reach of the federal courts" (slip op. at 30).

3. John Locke, *Two Treatises of Government* (1689), ed. Peter Laslett (Cambridge: Cambridge University Press, 1960), *Second Treatise,* § 96, p. 331f.

4. Thomas Hobbes, *Leviathan* (1651), ed. Richard Tuck (Cambridge: Cambridge University Press, 1991), chap. 16, p. 114.

5. The Marquis de Condorcet, *An Essay on the Application of Analysis to the Probability of Decisions Rendered by a Plurality of Votes* (1785), excerpted and translated in *Classics of Social Choice,* eds. Iain McLean and Arnold B. Urken (Ann Arbor: University of Michigan Press: 1995), pp. 91–112; Kenneth Arrow, "A Difficulty in the Concept of Social Welfare," *Journal of Political Economy* 58 (1950), pp. 328–346.

6. Consider an election with three candidates, A, B, and C. A is the first choice of 34 percent and the last choice of 66 percent, B is the first choice of 33 percent, and C is the first choice of 33 percent. Then A will win the three-way race, though A would have lost by 32 points to either B or C in a two-way race.

7. This is not strictly so: representatives could argue both for and against legislative proposals, and be granted multiple votes to be cast in conflicting ways. Unless, however, the representative had a distinct argument and a distinct ballot for each constituent, the problem of misrepresentation persists. Alternatively, a legislator who was empowered to speak and vote separately for each separate constituent, and did so, would function as a clerk, not a representative.

8. On the all-affected principle, see Robert Goodin, "Enfranchising All Affected Interests, and Its Alternatives," *Philosophy and Public Affairs* 35 (2007), pp. 40–68.

9. For a sampling of views on this growing topic, see Charles Beitz, "Rawls's Law of Peoples," *Ethics* 110 (2000), pp. 669–696; Michael Blake, "Distributive Justice, State Coercion, and Autonomy," *Philosophy & Public Affairs* 30 (2001), pp. 257–296; Thomas Nagel, "The Problem of Global Justice," *Philosophy & Public Affairs* 33 (2005), pp. 113–147; and Mathias Risse, *On Global Justice* (Princeton: Princeton University Press, 2012).

10. The classic exposition of speech act theory is J. L. Austin, *How to Do Things with Words* (Cambridge, Mass.: Harvard University Press, 1962, second edition 1975).

11. *Second Treatise,* § 210, p. 405.

12. *Political Liberalism,* p. 217.

13. South v. Peters, 339 U.S. 276, 279 (1950) (Douglas, J., dissenting).

14. Gray v. Sanders, 372 U.S. 368, 381 (1963).

15. Baker v. Carr, 369 U.S. 186, 300 (1962) (Frankfurter, J., dissenting).

16. Some of the following variations on districting are taken from teaching materials prepared by and with Frederick Schauer. The hypothetical is loosely based on the fact situation in *Shaw v. Reno*, 509 U.S. 630 (1993).

17. See her opinion in *Shaw v. Reno*, 509 U.S. 630, 642 (1993): "What appellants object to is redistricting legislation that is so extremely irregular on its face that it rationally can be viewed only as an effort to segregate the races for purposes of voting, without regard for traditional districting principles and without sufficiently compelling justification."

    Contrast the dissent of Justice Stevens, at 677: "[T]wo critical facts in this case are undisputed: First, the shape of District 12 is so bizarre that it must have been drawn for the purpose of either advantaging or disadvantaging a cognizable group of voters; and, second, regardless of that shape, it was drawn for the purpose of facilitating the election of a second black representative from North Carolina. These unarguable facts, which the Court devotes most of its opinion to proving, give rise to three constitutional questions: Does the Constitution impose a requirement of contiguity or compactness on how the States may draw their electoral districts? Does the Equal Protection Clause prevent a State from drawing district boundaries for the purpose of facilitating the election of a member of an identifiable group of voters? And, finally, if the answer to the second question is generally 'No,' should it be different when the favored group is defined by race? Since I have already written at length about these questions, my negative answer to each can be briefly explained."

18. Reynolds v. Sims, 377 U.S. 533 (1964).

19. Purcell v. Gonzalez, 549 U.S. 1 (2006) (Stevens, J. concurring).

20. Justin Levitt, "A comprehensive investigation of voter impersonation finds 31 credible incidents out of one billion ballots cast," *The Washington Post*, Wonkblog, August 6, 2014.

21. Michael P. McDonald, "2016 November General Election Turnout Rates," United States Election Project, http://www.electproject.org/2016g.

22. For estimates of voters without government-issued identification, see United States Government Accountability Office, "Elections: Issues Related to State Voter Identification Laws," GAO 14–634 (September 2014), pp. 21–25 (average of ten surveys); for voter purges, see Jonathan Brater et al., "Purges: A Growing Threat to the Right to Vote," Brennan Center for Justice at New York University School of Law, 2018, p. 2, n. 11.

23. Increase Mather, *Cases of Conscience Concerning Evil Spirits Personating Men, Witchcrafts, Infallible Proofs of Guilt in Such as are Accused With That Crime* (Boston: Benjamin Harris, 1693), p. 66.

24. Joshua L. Kalla and David E. Broockman, "Campaign Contributions Facilitate Access to Congressional Officials: A Randomized Field Experiment," *American Journal of Political Science* 60 (2015), pp. 545–558.

25. Carl Hulse, "Behind New Obamacare Repeal Vote: 'Furious' G.O.P. Donors," *The New York Times*, September 22, 2017.

26. Cristina Marcos, "GOP lawmaker: Donors are pushing me to get tax reform done," *The Hill*, November 7, 2017.

27. Center for Responsive Politics, "Most Expensive Midterm Ever: Cost of 2018 Election Surpasses $5.7 Billion," February 6, 2019, https://www.opensecrets.org/news/2019/02/cost-of-2018-election-5pnt7bil/.

28. I thank James Brandt for raising this point.

29. See John Rawls, "The Idea of Public Reason Revisited," in *Collected Papers*, ed. Samuel Freeman (Cambridge, Mass.: Harvard University Press, 1999), pp. 573–615.

30. One might say that the size of the donation expresses the strength of belief in the political position Donor is advocating, and so has epistemic value. For this to be so, Candidate would need to consider the strength of Donor's beliefs to have content-independent epistemic authority and also be able to infer strength of belief from the size of the contribution. Neither strikes me as a plausible assumption. I'm grateful to James Brandt for raising this point.

31. The cases of McGrail and Johnson are paraphrased from teaching materials prepared by Martin Linsky and Herman Leonard. See "Senator McGrail and the Death Penalty / Senator Johnson and the Death Penalty," Harvard Kennedy School of Government Case Program.

32. So I disagree with Alex Guerrero's view that the normative mandate of a candidate can be stronger or weaker, depending on the degree of support the candidate has. See Alexander A. Guerrero, "The Paradox of Voting and the Ethics of Political Representation," *Philosophy & Public Affairs* 38 (2010), pp. 272–306.

33. Christian List and Philip Pettit, "Aggregating Sets of Judgments: An Impossibility Result," *Economics and Philosophy* 18 (2002), pp. 89–110. See also Lewis A. Kornhauser and Lawrence G. Sager, "Unpacking the Court," *Yale Law Journal* 96 (1986), pp. 82–117.

34. So I don't share Eric Beerbohm's view that it is so difficult for a candidate to announce intentions without inducing a reliance that amounts to promising. That many voters will be infuriated by the refusal to promise does not justify the *ex ante* disempowerment other voters, who have more reason to be infuriated. See Eric Beerbohm, "The Ethics of Electioneering," *Journal of Political Philosophy* 24 (2016), pp. 381–405.

7. Wantonism

1. Harry G. Frankfurt, "Freedom of the Will and the Concept of a Person," *Journal of Philosophy* 68 (1971), pp. 5–20.
2. For childhood as a problem in nonideal theory, see Tamar Schapiro, "What Is a Child?" *Ethics* 109 (1999), pp. 715–738.
3. See Christine M. Korsgaard, "Taking the Law into Our Own Hands: Kant on the Right to Revolution," in *The Constitution of Agency: Essays on Practical Reason and Moral Psychology* (Oxford: Oxford University Press, 2008).
4. William Shakespeare, *King Henry IV Part 1*, 5.4.
5. William Shakespeare, *Richard III*, 1.1.
6. William Shakespeare, *Hamlet*, 3.1.
7. Dr. Seuss, *Horton Hatches the Egg* (New York: Random House, 1940).
8. Dr. Seuss, *The Sneetches and Other Stories* (New York: Random House, 1961). Note that the plural of Zax is Zax.
9. *Horton Hatches the Egg.*
10. Hearing before the Select Committee on Intelligence of the United States Senate, 113th Congress, First Session, Tuesday, March 12, 2013, p. 66. Emphasis in original video.
11. Ron Wyden and Mark Udall, "How Can Congress Debate a Secret Law?" *Huffington Post*, May 25, 2011, http://www.huffingtonpost.com/sen-ron -wyden/how-can-congress-debate-a_b_866920.html.
12. United States Foreign Intelligence Surveillance Court of Review, *In Re: Sealed Case No. 02-001* (2002).
13. For an extended treatment of adversary roles, see Arthur Isak Applbaum, *Ethics for Adversaries: The Morality of Roles in Public and Professional Life* (Princeton: Princeton University Press, 1999).
14. 50 United States Code § 1801(k).
15. Richard E. Neustadt, *Presidential Power and the Modern Presidents* (New York: Free Press, 1990).
16. Ronald Dworkin, *Freedom's Law: The Moral Reading of the American Constitution* (Cambridge, Mass.: Harvard University Press, 1997), p. 17.
17. For example, see James S. Fishkin, *Democracy and Deliberation: New Directions for Democratic Reform* (New Haven, Conn.: Yale University Press, 1991).
18. Thomas Hobbes, *Leviathan* (1651), ed. Richard Tuck (Cambridge: Cambridge University Press, 1991), chap. 16, p. 114.
19. This is one way to interpret differences between Habermas and Rawls. See Jürgen Habermas, "Reconciliation through the Public Use of Reason: Remarks on John Rawls's *Political Liberalism*," *Journal of Philosophy* 92 (1995), pp. 109–131, and John Rawls, "Reply to Habermas, *Journal of*

Philosophy 92 (1995), pp. 132–180, reprinted in *Political Liberalism: Expanded Edition* (New York: Columbia University Press, 2005), pp. 372–434.

20. Amy Gutmann and Dennis Thompson define deliberative democracy as "a form of government in which free and equal citizens (and their representatives) justify decisions in a process in which they give one another reasons that are mutually acceptable and generally accessible, with the aim of reaching conclusions that are binding in the present on all citizens but open to challenge in the future" (*Why Deliberative Democracy?* [Princeton: Princeton University Press, 2004], p. 7). On their view, substantive constitutions that remove basic rights and liberties from the legislative agenda might not be sufficiently open to future challenge, and so might fail the test of mutual acceptability. See also their "Moral Conflict and Political Consensus," *Ethics* 100 (1990), pp. 64–88, and *Democracy and Disagreement* (Cambridge, Mass.: Harvard University Press, 1996), chap. 1.

21. John Locke, *Two Treatises of Government* (1689), ed. Peter Laslett (Cambridge: Cambridge University Press, 1960), *Second Treatise*, § 96, p. 331f.

22. For the literary allusion, I'm grateful to Agnieszka Jaworska, *Rescuing Oblomov: A Search for Convincing Justifications of Value,* Dissertation, Harvard University, 1997.

23. See Christine M. Korsgaard, *Self-Constitution: Agency, Identity, and Integrity* (Oxford: Oxford University Press, 2009).

24. See Arthur Isak Applbaum, "Democratic Legitimacy and Official Discretion," *Philosophy & Public Affairs* 21 (1992), pp. 240–274; also in *Ethics for Adversaries,* pp. 207–239.

Conclusion

1. As noted in Chapter 4, Kant's discussion of the reconstitutive opportunities afforded by natural disasters suggests that his *as if* has a lower bound. For an illuminating reconciliation of Kant's apparently conflicting views on revolution, see Christine M. Korsgaard, "Taking the Law into Our Own Hands: Kant on the Right to Revolution," in *The Constitution of Agency: Essays on Practical Reason and Moral Psychology* (Oxford: Oxford University Press, 2008).

2. John Locke, *Two Treatises of Government* (1689), ed. Peter Laslett (Cambridge: Cambridge University Press, 1960), *Second Treatise*, § 240f, p. 426f.

3. See J. L. Austin, *Sense and Sensibilia* (Oxford: Oxford University Press, 1962), p. 8, and Harry Frankfurt, *On Bullshit* (Princeton: Princeton University Press, 2005).

Acknowledgments

The bastard Edmund, quips his father, came something saucily to the world before he was sent for. Not so this book. Over the course of its long gestation, I've incurred debts of gratitude to many good people who have been insightful, generous, and patient.

At Harvard University Press, my editor, Ian Malcolm, wisely shaped, suggested, and encouraged. In a welcome role-reversal, James Brandt, my former star teaching fellow, now an HUP editor, gave an astute read of the whole manuscript. The three anonymous readers for the Press were exacting, and, I confess, usually right. Jill Breitbarth, Lisa Roberts, Mary Ribesky, and Patricia Kot handled the design and production with artful eyes and keen ears. Don Olander, my Kennedy School assistant, tracked down citations, proofread copy, and prepared the index with conscientiousness and good cheer.

Three exceptionally talented undergraduate ethics fellows—Sophia Caldera, Matthew Mandel, and Rebecca Sadock—scoured the manuscript argument by argument in weekly meetings. Eric Beerbohm, on top of numerous reads of various chapters over the years, gave the whole one last pass. Michael Ignatieff, amidst defending his university from authoritarian threat, found the time to read the manuscript closely. Dennis Thompson, my sharpest critic and strongest supporter, gave me detailed and searching comments. As I've said in print before, I owe my calling to Dennis, who took a chance on me thirty years ago.

Danielle Allen, director of Harvard's Edmond J. Safra Center for Ethics, hosted a timely manuscript workshop. The panelists—Danielle, Eric Beerbohm, Nien-hê Hsieh, Frances Kamm, Jenny Mansbridge, Zeynup Pamuk, Tomer Perry, Mathias Risse, Lucas Stancyzk, Dennis Thompson, and Winston Thompson—provided probing responses. I'm especially grateful to Tomer for organizing the workshop. My colleague Michael Rosen encouraged me to send off the manuscript.

Versions of what have become Chapters 1 and 2 were presented at the Society for Applied Philosophy, the University of Bern in Switzerland, the Wharton School at the University of Pennsylvania, UC Berkeley School of Law, Yale Law School, Washington and Lee University School of Law, and, initially, as the Gross Memorial Lecture at the University of Toronto Faculty of Law in 2001. I am grateful to the participants at these talks, and for the helpful comments of Bruce Ackerman, Michael Blake, Cory Brettschneider, Ronald Daniels, David Estlund, Alon Harel, Frances Kamm, Erin Kelly, Christopher Kutz, Daniel Markovits, Lukas Meyer, Joseph Raz, Arthur Ripstein, Mathias Risse, Pranay Sanklecha, Frederick Schauer, Scott Shapiro, Alan Strudler, Dennis Thompson, Alec Walen, Bradley Wendel, and Alan Wertheimer. Parts I to IX of Chapter 2 were first published as "Legitimacy without the Duty to Obey," *Philosophy & Public Affairs* 38, no. 3 (2010), pp. 215–239. I thank Wiley Periodicals, Inc. for permission to reprint the text here.

Versions of what have become Chapters 3 and 4 were presented at the department of linguistics and philosophy at MIT, the University of Graz in Austria, the department of bioethics at the National Institutes of Health, the University of Bern, the Humboldt University in Berlin, the British Academy in London, the University of Vermont in honor of Alan Wertheimer, the Intervention Seminar jointly sponsored by the Carr Center for Human Rights Policy and the Edmond J. Safra Center for Ethics at Harvard, and initially at Indiana University's Poynter Center for the Study of Ethics and American Institutions in 2004. I am grateful to the participants at these venues, and to Brian Barry, Michael Blake, Allen Buchanan, Ezekiel Emanuel, David Estlund, Melissa Seymour Fahmy, Chaim Gans, Richard Holton, Michael Ignatieff, Frances Kamm, Arthur Kuflik, Rae Langton, Julia Markovits, Lukas Meyer, Richard B. Miller, Joseph Raz, Mathias Risse, Nancy Rosenblum, Pranay Sanklecha, T. M. Scanlon, Frederick Schauer, Dennis Thompson, Alan Wertheimer, and Kenneth Winston for their helpful comments. The intrepid Duncan Pickard travelled to Libya to write the case study on which Chapter 3 is based, and my colleague Tarek Masoud joined me in supervising the effort. Versions of the first four chapters were presented at a National Endowment for the Humanities seminar at Washington University in St. Louis, and I'm grateful to Kit Wellman and Andrew Altman for both their invitation and their useful responses. Much of the text of "Forcing a People to Be Free," published in *Philosophy & Public Affairs* 35, no. 4, pp. 360–400, appears in Chapters 3 and 4. I thank Wiley Periodicals, Inc. for permission to reprint the texts here.

Chapters 5, 6, and 7 have their origins in talks I gave in 2014 and 2015 at the Centre for Ethics at the University of Toronto, the Edmond J. Safra Center for

Ethics at Tel Aviv University, the philosophy department of the University of Vienna, and a conference on human rights at Fudan University in Shanghai. I am grateful to my hosts at these events, and for the comments of Tongdong Bai, Joseph Heath, Louis-Philippe Hodgson, Shai Lavi, Herlinde Pauer-Studer, Arthur Ripstein, Mathias Risse, Jacob Weinrib, and Melissa Williams.

Kalman Applbaum, Marc Cohen, Richard Fallon, Archon Fung, Tweedy Flanigan, Ingrid Jordt, Jessica Levy, Alan Mayer, Marie Newhouse, Christopher Robichaud, and Rory Stewart provided me with helpful commentary and encouragement at various stages. The influence of my colleagues Christine Korsgaard and Tim Scanlon is evident throughout.

My dear friend Alan Wertheimer did not live to see the book, but many long conversations with him over many years shaped it in countless ways. In our last exchange, a week before he died, we were still talking about moralized conceptions of coercion.

There is some truth in the jibe that professors don't really work. If you are married to one, however, you are more likely to lament that professors can't stop working. When one's mind is in the grip of an unsolved puzzle, when the glimmer of an idea dulls on the flat page, the days can stretch into evenings and the weeks into weekends. My one true love, Sally Louise Rubin, has supported this odd pursuit of mine with grace and understanding over the evenings, weekends, and years.

Sally and I have shared the wonder and joy of watching two little wanton creatures grow up to become reason-responsive persons. Emma Rubin Applbaum and Sophie Rubin Applbaum are our world. *Legitimacy* is dedicated to them in the hope that their generation will do a better job than ours at protecting democracy from wanton misrule.

Index